SO-BED-438

THE
TEN DANGEROUS
YEARS

WMS Mini Library

THE
TEN DANGEROUS
YEARS

By
MRS. GORDON H. SMITH

MOODY PRESS
CHICAGO

Winona Lake
Free Methodist Church
Library

© 1975 by
THE MOODY BIBLE INSTITUTE
OF CHICAGO

All rights reserved

Smith, Laura Irene Ivory.
   Ten dangerous years.
   1. Missions—Vietnam.   I. Title.
BV3325.A6S6   266'.009597   75-14145

ISBN 0-8024-8582-0

Printed in the United States of America

Contents

Mrs. Gordon H. Smith stands beside battle-scarred marine helicopter.

Gordon H. Smith wears helmet and flak jacket to drive to marine outpost to preach. Chaplain's office is below ground in fortified bunker.

6

1

"And the Gates Shall Not Be Shut"

FOR THE SIXTH NIGHT in a row, I put on my hat and coat, closed my two packed suitcases, and waited for our son Stanley to drive me the fifty yards across our mission compound in Da Nang to his house. If I had been seen walking over there by the trigger-happy Vietnamese soldiers on full alert everywhere, I might have been shot. At eleven o'clock Stan, Ginny, their three children, and I would all sleep in the safest corners we could find in their house. We thought the Communists might come jumping over the back fence of our property, swarm into the main mission house where I was living, and attack the school for Vietnamese police detectives directly across the street.

Gordon was in Florida visiting our new board, the United World Mission, and would be returning via England and Holland, where he would be meeting some new missionary candidates.

This was the Tet Offensive of 1968. Fighting raged in all the big cities of South Vietnam. Our home city of Da Nang was in grave danger because the city of Hue, sixty miles north, was occupied for a month by the Communists.

On the seventh night we received word that all foreigners had to go to the big CORDS hotel, a five-story apartment building for American Aid personnel, who called it "the Alamo."

Our family got into Stan's car with our suitcases, mosquito nets, and some bedding and drove to "the Alamo," two blocks away. We wondered if that night we'd be taken out to one of the U.S. Navy warships of the Seventh Fleet standing offshore.

The next morning as we returned safely to our homes, we heard over the radio that six of our former missionary col-

7

leagues of the Christian and Missionary Alliance (C&MA) at Banmethuot, where we had pioneered for over twenty years, had been massacred by the Communists and two other missionaries had been captured.

Ten dangerous years? We have known hardly anything but danger since 1941 when the Japanese poured in to make Indochina the springboard for their lightning conquests in the Pacific.

God not only brought us through those earlier years of prolonged fighting between the French and the Vietminh, but also through this, America's longest war.

This book's theme is that despite all the terrible dangers of those years, God's work went on successfully.

With Gordon's first book, *The Blood Hunters,* this makes the fifth book in the series that narrates the wonderful workings of God from 1929 to the present. It begins where *Victory in Viet-Nam* stopped in 1963.

God still speaks to Gordon and me in our life verses of Isaiah 45:1-3, "I will loose the loins of kings . . . and the gates shall not be shut; I will go before thee, and make the crooked places straight: I will break in pieces the gates of brass, and cut in sunder the bars of iron: and I will give thee the treasures of darkness, and hidden riches of secret places." He is continually fulfilling these marvelous promises!

Vietnam was long in world focus. This strategic corner in Southeast Asia has held the key to the survival of freedom in that part of the world.

America's might, as well as that of Australia, New Zealand, Korea, the Philippines, and Thailand, were staked on holding this land against the advance of Communism. Vietnam held the stage for over ten long years.

For years we missionaries in Vietnam watched the progress of the American forces there. It was unusual that missionaries were able to stay while a major conflict raged. We weren't able to travel far on the roads to visit country places, but we were able to continue missionary work in the large coastal cities, all of which were heavily guarded by large American bases surrounding them.

Vietnamese and tribal national workers were able to work in many of the interior sections or to lead the Christians out, after their churches and stations were burned by the Communists, to safer refugee areas where they could keep on working for the Lord.

We'll never forget the arrival of the "Screaming Eagles," the 101st Air-Borne Division, in 1964. As the first United States transport ships neared the dock of Camranh Bay off Nhatrang, a cry went up from the 3,700 paratroopers, "Vietnamese, take a break! We're here!"

Astounding accounts followed these "Screaming Eagles." One was on July 8, 1966, when Captain William Carpenter of the 101st Airborne Division was fighting in the Kontum District of the central highlands of South Vietnam. Carpenter and his men fought a terrible battle in the Dak-Ta-Kan River valley, forty miles north of Kontum near Dak To. Our missionary son, Stanley, and his family worked there among the Sedang and Jeh tribal people. Then, because of the war dangers, they had to move to Kontum.

Through the years, the Communists gained many victories in the country places all over the land. It was a long period of great chaos and war.

Our missionary work suffered greatly. John Haywood, a young missionary who arrived from Birmingham, England, in 1963, was interested in our leprosy work. He was killed in a Vietcong ambush in 1966 while driving on the mountain road to Hue from Da Nang to get some young pigs and chickens for the patients to raise at the leprosarium. His young wife, Simone, from Switzerland, with their baby, Jacqueline, born a few days after her father's death, are still in the leprosy work today.

There were other martyrs among our national evangelists and Christians through those years. How young they were and how greatly needed!

Thousands of Christians in America and other parts of the free world have been standing firmly on these promises of God in regard to Vietnam:

Jeremiah 33:3, "Call unto me, and I will hear thee and answer thee, and shew thee great and mighty things."

Revelation 12:11, "They overcame him [the great enemy] by the blood of the Lamb, and by the word of their testimony."

1 Corinthians 16:9, Paul said, "A great door and effectual is opened unto me, but there . . . [will be many difficulties and] many adversaries."

Romans 8:31, "If God be for us, who can be against us?"

Matthew 16:18, "The gates of hell shall not prevail against [the Church of Christ]."

These friends have been praying the prevailing prayer of faith in the name of the Lord. God is sufficient for all the difficulties in Vietnam. He will surely make His promises come to pass.

> I will not be afraid, I will not be afraid,
> I will look upward and travel onward
>   And not be afraid.
>
> He says He will be with me, He says He will be with me;
> He goes before me and is beside me,
>   So I'm not afraid.
>
> His Word will stand forever, His Word will stand forever,
> His truth it shall be my shield and buckler
>   So I'm not afraid.
>
> He says He will do marvels, He says He will do marvels,
> Above our asking or even thinking,
>   So look up, and praise!

AUTHOR UNKNOWN

2

Reaching Twenty-four Tribes for Christ

WE DEARLY LOVE Indochina, the country, and its peoples. Gordon and I have worked here since 1929. We spent our first four years in Cambodia, where we contacted the Pnong tribe and reduced their language to writing. Our first book *Gongs in the Night* tells this story.

Then God called us to be the first full-time pioneer missionaries using some of the tribal languages to begin the work among the Annam tribespeople, in the area now called South Vietnam. The story of our twenty-one years working out from Banmethuot is told in our two books, *Gongs in the Night* and *Farther into the Night*, and Gordon's book, *The Blood Hunters*.

Who are these tribal people living in the interior mountains and jungles of Vietnam? The French called them *Montagnards* (mountaineers), and the American soldiers called them "mountain yards" after the French name. They are the brown-skinned aboriginal people of Indochina who were here long before the time of Christ. They were the first to own the land centuries ago, just as the many tribes of Indians were the first to own North America. The tribespeople have reddish brown skin, deep-set eyes, flat noses, and large mouths. The men are naked except for their hand-woven loincloths, and the women wear hand-woven wraparound skirts, short or long, according to their particular tribe.

Then, centuries ago, before the time of Christ, yellow-skinned people came down from a province in south China called Viet. These people followed the coast of the South China Sea and took all of the rich land along the sea away from the aborigines, the brown-skinned tribespeople. They drove the tribes back into the mountainous jungles of the interior. They formed the countries of Tonkin, Annam, and Cochin-China. Today Tonkin is called North Vietnam, and part of Annam and Cochin-China is called South Vietnam.

These Vietnamese people, cousins to the Chinese, have yellow skin, slanting, surface-set eyes, and high cheekbones. They are small-boned, slight, and average about five feet two inches in height.

Also, many centuries ago, brown-skinned people from India came over and took the country away from the aboriginal tribes on the west side, driving them into the interior mountains. They formed the lands of Cambodia and Laos. The Cambodians may have been of Hindu origin, for their languages were made up of characters based on the Sanskrit and Pali of India. They are called Cambodians and Laotians.

The French, who arrived to rule the land one hundred years ago, called the country "French Indo-China." "Indo" was for the people of Indian origin, that is, the Cambodians and Laotians; "China" was for the Vietnamese people of south China origin; and "French" was added because France had taken over, defending Cambodia and Laos from the Siamese on the east, and Tonkin, Annam, and Cochin-China from the Chinese on the north.

Gordon and I entered Banmethuot, the strategic center for work among the southern tribes of Vietnam, in 1934. We lived in the jungle town of Banmethuot for over twenty years, opening up the work of Christ among the large Raday tribe; the Mdhur of Mdrak; and the Krung tribe between Buon Ho and Pleiku. We began the work with the Jarai tribe at Pleiku and Cheo Reo; the Mnong Bandon wild-elephant trainers, forty miles from Banmethuot; and the Mnong Rolum, Bih and Mnong Gar in the wild jungle country of the Darlac Lake District. It was a fairyland teeming with royal Bengal tigers, leopards, wild elephants, gaurs, snakes, and thirty-foot pythons. There were also gibbon apes, monkeys of all kinds, mynah birds, parrots, and wild peacocks.

We began the Gospel work with the Mnong Preh tribe at

Dak Song, sixty miles southwest of Banmethuot, and the Mnong Dip, whose men wore long tail feathers of birds in the knobs of their hair. We worked down to eighty miles north of Saigon, also opening the Gospel work among the Stieng tribe at Nui Bara and Bu Dop. The stories of all this work are told in the two books, *Gongs in the Night* and *Farther into the Night*.

The book *Victory in Viet-Nam* tells of our beginning work among the tribespeople in central Vietnam in 1956, with our headquarters in the city of Da Nang on the coast. The extent of our mission field was from 200 miles to the north of Da Nang to 200 miles to the south of Da Nang. In 1956 there were great gaps to be filled in this tremendous area, so we started to work absolutely from scratch.

We followed roads leading from twenty to fifty miles from the main coastal highway into the tribal territories and the frontier villages of the backcountry Vietnamese. We began stations among the Bru tribe at the 17th Parallel, which became the demarcation line between North and South Vietnam after the Geneva Accord of 1954. These Bru centers were at Cam Phu and Cam Lo.

We began work among the Pkoh tribal people behind the city of Hue, reaching over to the Laotian border at A-Lui and A-Shau. Three centers were soon making good progress among the Katu tribespeople in the Vietnamese frontier villages of

Hrey Christians with Pastor Tin assemble at Xuan Phuoc
near Qui Nhon

13

Phu Hoa, Thanh My, and Nam Dong. An unsubdued, uncivilized mountain tribe called the Ka Yong was being reached from a backwoods settlement of Phuoc Son. The Cua tribespeople were responding to the Gospel in the frontier post of Tra Bong.

Several thousand of the Hrey tribespeople had turned to Christ in the backcountry hamlets of Son Ha, Gi Liang, Ha Bak, Ba To, and Gia Vuc. Flourishing stations for the spreading of the Gospel among the rural Vietnamese were in Dong Ke, Son Nam, and Tu My, all located about twenty miles behind the coastal city of Quang Ngai.

An Lao and Kim Son of Binh Dinh Province, to the south of Quang Ngai, were good jumping-off centers for reaching thousands of Hrey and Bahnar tribespeople, far into the interior mountains.

In the central highlands of the Province of Kontum, we opened a church in the city of Kontum for the Vietnamese and tribespeople of that area. The important settlement hamlets of Dak Psi, Dak To, Tan Canh, Dak Sut, as far as Dak Pek, one hundred miles to the north of Kontum, were all opened to reach the great Sedang and Jeh tribes. Several thousand of the Jeh people soon accepted Christ in these big resettlement areas. There were three tribes yet to be reached: the Mnom, Halang, and Roglai.

We started work in the flourishing Vietnamese town of Ankhe in the Bahnar tribal area. Also we went to Phuoc Lanh, a pioneer hamlet fifteen miles behind the coastal city of Qui Nhon, reaching the Cham Bahnar and Hroy tribespeople.

We also began to take the Gospel to the two islands off the coast of Vietnam in that section of the country, Cu-Lao Cham Island, thirty miles by our motor launch *Hope* from Da Nang; and Ly Son Island, one hundred miles south down the coast from Da Nang and twenty miles out in the sea, opposite Quang Ngai.

As we began opening these thirty or more new stations in strategic places among the different tribes of central Vietnam and also among unreached Vietnamese people, we knew that we must train national workers immediately to man these evangelization posts. So we soon opened a Bible training school in Da Nang and began teaching some new converts in the Word. Among these were some Cua, Hrey, and Katu tribespeople who believed on Christ from almost the first time we told them about Jesus, the Saviour. Of these, Quang, a Cua, and Trien, a Katu, have become valuable workers among the tribespeople.

God sent us fine Vietnamese Bible teachers and students. Mr. Nhut, our Bible school principal from the beginning in 1956, is still with us today and is greatly used of the Lord.

So despite the fact of a terrible conflict going on all these years in Vietnam, our missionary work as well as that of the other societies, has been progressing well, especially in the medical work in the leprosariums, and in the social work of the orphanages. Many souls have been saved in the numerous refugee camps, in the crowded hospitals, and in the prisons. War plows up hearts and makes an opportune time for sowing the Gospel seed.

The work of missions was not stopped by the war. The main reason was because America had command of the air, so the enemy could not bombard us. If the Communists had had strong air power, we missionaries would have been obliged to leave. Now we can tell how the missionaries and national workers have been able to carry on, under strain and difficulty, of course, but with tremendous success.

3

The Captive Tribes

DURING THE YEARS of raging war with the Communists, there were some martyrs among our national preachers, and many Christians were killed. Great numbers of people were taken captive by the North Vietnamese and the Vietcong.

What do these names Vietcong and North Vietnamese mean? Who is this enemy in South Vietnam?

In 1954 the country of Vietnam was officially divided into two parts, North and South Vietnam, by the Geneva Accord after the French, who were in French Indochina as colonists for one hundred years, were defeated at Dien Bien Phu by the communist Vietnamese, who were then called Vietminh. Ho Chi Minh, the Vietminh communist leader, took over North Vietnam for the Communists after the accord. South Vietnam stood firmly for freedom against Communism. They asked the Americans to enter South Vietnam to block communist enslavement.

The South Vietnamese in 1959 asked the Americans to come in to save them from the threatened slavery by communist North Vietnam. The Americans responded to this urgent appeal by arriving to assist South Vietnam. They were in Vietnam by request, because of the SEATO treaty, by obligation, and by commitment—just as they had been in Greece and Korea fighting against the Communists, and as the British had fought them in Malaya. If they had not given timely aid, the determined Communists would have taken these countries and held greater power in the world today.

In 1954 when the country was divided, nearly one million North Vietnamese came south, seeking liberty from the Communists. They all settled there and are loyal to South Vietnam today. But a large number of Vietminh Communists, who were supposed to join their fellow Communists in the north, stayed on in the south, forming hidden cells of Communism. After about five years, in 1959, these Vietminh came to the surface as terrorists and leaders of communist aggression. They were then called the Vietcong. "Cong" in the Vietnamese language, with the proper accent, means "Communist."

Soon the North Vietnamese troops infiltrated down into the south over the Ho Chi Minh Trail through Laos and Cambodia, and across the 17th Parallel at the Demilitarized Zone (DMZ). Northern political advisers, economic counselors, and leaders for the communist army also infiltrated. Attacks began on South Vietnam outposts.

Of the Katu tribe of primitive people in the mountain country behind Da Nang, four Christian village chiefs were killed by the Communists, and 10,000 Katu tribespeople were taken captive by the Communists to work and fight for them. Only about sixty of them escaped and are free in the south today.

Katu tribesman in frontier village

Women of Jeh tribe near entrance to underground home

The same thing happened to the Pkoh tribe behind Hue. Our first Vietnamese preacher to this tribe, Mr. Hiep, was captured and buried alive by the Communists in 1960. A lovely young Pkoh Christian tribes girl, Mua, was captured at the same time and also was buried alive. Mua's Christian grandfather, the chief of the first Pkoh village to receive Christ, was choked to death by the Red soldiers. All three were martyred simply because of their stand for Jesus Christ.

A few weeks later the whole Pkoh Christian village of Khe Tranh was captured by the Reds and marched away into the wild jungle and mountain territory and perhaps over the Laotian border at A-Lui, five days' walk away.

The Vietcong and North Vietnam Communists openly used Laos and Cambodia as sanctuaries for organizing their forces and infiltrating into South Vietnam.

In a few months' time the whole Pkoh tribe of around 10,000 people was taken away by the Communists. They have been held in the dense jungle mountains for thirteen years now. No word from them ever gets out from behind the iron curtain.

The communist Vietcong also captured the whole Ka Yong tribe, poor, primitive tribespeople from far back in the interior jungles behind our Phuoc Son center. No word has been heard from them either during those twelve or thirteen years. They simply became communist slaves and as the enemy armies captured these different tribes of people they became masters of great sections of mountain jungle country. There are no cities or towns in these mountain territories, but the Communists could hide large numbers of guerrillas, food, and army supplies in the caves and mountains of these huge tribal areas.

All but about 2,000 Cua mountaineer tribespeople have been captured by the Vietcong behind the center of Tra Bong. All of the Cua country now, with nearly 8,000 Cua tribespeople, is under communist control.

Thousands of the Hrey tribe of 80,000 people have been taken over by the Vietcong and North Vietnamese behind our Son Ha, Gi Lang, and Bato, Gia Vuc centers. These vast sections of wild mountain country and these large numbers of bright tribal people all have been under communist control for a number of years. Even the centers of Gi Lang and Bato in the beautiful Son Ha River valley, with its rich rice fields, have now fallen to the Communists.

The Bahnar tribe and their mountain country behind An Lao and Kim Son also have been taken over, and all the tribal country behind Ankhe has gone to the Vietcong.

The Cham Bahnar and Hroy tribal country behind Phuoc Lanh, with thousands of these mountain people, have been in communist hands for years. A few thousand of them fled as refugees into the Government of Vietnam (GVN) areas, and a number are being reached with the Gospel today.

Thousands of Jeh, Sedang, and Halang tribal people also have been captured by the Communists. There were many hundreds of Christians among these captives.

All of these hardy mountaineer prisoners have been used by the Communists throughout these war years, to show the North Vietnamese the trails of their mountain country and to carry guns and heavy war supplies for them over the long, hard mountain paths. They've had to make gardens for the enemy in places in the jungles well hidden from the view of searching planes; raise pigs and chickens; dig deep trenches, dugouts, and barracks, camouflaged with branches, for the communist armies. They've had to show the enemy where to find long tunnels in the mountains for their excellent guerrilla hiding places.

As the cease-fire pacts are signed now, will these precious tribespeople and their vast interior tribal territories be set free from the Vietcong and the North Vietnamese? So far, they are still captives!

4

The Red and Green Berets

THE GOVERNMENT of South Vietnam built thousands of re-settlement hamlets, beginning this large project in 1961-62. These villages were to house the tribal people or backcountry Vietnamese who had to be moved away from the Vietcong communist-threatened areas.

The United States spent thousands of dollars on each hamlet to improve the economy of these refugees. They have established large pig-raising programs, introducing American pigs which are larger than the Vietnam or tribal wild-pig species. They also have brought in American hens, which are bigger than the Vietnam hens and produce eggs which are larger and much more numerous.

The Americans sent in many agricultural experts who taught the people new ways of fertilizing and of growing rice, two to three crops a year. They helped in improving their gardens of manioc (tapioca), sweet potatoes, pumpkins, onions, cucumbers, tomatoes, and corn. USOM, now USAID, and other big American aid organizations have built up these hamlets with 600 to 700 people in each resettlement village.

The American men worked hard with the Vietnamese and tribespeople in building these living places. They also helped establish schools and medical centers.

But over and over again the Vietcong Communists, who infest the mountain areas and backcountry places, would make terrorist attacks on a hamlet, torture and kill the village chief and security chief, burn the village, killing and wounding men, women, children, and all the cattle, pigs, and chickens.

So the U.S. Special Forces, President Kennedy's elite guerrilla-warfare trained troops, with their American-trained Vietnamese and tribal strike forces of marines and rangers, set up many strong border-surveillance camps in remote centers throughout the country. One was at Khe Sanh to protect the Bru tribespeople in the Demilitarized Zone (DMZ) from communist forces coming over the border from North Vietnam and Laos.

Another strong camp was in the A-Shau Valley behind Hue, near the Laotian border. A third was at Nam Dong in Katu tribal country. A special forces camp all through the war years was at Tra Bong to help guard the 2,000 Cua tribespeople in their settlement area. At Bato and Son Ha, big camps watched over the Hrey tribal country. Camps in Binh Dinh Province at An Lao and Kim Son, guarded the Bahnar tribal area.

The Jeh, Sedang, and Halang tribes in the Kontum Province were protected by special forces and marines at the outposts of Dak Pek, Dak To, and Tan Canh, centers not far from the Laotian border and the Ho Chi Minh Trail.

Camps were in Pleiku Province at the Cambodian border caring for the Jarai tribe. Near Banmethuot, strong camps protected the Raday and Mnong tribes against the Cambodian border.

Many other special forces camps and marines were in the various provinces along the primitive border areas of South Vietnam. They were in communist heartlands, the important staging areas for the Vietcong guerrillas.

Gordon and Stanley visited many of these camps by helicopter, especially in the Jeh tribal area at Dak Pek and in camps near Da Nang. Each camp had sandbagged heavy log walls, barricaded by barbed wire and sword-sharp bamboo pungee stakes planted thickly in the ground and pointing outward. Mines and booby traps were hidden in tall grass along paths leading to the camps.

Inside the walls were bunkers made of logs and sandbags, with tin roofing to keep out the rain. Some bunkers were strongly reinforced with concrete. There were sandbagged mortar emplacements, and claymore mines, triggered by trip wires set up in front of the bunkers to face the enemy. Some camps had rocket launchers.

The special forces men and the American-trained South Vietnamese Rangers, all wore the same jungle camouflage fatigues called "tiger suits" because of their black stripes. The special forces wore their famous green berets, while the rangers wore dark red berets. They carried combat packs and had pistol belts and harness, hung solidly with ammunition pouches. In battle they had many grenades hanging loosely from their harness and belts ready for instant plucking.

The Vietcong were dressed in black calico pajamas. Many were veteran battle groups. They were the Vietminh who had fought against the French for nine years or more, and they were under good leadership and had many hard-core battalions.

Some of the North Vietnam officers wore khaki, but they, too, were mostly black-clad, flat-helmeted, carrying machine guns. Many hard-core North Vietnam cadres had trained tribesmen to fight with them. These tribesmen had been terrorized and forced into fighting with the enemy.

Terrible battles raged at these camps. The Communists sometimes threw two or three battalions into one attack on a

These young Christians who grew up at the China Beach Orphanage wear the South Vietnamese Ranger "tiger suits." Ca Rop, *left,* later was killed in action. Cong, *right,* served as a paratrooper, was wounded seriously, and then became an army chauffeur.

special forces camp. Mortar shells would come rocketing in, splitting the night with eerie whooshes, followed by shattering explosions. There would be agonized screams from soldiers hit by the searing blasts. The smell of powder and explosives would be strong.

The enemy would send shells crashing into the barbed wire, opening rents in the barricades, and then the Communists would rush through. The special forces would rake the first wave of Vietcong with machine gun and rifle fire and grenades. But another wave of black-clad Communists would charge forward, carrying ladders which they threw over the wire. The Vietcong mortar fire never ceased.

Only the sandbagging saved the special forces. By radio they would call in air force planes from the nearest city base, and the planes would soon be there, dropping high-intensity flares of white, green, and red stars, turning the battlefield into high noon.

The bunkers furiously returned the fire, even using Claymore mines, with their blasts of steel fragments.

Sometimes a platoon of screaming South Vietnam Strikers with American special forces would climb over the walls from inside the camp and charge the Vietcong hordes in hand-to-hand fighting.

Slowly our forces cleared the way and the Vietcong, hauling as many of their dead and wounded as they could, retreated. Many of our side would be killed, and nearly all would be wounded.

Just as they would think the battle was quieting down, another horde of black-uniformed, ferocious, suicidal Communists would attack a different side of the camp. Machine guns and grenades would defy them!

Suddenly six or more fighter planes would be roaring overhead, whipping low over the camp. Bombs would tumble from the planes on to the Communist attackers. The Vietcong would turn tracer bullets on the American planes, and perhaps one or more of the fighters would burst into flames and crash in the mountains. Then the last Communist battalion would flee. The camp was saved!

In early dawn, the wounded defenders had to be taken out to the main military hospitals at Da Nang or Hue; or if the camp was in the south, to Nha Trang or Saigon.

The officers would radio for helicopters to come in, and soon these would be seen, whirling and choppering through the morning skies, over the wooded mountains, to land on some small landing zone built in the jungle near the camp. This was a great help, but often enemy bullets would hit the metal choppers as they came swirling down. Pang! Pang! Pang! The choppers would list, plummet, the whirling rotors would dig into the ground, and the machine would be wrecked! The men inside would be wounded or killed.

The forces would call in more helicopters to get out the wounded. Soon they would be seen coming through the red sky of dawn. Slashing the air with tremendous downdraft, they would come down. The soldiers would slip the litters aboard onto the chopper floor, with the wounded men tied securely on them. The choppers would leap skyward in strong, wild swirls of dust again, and soon they would be up and out of gun range!

But sometimes the choppers were hit very badly by the Vietcong snipers and would be so riddled and torn that they could barely make it back to a military hospital.

5

Leprosy Can Be Cured!

WE HAVE MINISTERED to people with leprosy in Vietnam for over twenty years. In 1950 we opened a leprosarium at Banmethuot among the Raday and Mnong tribes in the southern highlands of South Vietnam. This work has been carried on by missionary medical personnel of the Christian and Missionary Alliance ever since.

In 1957 the care of the people with leprosy in central Vietnam, from the Da Nang, Hue, and Quang Ngai areas, was laid upon our hearts. Government officials said they would be pleased if we could establish another leprosarium, saying that this would ease the burden considerably of the leprosy problem which rested upon the government's shoulders.

They gave us a beautiful site at the foot of mighty 5,000-foot Bana Mountain, twelve miles from Da Nang. Gordon and faithful Vietnamese Pastor Lich and Pastor Yen, all eagerly interested in helping the people with leprosy, reveled in making these wooded foothills into a "Happy Haven" for the afflicted ones! Pleasant waterfalls and streams rushing down the mountainsides were harnessed to become a fine running-water system through two-inch pipes for the camp. Buildings were put up, some quickly with mud and bamboo with grass-thatched roofs, and some permanent buildings of cement.

All was going well in establishing this base, and we found that we were truly in the day of healing for the people with leprosy. A great major breakthrough has come for these afflicted ones throughout the world. Leprosy can be cured! This is the day of opportunity for the leprosy sufferers.

The treatment is Dapsone, one of the derivatives of D.D.S.

(Diamino-Diphenyl-Sulphone). It is in the form of small pills to be given carefully and in regular doses. This is great drama in the treatment of this age-old disease, and there is wonderful success in healing it today.

Dr. Stanley G. Browne, director of the Leprosy Study Center in London, England, declares in his book on leprosy control: "If existing knowledge about leprosy were conscientiously and persistently applied, the disease could be *controlled* in our generation and *eradicated* in the next!"

How wonderful to be having a part in helping to control and eradicate this dread disease! The drug Dapsone has been available for over twenty years now, and during this time millions throughout the world, in leprosariums, hospitals, and out-patient clinics, have been cured of leprosy.

Dapsone, given by mouth, is simple and cheap, about $4.00 a year per patient. Usually after eight or nine months of carefully supervised, regular treatment of Dapsone pills, the patients cease to give the disease to others. So if we can regularly treat everybody who has the contagious kind of leprosy, this will solve the problem of leprosy.

We were seeing good results of healing among our patients. The microscope revealed that many had become "negative," free from any sign of active leprosy. But they would have to

The new leprosarium at Cam Hai had to be abandoned because of Communist terrorism.

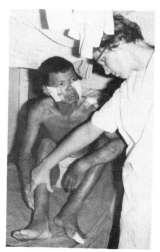

Swiss nurse, Simone Haywood, treats leprosy patient.

26

be examined at regular intervals to see that the leprosy bacilli were not reactivating. Maybe some germs might be hidden and the medicine had not reached them. Then these germs would start to work after lying asleep for a long time. But more treatment of Dapsone would soon reach them.

Also, our patients were being given the wonderful fellowship of Jesus Christ. It would not be a true victory unless the patient had spiritual regeneration too! Jesus showed great concern for the hungry and sick, bringing them help and comfort. But He also said, "What shall it profit a man, if he shall gain the whole world, and lose his own soul?"

The physical aid is a great instrument in bringing the leprosy patient to God. Practically the whole colony at Bana had accepted Christ as Saviour and Lord.

Then in 1960 the Vietcong Communists from their mountain hideout began terrorist attacks on our Bana Leprosy Settlement. The Christian village of An Loi, next to the leprosarium, with its little church built by the people, was destroyed. The Communists would come, demanding food and money, and if it was not given to them, they would kill the people. So the villagers in all this Bana section were fleeing closer to Da Nang for protection.

It was too dangerous to keep our patients in this Vietcong infested area, so we rejoiced when the South Vietnam government gave us a new site for our leprosarium at a place called Cam Hai. This was a sandy stretch of land near the sea, two miles from the Marble Mountains on the outskirts of Da Nang.

Then came the colossal task of building again! It took great courage to start anew after seven years of careful, patient planning, building, and getting settled in the beautiful Bana foothills! The patients had been so happy there.

But in six months' time, ten buildings were erected in the new "Happy Haven" at Cam Hai. There was a large hospital with two long dormitories, toilets and baths, storehouse, kitchen, dining room, and two bungalows for the nursing staff.

We did not employ an architect or contractor, but Gordon and Mr. Lich, who is now superintendent of the leprosarium, did all the planning, along with forty-six leprosy patients and twenty other Vietnamese workmen helping. They put up many substantial structures at low cost.

Some of the buildings and rooms were built with funds sent as memorials to loved ones, and small marble plaques with the memorial names on them, were placed over the respective doors.

The building materials were of hard wood from the Bana mountain forests cut by some of the patients. The walls were made of cement blocks, plastered over smoothly with cement. The roofs were made of heavy cement tiles, colored a dusty rose. The wooden doors and window frames of all the buildings were painted french blue, and the cement walls were whitewashed a light cream.

This Happy Haven Leprosarium nestled amid a forest of long-leaf pine trees and overlooked the turquoise blue South China Sea only a few hundred yards away. There were continuous breezes, and everyone who visited the spot exclaimed at its beauty.

It was not long until supplies of medical equipment arrived from the government health departments, and some more buildings were completed. The Minister of Health and other high Vietnamese officials were invited for the dedication service.

We brought in all of our patients from Bana, people from all over the province, and 150 leprosy patients who had been waiting so long in poor, miserable accommodations at the Da Nang and Hue City hospitals. It was a joy to start caring for them in this new, happy home.

When Jesus was here on earth, He was moved with compassion every time He saw a person with leprosy. It says in Luke 5:12-13 that "a man full of leprosy" came to the Master.

What does "full of leprosy" mean? It means that the man's face is distorted by large, fleshy tumors, and is puffed up and deeply furrowed. His nose is sunken in and his lips are swollen and cracked. His ears have enlarged and are covered with beady nodules. His hands have lost fingers and are swollen and covered with sores. His toes are mostly gone and he has ulcers on his feet.

This caricature of humanity catches the Master's eye and in

Jesus' look, he sees love and an invitation to "come"! So this poor, wretched man edges toward the Master. No man dares touch him, to stop him. As he prostrates himself on the ground at Jesus' feet, he cries, "If You want to, Lord, You can make me clean!"

We are startled by Christ's reply, "Of course I want to!" Then the Lord places His hand on this poor man and His confident words ring out, "You are clean!"

We can hear the gasp of the crowd, "Look! Look! He touches him!"

And then, the stunned amazement! With one stroke of divine, artistic genius, Jesus restores that man to his former beauty! The man with leprosy arises *whole!*

Jesus commands *us* to "Heal the sick, cleanse the lepers . . . freely ye have received, freely give." "Comfort ye! Comfort ye my people, saith your God" (Mt 10:8; Is 40:1).

On the gateposts to our "Happy Haven" were carved on marble plaques the words in Vietnamese and in English: "WHERE LEPERS ARE CLEANSED AND THE POOR HAVE THE GOSPEL PREACHED UNTO THEM" (see Lk 7:22).

The patients were happy in their fine new living quarters. Kind Vietnamese nurses were there in their white uniforms, binding up the hideous sores of leprosy, evil-smelling and nauseating.

A young registered nurse from Switzerland, Simone DuBois, and her fiancé, John Haywood from England, came to head up the leprosarium work. Soon they were married in our chapel at Da Nang and over a hundred guests, Vietnamese and missionaries, were at their lovely wedding. They then went to the Happy Healing Leprosarium on Hay Ling Chau Island near Hong Kong and took the special training course there on the treatment of leprosy. This was of great value to them in helping in our leprosarium work.

But the communist Vietcong began coming in from the jungle mountains here also, infiltrating this whole area south of Da Nang! Two years previously, in 1962, Dr. Eleanor Vietti and a missionary practical nurse the Reverend Archie

Mitchell, both of the Christian and Missionary Alliance, and a helper from the Mennonite Central Committee, Dan Gerber, were all captured by the Communists in the Banmethuot Leprosarium and carried away, perhaps over the mountains and up to North Vietnam. No word was ever heard of them throughout the years.

Now Simone and John did not dare go out to our Cam Hai Happy Haven Leprosarium for fear they would be kidnapped like those at Banmethuot.

The American marines and Vietnamese soldiers were out in this section now, raiding the communist underground dugout camps every week.

Once a whole group of Communists poured into Happy Haven for shelter from an attack by the American and Vietnamese troops nearby. The marines and Vietnamese spotted them by helicopter from the air, and paratroopers were dropped into our leprosarium. They caught fifty Communists, but about twenty others jumped into the leprosy patients' beds and covered themselves up with the patients' blankets, some even quickly putting on fake bandages! Our patients feared the Communists so they didn't dare tell the Americans. However, a count of the patients was given to the marines, and the Communists were not able to play this trick again.

When Jesus was here on earth, the people asked Him, "Who is our neighbor?"

Jesus answered, "These poor, suffering, hurt ones—they are your neighbors! Go like the good Samaritan did—go where the patient is; pour in oil and wine: bind up his wounds; lift him up and care for him. Do likewise!" (See Lk 10:29-37).

We must put out our hands like Jesus did and touch these people with leprosy.

We sent out urgent calls for friends in America and England to pray fervently for our leprosarium in this time of war, for our nurses and national evangelists working among the patients, and that many would "touch" these needy ones through their sympathy and gifts. We must each *do* something!

We, with the gifts from you friends at home, build their houses and make their beds. You send us bandages and some of these poor ones had never seen a nice, white, soft, clean bandage before! You help us give them soap and some of them never had a cake of soap in all their lives before! They are overjoyed to receive the lovely clothing you send in boxes. Your gifts help us to buy cooking pots for them and to put some food into their cooking pots for their poor, thin, emaciated bodies.

It is so wonderful to share in all this work!

> I can hear my Saviour calling,
> I can hear my Saviour calling,
> I can hear my Saviour calling,
> Take your cross and follow,
>   follow Me!
>
> Where He leads me, I will follow,
> Where He leads me, I will follow,
> Where He leads me, I will follow,
> I'll go with Him, with Him,
>   all the way!
>
> E. W. Blandy

6

The Jeh Turn to Christ

IT WAS THE FIRST FURLOUGH TIME for our son and daughter-in-law, Stanley and Ginny, and their two children, Kenny, then two years old, and Karen, two months old. They had been missionaries for four years in the Kontum District, pioneering at Dak To. Now they were going home to America in July, 1964.

So before they left, Gordon and I visited with them in their new house they had built at Dak To. They, with our other missionaries had been at Da Nang for a national workers conference, and we accompanied them back to Kontum on an Air Vietnam plane.

It was dangerous now to go by road from Da Nang to Kontum, as there were many Vietcong ambushes and kidnappings on the roads, especially going from Qui Nhon up into the mountains of An-Khe, Pleiku, and Kontum.

It was cool and rainy in the highlands, which felt good to us after the torrid heat of the dry months of June and July in Da Nang.

We had good fellowship and a Vietnamese meal with our national workers, Mr. and Mrs. Kinh, at Kontum. This is the important frontier town of the Sedang, Halang, Bahnar, and Jeh tribes. They were starting a Christian public school next to the church which God would use to His glory in the future days.

Then Stanley drove us in the afternoon in their old Land Rover to their station, thirty-five miles north at Dak To. The road was well paved most of the way, but Vietnamese military trucks came driving at high speeds, and Stan would have to quickly pull off the road to get out of their way. Also the Rover's old tires were very worn.

Here in the heart of Sedang tribal country, we were delighted to see the new house, just completed by Stan after much hard work. He built it like an old-time French plantation house, high up from the ground on cement pillars with a garage underneath. It was nice to be up high after our low tropical bungalow at Da Nang, and we drank in the sweet, cool mountain air. Dak To is 2,200 feet high, and eddies of perfume floated in from the surrounding mountainsides and forests. The house had wide windows and doors opening onto verandas, facing ranges of green, blue, and purple mountains rolling off into the distance. Dry rice fields of Sedang tribespeople sloped down the hillsides in the foreground. Gibbon apes called from the jungle, and early in the morning their hooting resounded from every side.

Tribespeople walked down the road in front of Stan's house all day, carrying baskets on their backs loaded with things to trade for salt, brown sugar, copper wire for bracelets, and many other goods at the Dak To market. In their baskets were horns of deer, a skin of a leopard or a tiger, wild honey, sweet potatoes, manioc, and other jungle produce. Some of the tribeswomen walked at such a brisk pace that their baskets seemed to float on their backs.

It was a fascinating scene, but we were brought up quickly when we thought of the Communist guerrillas roaming the jungles not far away. Stan and Ginny's house stood isolated several miles from any protecting fort. It was dangerous to drive north on the roads past Dak To to visit the many tribal villages in their district and to go on to the Jeh tribal centers of Dak Sut and Dak Pek. Mines were often laid by the Communists in the roads, and cars and trucks were blown up.

Military trucks loaded with Vietnamese soldiers and equipment were continually roaring by on their way to a big operation. The sky was full of helicopters whirling along, while fighter bombers outsped them higher in the sky.

The next day the trucks returned empty, and we knew the helicopters were probably carrying back the wounded and dead.

Nevertheless, we enjoyed our week with our dear ones. They

were busy packing everything away before leaving for furlough in ten days' time, so I spent a lot of the time entertaining little Kenny with stories and motion songs. I couldn't tell him enough. We'd talk over everything in both English and Vietnamese. He understood many of the things more clearly in the Vietnamese language.

It was also a joy to hold little rosebud Karen, sitting on the high veranda facing the west, watching some wonderful sunsets glowing beyond the blue mountains.

It was sad for us to say good-bye as we left the Kontum airport. We missed them greatly as they were home in America for a year of deputation work. They made their headquarters at the home of Ginny's parents, Mr. and Mrs. Ed Scull of Wheaton, Illinois. They had many challenging meetings over the States, with messages and pictures showing their work among the Jeh and Sedang tribes.

Shortly after Gordon and I returned to Da Nang from Kontum, our Bible evangelistic car, a gift from our cousins, the Vernon Hedderlys and other friends in England, started off to Kontum with a team of four national preachers and our Vietnamese chairman, Mr. Nhut.

Although it was very dangerous for cars to use the main highways in those war days, yet the valiant Vietnamese evangelists were willing to go for God, trusting in His protection. On this trip they especially claimed the 23rd Psalm: "Yea, though I walk through the valley of the shadow of death, I will fear no evil, for thou art with me." His power is mightier than the power of the Communists.

It was a long trip from Da Nang down the main coastal highway 200 miles to Qui Nhon. Near Mo Duc and Duc Pho, just past Quang Ngai city, the Bible car ran by a battle raging fairly close to the road. A sudden, nerve-jangling thunderclap of shooting broke out, and Tri, the driver, heard a bullet "ping" past the car as he tore along.

At Bong Son, farther along the coastal road, the evangelists met preacher Soc and his twenty Christians. Our station of Kim Son in this section, twenty miles back in the mountains among the Bahnar tribespeople, had been overrun by the Com-

Preacher Trien looks over Jeh villages at Dak Pek before they went underground. He was captured in 1972, and no word has been heard of him since.

munists even then in 1964. Soc was still able to go into An Lao, another backcountry station, to meet with a few Christians once a week. But the Communists were closing in from the mountains and gradually taking over these villages.

While the Bible-car band spent the night with preacher Soc, the Vietcong stole into Bong Son and murdered the village chief in his house, quite near Soc's place. Our workers heard the sad death wails of the stricken family all night long.

The preachers left the car at the coastal city of Qui Nhon and took the local train fifteen miles to the station of Phuoc Lanh in the foothills among the Cham Bahnar and Hroy tribespeople. The train ride was risky for fear of Communist mines and attacks, but to go by car would have been more dangerous. Almost every day the road was mined. A truck had been blown up near Phuoc Lanh just the day before.

Pastor Vui was working there among the Bahnar-Cham tribespeople who met regularly in a chapel. Later on, the Communists came in and several thousand of these tribespeople fled as refugees out near the coast. Over 200 of them have become Christians, and our workers are caring for them today at Tuy Hoa and Dong Tre.

From Qui Nhon, the workers turned west from the coast and drove into the mountains sixty miles to An-Khe where they had three days of special meetings with the An-Khe evangelist and a group of Christians. Then they went to Kontum and had meetings with the workers in the church and school there.

Arriving at Dak Sut at noon, they wanted to go twenty miles farther to Dak Pek for their noon meal. But they decided that since Mr. Thuong, the worker at Dak Pek, was a bachelor, and food was hard to find there in the interior, they would stay with the preacher, Mr. An, and his wife at Dak Sut for lunch.

During the noon hour a soldier arrived to tell them that the civil guards, who were scouting the road, found two automatic mines recently laid between Dak Sut and Dak Pek! The Bible car would have been the first vehicle to use the road and hit the mines freshly hidden in the car tracks! So God had led them to stay behind for lunch while the civil guard scouted the road.

The mines were taken to the authorities at Dak Pek, and the guards were rewarded $15 for finding them.

With this testimony of God's care, and feeling greatly strengthened in their faith, the band went on their way rejoicing. When they reached Dak Pek, they found that Mr. Thuong was away on an eight-day trip preaching in the Jeh tribal villages. Mr. Nhut was told that many of the Jeh people had turned to God and were meeting in the Dak Pek chapel with Thuong every Sunday.

The Bible-car party set out to find Thuong in the Jeh territory, calling at Ben Sial.

Yes, Thuong had been there, the Jeh village chief said, and he had preached to the people, but then he had gone on to another Jeh village. They drove on to the next place and Thuong had been there too, but had gone on farther.

They then came to the Dak Ro Tah center where our missionaries, Dr. Harverson and Oliver Trebilco, had begun work among the Jeh several years previously and then had to leave because of the Communists coming in. Soon after that, two of our Vietnamese workers, Tri, now the Bible car driver, and An, the preacher at Dak Sut, had been captured by the Communists when the enemy came in to Dak Ro Tah and burned down the fort and tribal villages. A battle had raged for several hours. But An had been able to escape from the Communists by hiding behind a rushing waterfall; and after they had marched Tri six days into the mountain jungles, the Communists let him and some of the other prisoners go again, a miracle of God. (These stories are told in *Victory in Viet-Nam*.) Now Thuong was back preaching in this center again.

"He preaches wonderfully in the Jeh language," the chief of Dak Ro Tah said.

All the Jeh villages were enthusiastic over Thuong, and the district chief told Mr. Nhut, "We would like you to send us another preacher just like Thuong. There are two or more Jeh villages here, near Dak Ro Tah, that want to believe on the Lord Jesus Christ right now, but they must have a preacher to help them. The government leaders were going to call in a Roman Catholic priest to preach to them, but the people refused. Then the government said they would send a Buddhist priest, but the villagers cried, 'No, we want a preacher of your Protestant mission.'"

Mr. Nhut wept as he told us this on his return to Da Nang. He is so thrilled at the earnest way Mr. Thuong, this solitary pioneer in a harsh, war-torn land of mountains and jungle, is giving himself wholeheartedly to the Jeh people.

They drove on for a half hour farther from Dak Ro Tah to Dak Ru Dak, a walk of two hours for Thuong, for they now found out that he was visiting all these villages, on this eight-day trip, by foot. There they found Thuong.

This village is on the new highway from Dak Ro Tah leading through the mountains to Phuoc Son and Thanh My, a tribal territory closed to us at that time by the Communists, who are still hiding there.

Thuong, a frail little man of ninety pounds, was thinner than ever, and his heart was bothering him after so much climbing in the mountains. But he found it easier to walk than to pump his bicycle up the steep inclines. We prayed that we might be able to buy him a motorcycle.

Thuong joined the evangelistic party in the Bible car and they all drove back to Dak Sut. There was a big fortified re-settlement village called Plei Bom near this Dak Sut center, and Stanley, Ginny, Gordon, and I and a Vietnamese evangelist, Mr. Tuu, had visited there over a year before. We remembered its fortifications against the Communists: four high fences of sharpened stakes and bamboos, interlaced with sword-sharp pickets and barbed wire. Each house had a dugout under it, for this was enemy territory.

At the time of our visit a Christian Jeh schoolboy, about thirteen years old, had died, and his family was preparing a big funeral for him. Tuu preached to the people that day and challenged them all to believe in Christ as this schoolboy had done. Several families in this village soon accepted Christ under the ministry of Tuu and his Jeh Christian worker, Ngo, and Stanley and Ginny. Thuong also had been visiting here with Preacher An, of Dak Sut.

When the evangelistic car and party arrived and held more meetings, the *whole* village of 347 people said they wanted to accept Christ! This was the first big break among the Jeh tribe of 8,000 people who today have all accepted Christ except for 500 people who we believe will soon join the others. This means that practically the whole Jeh tribe is Christ's today, and the village of Plei Bom was among the first to catch the revival fire in this area.

The villagers came forward in a great mass, holding up their hands at the invitation to follow Jesus! Soon they brought heaps of their old sacrificial altars, buffalo heads and other animal skulls, stones, beads, little models of Jeh coffins "that hold the spirits of the dead," and pieces of poison wrapped in cotton!

They called to the preachers, "Come into our longhouses and help us gather up all the remains of our old devil-worship stuff! We want to 'cut all the ropes' that hold us to the old life. We shall always be slaves to these devil spirits while we have their charms in our houses. So we want to gather them all up now and have you help us burn them."

Even the sorcerers came, believing in Christ, along with all the village people. When sorcerers give up their authority, their hold over the ignorant, and all the gifts they take because of their lies and deceit, this is truly a miracle!

So the Vietnamese preachers, with the Jeh tribespeople, gathered all the old skulls, stones, beads, altars, certain sacred tree branches, and feathers, and they filled the back of the Bible car with their collection.

Mr. Nhut preached some more, and Thuong, An, Tuu, and Ngo all gave stirring messages. Then they had a great bonfire. On top of a big heap of dry branches they threw the old gourds, masks, vertebrae bones of snakes, all the foolish, old things by which the sorcerers had told gigantic lies, pretending to see the future. Then a firebrand was set to the pile. There was a crisp, crackling sound as flames leaped several feet high. The place was still with awe! This was defiance of the evil spirits. Some trembled and wondered what the demons would do. But the evangelists broke out into their favorite chorus, which they always sing as souls are coming to Christ: "Hallelujah! Thine the glory!" and soon all the Jeh joined in singing to God, "Hallelujah! Amen! Hallelujah! Thine the glory! Revive us again!"

The spell was broken! They had burned their links with the past and had defied the evil spirits. And nothing had happened! God Almighty was stronger than the demons! They had put their trust in Him! Now they were free!

Many more Jeh villages were to follow Plei Bom in receiving Christ as their Saviour. The break had begun. The fires were spreading!

Tri, the driver-evangelist, saved a few of the devil-worship things for me as he usually does. I take some home with me to America on furlough to show to the people. From the village of Plei Bom, Tri brought me a fancy stone of pointed quartz that looked like a crystal flower. To the heathen tribesmen any object out of the ordinary is considered supernatural, with a spirit living in it. He brought a string of old, odd-shaped stone beads, and little quills that held bits of shining micah, which they offered to the spirits as they sacrificed. There were small bamboo tubes to "hold part of the soul" of someone who had died; a little model Jeh coffin, also holding "part of a soul," and a piece of poison, used to murder their enemies, wrapped in cotton dyed in blood! The Jeh had also given Tri one of their old sacrificed buffalo skulls with its huge horns for me.

How wonderful it was to see these poor, primitive Jeh tribespeople give up these awful superstitions of heathen darkness and come into the light of life through the power of our Lord.

When Gordon first saw these Jeh people in 1937, he thought they were about the lowest, most primitive people in all Vietnam. Surely they would be the *last* that could ever be reached by the Gospel. But these people, hidden far off in high mountains and down in deep secret valleys, had been brought in by the South Vietnamese government because of the war, to big fortified resettlement camps. So they could hear the Gospel at last after all those dark centuries, and they were responding to God in this marvelous way! "Surely the wrath of man shall praise thee" (Ps 76:10).

In 1964 and continuing to the present, God was again fulfilling His wonderful promise to us in our life verses of Isaiah 45: 1-3, that in spite of the war and "crooked places," He would give us "the treasures of darkness, and hidden riches of secret places."

7

Forsake Not the Children

"WHERE IS MY MOTHER?"

"I want to go home."

"I saw my mother get killed in the battle."

"My father was shot dead!"

"What are they going to do to us here?"

They were twelve little Katu tribes children whose parents had been killed in battle. They ranged from about two to seven years of age.

As the American officers brought them to our orphanage, the kiddies clung to the soldiers' legs for they already loved these men. The children were decked out in oversized GI shirts and pieces of clothing. Their faces were clean and their hair combed. Their great dark eyes were afraid of us, and they didn't want to leave the American officers.

None of these Katu tribes children spoke Vietnamese. We quickly placed our Katu tribes preacher, Mr. Trien, at our orphanage for a month or so, to help them get settled and to calm their fears. They were asking Trien questions now in the Katu language, and he was comforting them.

Some American officers in Vietnam, U.S. Special Forces advisers, with a team of Vietnamese soldiers, had been patrolling in the jungle forty miles from Da Nang. Suddenly they were attacked by a staccato burst of machine gun fire from a Katu tribal village under the control of the Communists. The place was strongly fortified with high fences of sharpened bamboo stakes. Bamboo staves, that could cut like knives, poisoned at the tips, were stuck in the ground, bristling thickly all around the fences. A battle followed with both men and women of the Katu tribe firing at the Americans and the Vietnamese.

41

It was some time before the battle was over, and many from our side were wounded. The American officers entered the village and found Laotian, North Vietnamese, and Katu Communists there, mostly lying dead on the ground. All the others had fled.

There was one wounded Katu man whom they took as a prisoner, and just one living Katu woman was left. Her baby had been killed in her arms as a bullet went through her wrist. Another of her children was dead and a two-year-old little girl clung to her skirt alive. This woman, with her children around her and one in her arms, had fought as savagely as the others, having been trained to shoot by the Communists.

Now, in the midst of the dead, stood twelve little Katu children. One was a small three-year-old girl who had a piece of shrapnel through her thigh, and her face was laid open by a grenade. Another little girl had been desperately ill before the battle. The soldiers found her with mastoid trouble, a suppurating hole behind her ear. Others had wounds in their arms or legs.

The officers told us, "At first they were like little wild animals. We picked them up from among the dead Communists, and we led them down the jungle path to where we had our helicopter pad. As we tried to put them into the helicopter, they would speedily climb out again as fast as little monkeys. They were terrified of the slashing rotor blades and the roaring engine."

But finally the American soldiers got the wounded woman and her little girl and the other twelve children into the helicopter and off they whirled, taking the wounded and sick to the Da Nang hospital. They kept the well children in their own military fort for a couple of weeks.

"We finally got them housebroken," one officer told us. "It was fun seeing them march out to the washhouse in a single file every morning, like a line of ducklings."

Now they had brought them to our China Beach Orphanage, and we gave each child a new bed. The beds are double-decker iron beds, and the Katu liked being near each other. We fitted them all out with new clothes and shoes from boxes sent by

American friends. Until they received the GI shirts, they had only known tiny loincloths for clothing in the jungle. Now they were pleased with their nice American children's clothes and shoes! They had never worn shoes in their lives before! Also they received a blanket each.

But for the first night or two they cried themselves to sleep, longing for their dead loved ones. Then they grew more cheerful and began to play on the swings, slides, and teeter-totters that the American military men had put up for the orphans. They especially liked the slide; even the two-year-olds wanted to climb up and slide down into the soft sand.

Forty other children were in the orphanage at that time in 1964. So the Katu tribes children soon were learning Vietnamese words. The older children went to the primary class in the orphanage school and learned to read and write in Vietnamese.

As they lived at the orphanage, they learned of Jesus. After a year's time, they all became Christians. Some of the older ones were baptized in the ocean at our Easter sunrise service in 1965.

I called one of the little Katu girls "My Little Girl." She has great brilliant black eyes and a merry smile. Her name is Phia. Now, eight years later, she has been adopted by the Minister for Mountaineer Affairs, representing the tribes in the South Vietnam government of Saigon. He is a Jarai tribesman and a Christian, so Phia has a nice home in Saigon and is being well educated.

The American special forces men who brought the Katu children, came occasionally to the orphanage, rigged up four huge nylon parachutes on the beach for shade, and brought hot dogs, hamburgers, chicken, and hundreds of cans of soda pop, making a picnic for the orphans. Afterward, just two of the Katu children had "hangovers." It was a bit more than these jungle children were used to eating and drinking. The barbecued chicken especially had gone over big with them because they could eat it with their fingers, as they were used to doing in the jungle.

The wounds of the Katu orphans soon healed, and they

grew happy and loved to romp and play with the others. They were very affectionate children and liked to be held and hugged.

That is what our orphanage exists for: to help the fatherless and homeless. It is a tremendous joy to take on this responsibility.

We had to keep putting up new dormitories for there were hundreds of children who needed help. Do you think it would be easy and right to turn them away? Jesus said, "Whosoever shall receive one of such children in my name, receiveth me" (Mk 9:37), and "Take heed that ye despise not one of these little ones" (Mt 18:10). The value of a little child is given great emphasis in Scripture.

At this time a doctor and his doctor wife, Dr. and Mrs. Archie Dillard, from Seattle, Washington, both working in Medical Aid under USOM, now USAID, asked us to take a fourteen-year-old boy called Thao. He had had a terrible cancerous growth on his forehead, hanging down over one eye. Dr. Dillard, working in the Da Nang hospital, performed a skillful operation on Thao, removing the tumor and sewing up the wound around his eye. The boy was abandoned by his relatives when he had the tumor because they believed this growth was caused by an evil spirit. So we took Thao into our orphanage. Dr. Dillard feared the cancer might grow again and spread into his brain, but God worked a great miracle in healing Thao.

For some days Thao was very hostile to the Gospel and the meetings at the orphanage. But soon the children's Vietnamese leaders kindly and gently won him to Christ. He became happy and peaceful and was with us for five or more years. He grew into a tall, fine youth, and became a good Christian, surrendering his life fully to God. He has trained as a nurse's aid in two Da Nang hospitals and now helps as a practical nurse on some of our mission stations. He has learned how to clean up badly neglected diseased skin, and has given hundreds of injections without causing a needle abscess. He is being used of the Lord as a young people's worker today.

Around that time, a twelve-year-old Vietnamese boy named Khanh came in from Son Nam, a backcountry village twelve miles behind Quang Ngai where over one hundred Vietnamese Christians had built a church and were meeting regularly. The Vietcong launched many attacks on this peaceful country village. It had prosperous green rice fields all around it, and the village was thickly planted with trees of delicious fruits. Each little home had its own garden for vegetables and its own poultry and livestock.

The Son Nam people were eager to go on learning of God under their pastor and meeting in their church. It had been a pleasure for us to visit this village in the past and to camp there with the people and help minister to them.

Then the Communists came and there was heavy fighting. Khanh's mother and three younger brothers and sister were killed. His father, tiny sister, and himself were the only ones left in the family.

Again war broke out as the Communists tried to capture the village with its rich rice fields. Planes came in to bomb!

"Run into the dugout hiding place!" cried Khanh's father. Khanh ran, but the father himself took the little girl and ran into his home.

"Father, hurry! Come here with me!" cried Khanh from the dugout shelter. But the father sat on in his house, holding his little girl on his lap and praying. Down came the bombs, bursting in shattering blasts!

When Khanh got out of the shelter hole a few minutes later, there was nothing left of his home, his father, or sister! It was a devastating tragedy for Khanh who was all alone now.

One of his little village friends, twelve years old like himself, had been badly wounded in the attack. Khanh bravely took this boy on his back and ran through the Vietcong lines, calling on God to take them through safely to Quang Ngai, twelve miles away. God did. Khanh, still lugging his friend on his back, came to the Medico Hospital founded some years before by Project Concern, associated with the Dr. Tom Dooley Association. They took in the wounded child for treatment, and Khanh told them, "I'm going on to the China Beach Orphanage up at Da Nang. Maybe they'll take care of me."

He came up the one hundred miles from Quang Ngai to Da Nang, tired and worn, with his sad little face.

"May I come here to stay?" he pleaded with the orphanage heads. The lonely child was welcomed in.

Khanh's father had been a deacon in the Son Nam church and was one of the first to believe in Christ in that backcountry area.

Khanh is still with us today, eight years later. He is just finishing high school. All through these years, he's been a fine testimony for Christ in the orphanage and has offered his life to God to train to be a preacher.

His village of Son Nam, with all the other villages in that prosperous rice farming area, came under communist control. We had several small churches there, and they all were destroyed. But the people fled with their Vietnamese pastors as refugees to the outskirts of Quang Ngai where they have set up refugee villages during the last seven or eight years. They have built five small temporary wooden churches with tin roofs in their different sections, and they long for the day when they can return to their own villages.

Our orphanage kept on expanding. We took in ten Cham-Bahnar tribal children from Phuoc Lanh, near Qui Nhon who had been orphaned in the war and were left destitute.

Then nine Jeh orphan boys were brought by Pastor An from Dak Pek. Later on, two of these, A-Ron and A-Yen, studied in our Da Nang Bible school three years. They are preachers today to their Jeh people in the Kontum District, and God is using them greatly.

More and more Vietnamese children whose parents were killed in the war entered our orphanage. We became busy building a long L-shaped building with a wide veranda facing the sea. Solidly made of cement with red cement tiles for roofing, it provided dormitory space for 125 children, with toilets and baths, several staff rooms, and a small apartment for a missionary nurse. We praised God for making all of this possible in two or three years' time!

The U.S. Armed Forces became more and more interested in our China Beach Orphanage. It was the American men who gave the orphanage this name. Its true Vietnamese name is My-Khe, named after the section of the ocean beach where it is located. But the Americans found this name hard to pronounce, so they called it "China Beach Orphanage," since it is on the shore of the South China Sea.

The American men gave us a lot of practical help in putting in electric wiring and pumps, and painting the rooms. Besides giving gifts of money to help run the orphanage, they sometimes brought American food, treats of oranges, apples, meat, milk and vegetables. They brought American soap, and games the children love, like Monopoly and Chinese checkers, and furnishings for the rooms.

Many of the men enjoyed visiting the children because they reminded them of their own children at home.

A gift of $1,000.00 was given to help build the long L-shaped building by the American consul at Hue. Mr. and Mrs. Helble had lost a beautiful two-year-old daughter when she drowned in their garden pool while playing with some tiny ducks. So part of this building is in memory of Cindy Ly Helble.

Substantial gifts also came from Oxfam in England. The orphanage was to be expanded until it could accommodate and train 350 children. Our next project would be to build a large chapel with many schoolrooms underneath.

8

Offshore Islands: A New Mission Field

TWO OFFSHORE CORAL ISLANDS waiting for the Gospel message! We were the only Protestant mission responsible for getting the Gospel to these unreached island people.

The war here did not reach these two islands out in the ocean, thirty miles offshore. They have been well guarded against the Communists by the Americans and Vietnamese. The door has been wide open the last ten years to take the Gospel to these free people. Many thousands of refugees fleeing from war zones on the mainland have flocked to these lovely islands for safety. It is a great mission field today!

Gordon and I with some Vietnamese evangelists went there by our first mission boat, the *Hope*, a fifty-foot motor launch with a deep keel and a seventy horsepower diesel engine. Nam, the pilot, and his helper, Tam, manned the boat, with Gordon occasionally taking the wheel or overseeing the engine. We had been preaching on these two islands from time to time for two years, ever since we had built the mission launch.

At Ly Son Island, one hundred miles south of Da Nang, with its population of 7,000 fishermen, a Vietnamese pastor and his wife, Mr. and Mrs. Huk (pronounced "Hook") were there at that time, and there was a small group of new Christians.

At Cu-Lao Cham Island, thirty miles across from Da Nang, the people were asking for an evangelist to stay with them and teach them more of the Gospel.

So on this trip we were taking preacher Bui Bao and his wife to place them as the resident evangelists on this island of 350 fishermen.

Our cook Anh Hai, was along. He had a wrinkled, lively face, like a quaint old faun and jumped gaily about as he cooked on our little primus stove in a spot sheltered from breezes at the back of the boat.

Our four-hour trip from Da Nang across the open sea to Cu-Lao Cham Island was a delight. It was a calm, warm morning and we enjoyed the smoothness of the motion as we glided down the Da Nang River and Bay, past the green mountains of the Son Cha Peninsula. American soldiers, in their huge radar station on top of the peninsula, named it "Monkey Mountain" because of there being so many species of monkeys there.

Then we were out on the broad ocean. The sky and vast waters were a pale, pastel blue and we gazed at the beauty of the rows of Vietnamese fishing boats gently rocking in the wide, smooth swells. We joined our Vietnamese workers in singing hymns, and they talked and laughed all the way.

The Cu-Lao Cham Island is made up of several great rocky mountains towering up into the sky. The 350 people on the island can only live in two or three sandy coves at the foot of the rocky cliffs. The mountainsides are covered with heavy undergrowth full of bamboo shrubs, wild banana plants, and giant trees of the forest. Vines tangle and festoon themselves madly over the trees and huge rocks. Monkeys and big snakes, pythons and cobras, are abundant on the mountains.

The waters approaching Cu-Lao Cham were a vivid green blue, crystal clear because of the white coral bottom all around the island. No rivers empty silt into these clear waters.

Nam steered the boat into a small bay. Before us lay a broad stretch of soft, warm sand over which hung graceful palm trees. The little thatched bamboo huts of the Vietnamese islanders were framed in among the palms. Many fishing boats with their great brown nets made of coconut fibers were drawn up on the beach.

The *Hope* had to anchor a little way offshore where the water was about fifteen feet deep. Some of the young islanders splashed out into the water and came swimming with dog-paddle strokes to see our motor launch and us.

Then, three at a time, we got into a little waterproofed basket coracle, which was the lifeboat for the *Hope*, and Tam sculled us with a wriggling motion of his paddle in to shore. We carried tracts, flannelgraphs, pictures, and Gospels to bring the message of life to these waiting islanders.

They have believed through the centuries in Buddhism .and ancestor worship, like the Vietnamese on the mainland, but they also believe in Taoism and animism. They greatly fear the demons and ghosts whom they think try to get into their homes, sailboats, and even into their bodies. They believe it is the evil spirits who make them sick. They call in Taoist sorcerers who they think have the power to drive away these evil spirits.

These sorcerers deceive the people with tricks and lies. They tie amulets, small packages of "magic" stones, bones, and feathers, around the people's necks and put cords on the babies' wrists, necks, and ankles to keep out the demons of sickness.

The people also worship a white whale and have some of its bones in shrines. They say that long ago this whale saved some drowning fishermen and it has very special magic for them.

The islanders had not been too friendly toward the Gospel, but this time they seemed to be a little more openhearted so we began to search for a house to rent for Bui Bao. The people all live in small bamboo shacks crowded together under palm trees in the sandy beach coves. It seemed impossible to find any extra space in a house for Bui Bao and his wife. But finally, one family moved out of their tiny shack and went to live in their parents' house, renting the shack to us for four months or so. In the meantime we looked to God to help us build a little home and chapel on the seashore for the Bui Baos.

Gordon led all of us in the party to the village chief's house and asked his permission to preach to the people. This was granted and the Vietnamese evangelist quickly set up some Gospel posters and a hymn sheet on the beach. We all began to sing and soon a crowd gathered under the coconut palms. We began to teach the people the hymn, "The Light of the World Is Jesus." Soon the boys and girls learned some of the lines by heart.

We preached Jesus then as the "Light of the World." One evangelist held up a large colored picture of Jesus standing in the darkness, holding in His hand a brilliant light. The evangelist told the people, "Jesus Christ is the only light to bring us out of our dark ways of fear and evil."

I showed a flannelgraph story of Christ healing the blind man in John 9. One worker, pointing to the pictures of the blind man, testified, "I was once blind like that man. Then my eyes were opened and I saw how I had been following lies and superstitions. Jesus is the truth and His light reveals the dark, false beliefs."

All the workers witnessed of how "the idols of Buddha, the tablets of the ancestors, and the whale bones here in Cu-Lao Cham cannot hear prayers. But Jesus, God's living Son, hears us. We can talk to Him, and He is beside us and gives us strength. He guides us with the light of His Word."

Gordon held up the Bible and proclaimed, "In this Book lies the light of God. Jesus says here: 'I am the light of the world: he that followeth me shall not walk in darkness, but shall have the light of life" (Jn 8:12). We all sang again, "The Light of the World Is Jesus."

Then we gave the people some Bible pictures and posters that they could put up on the walls in their homes, and we handed out many Vietnamese tracts and Gospel portions.

It was now suppertime so we were all paddled back to the boat. Anh Hai had a good supper for us of fresh fish he had bought from one of the fishing junks just returned with a catch. He had fried the fish, just five minutes out of the water into the pan, on the little stove and they were crisp and delicious with lime fruit drinks.

The Vietnamese workers, eating with their chopsticks, had their bowls of rice, bits of vegetables, pieces of fish, red peppers, all dipped into Nuoc Mam, their fish sauce.

We all had oranges and pineapples for dessert and drank shallow bowls full of hot, scented pale green tea from a teapot kept in a padded basket.

We had another meeting with the islanders that night by the light of lanterns on the shore. How we all rejoiced when two of

51

the island people came forward and accepted Jesus Christ as their own Saviour and the light of their lives.

It was so good to be free from the Communists over here on the island! Not many months later, 3,000 refugees fled here and 15,000 to Ly Son Island, to be safe from the Communists on the mainland. So Bui Bao had a big field in which to work.

He soon had built a tiny cement house, and ten Christians were added to his little congregation. A small whitewashed brick chapel was then built, and it is there today as a lighthouse in the darkness of Cu-Lao Cham.

We left the island the next morning at 4 o'clock as Nam said he could tell there would be a high wind later on in the day.

It is a eight-hour trip down to the next island of Ly Son. I went up on deck to watch the ocean. It was still night but our boat was lit up, and lighthouses were flashing from the Da Nang coast and the Son-Cha Peninsula thirty miles away. There was a bright moon going down in the indigo west with a shimmering pathway on the water. Now and then we'd pass a fishing boat, its big lateen sails dark in the moon's path, but lit up with red torch flares so that the fishermen could see to haul in their nets.

The waves were rather high and I was a bit scared up in the prow of the boat for fear I'd fly overboard! But Nam tied my wicker chair well to the mast, and I hung onto the pole when we galloped high upon the waves and then plunged down into the valleys again.

I saw a most dramatic and beautiful sunrise over the ocean. The sun shone great shafts of soft pink light up into an aqua green sky, and there were long belts of purple and rose clouds. The sun rays became more brilliant until at last, at 6:30, the great molten disc itself burst forth in power, glory, and majesty, illuminating the whole ocean floor. I was steeped in beauty!

Around 7 A.M. Gordon, below in the cabin, began to feel "the sea getting him down," so he, too, came up on deck in the cool morning air. We just ate fruit for breakfast as we sat on our chairs in the prow, for Anh Hai was now laid too low with the heaving of the boat to do any cooking and we ourselves would soon be ill if we tried to get the stove going to make coffee.

As we neared Ly-Son Island around noon, the waves were vast, rising up in crests of white foam, trying to sweep over the bow. Gordon and I still sat up in the prow, towering high on the hills of waves and crashing down and wallowing in the foaming valleys. We were indeed riding Thoreau's "galloping white Seahorses!" It was exciting and exhilarating, but I was also a little frightened and I hung onto the mast for dear life. The *Hope* took the crests and valleys well. But all of our Vietnamese workers were prone on the deck, and Anh Hai was groaning down in his bunk.

Turning around the coral reef, which was a mass of crashing, seething waves, we headed into a quiet bay. What great peace at last to drop anchor safely between the angry, boiling coral reefs! The water in the cove was a brilliant green blue, sparkling clear in the sun. We could see coral rocks lying twenty feet below the surface and colored fish swimming about.

We were soon out in our little round wicker coracle paddling in to shore, where the coral rocks come up close to the surface of the water. We were eager to visit with Mr. and Mrs. Huk and their children, who had been preaching on the island for about a year.

We had to walk two miles down the one main pathway of the island to the Huks' home, for we couldn't dock in front of his house because of the coral reefs.

Crowds of dirty, yelling children followed us, as usual, as we walked along, staring and pointing at us as if we were creatures from another world. Although we had visited this island a number of times, still our looks and clothing were strange to them. These children come to our meetings in great numbers as they love to hear the singing and see the pictures of Jesus.

We nearly roasted in the scorching heat of August! Out in the sun it would be over 120 degrees and in the shade, 96 to 98 degrees, devitalizing and suffocating.

But it was a joy to meet with the Huk family and to visit some of the Christians who came to see us.

The 7,000 inhabitants of this seven-mile-long island of Ly-

Son live in tiny grass shacks crowded together in a labyrinth of little winding lanes. All the main roads are hedged in by hibiscus, loaded with red bell flowers practically all year round. Over 15,000 refugees soon began to pour into this island during the dangerous war years, and it became very crowded.

That night we had a good meeting at one end of the island, preaching to a big crowd.

The next morning, Sunday, we again walked the two miles from the boat landing to Huk's house for the morning worship service. They had a little brick building which was used for a small chapel room and living quarters for the Huk family. Forty Christian men and women met every Sunday and on Thursday nights for services. I gave a flannelgraph lesson on one of Christ's parables, and one of the evangelists followed with a Bible message on the putting away of all idol worship.

This island, too, has been steeped in age-old Buddhism, Confucianism, and Taoism. Altars to Buddha, tablets with the names of ancestors, and all sorts of weird charms are in every home. But it was wonderful to see a Christian community growing in faith in Christ.

We ate a rather poor native meal with the Huks. We were sure that the meat was dog meat, as they gave Gordon and me eggs with our rice instead of meat. But the coconut juice was delicious. We could drink it right out of the brimful coconut. It was cool and very sweet, with lots of "soda water" tang.

On the beach two Vietnamese sorcerers were performing a ceremony of chasing evil spirits from a fishing junk. The men wore special red robes and bands around their heads. First they set up a sacrificial offering of fruit, rice, false paper money, and burning joss sticks. Then they went into the stern of the boat and chanted some long prayers. Next they opened up all the holds and boards covering the bottom of the curved junk. One sorcerer threw handfuls of powdered resin into these places and over the fishing nets, and the other held a burning torch to the powder. It exploded with great bangs, and the sorcerers shouted loudly at each fiery blast, "Oop! Pha!" (Get out, Devil!) "Go Con Ma! Con Qui!" (Depart bad spirits of the ocean and the ships!).

The Vietnam fishermen all along the coast have this ceremony performed over their junks so that they'll be kept from danger from the waves and so they'll catch many fish. They are deeply superstitious.

The next morning we left at 4 o'clock again because Nam feared a big storm was brewing. Also Gordon had to get back to his building program at the leprosarium and orphanage.

We had an easy trip home, with the ocean in long, smooth swells again, and I saw another unforgettable sunrise. I sat out on the prow as usual and sang for two hours as I watched the changing colors of violet, rose flush, and crimson. The ocean was like bolts of colored silk, rolling out smoothly and dyed with the sunrise. It took us twelve hours to get home from Ly-Son Island, a distance of about one hundred miles.

Just the next day a big north wind blew, and we got the tail end of the terrible typhoon "Winnie" that hit the Philippines, killing over one hundred people and leaving many homeless! Nam had gotten us home just in time!

We're glad for the few who are responding to the Gospel on these islands. But they are so *few* in comparison to the great number of people who are sinking into a lost eternity. We must get into these islands with young missionaries filled with the Holy Spirit.

May God grant us *action*, recruits of youth who will come crying, "This I will do!"

Our national workers are noble, ready to sacrifice, and have wonderful faith. But they often need the help of a missionary, living with them, and leading them in the hard, discouraging places if the work is to go forward. "How long are we *slack* to go in to *possess* the land?"

> Is it fair
> That others should have all the Light so long?
> We do not ask that they should have the night.
> But when will our turn come to have the Light?
>
> ANONYMOUS

9

At Home in Da Nang

ALTHOUGH GREAT BATTLES were raging around us and it was a hard, critical time, we missionaries lived peacefully in Da Nang. Over 50,000 Americans were around the outskirts of the city in huge marine, air force, army, and naval bases, with helicopter bases for each. Several American military hospitals made from Quonset huts were overflowing and busy night and day.

The United States white naval hospital ships, *Repose* and *Sanctuary*, were anchored in the big Da Nang Bay, especially for the wounded men, choppered in from the battlefields not many minutes after they had been hit. The choppers landed on the rear deck of the ships and the wounded were quickly whisked by hospital orderlies into the operating rooms, within minutes after being with the fighting forces under fire.

Soon the German hospital ship *Helgoland* was anchored in the Da Nang River, where it ministered especially to Vietnamese people. A whole village would be struck by Communist terrorists in the night, and sometimes thirty or more sufferers would be brought to the *Helgoland* afterward.

"How long will this carnage go on!" the German doctors would exclaim in horror as they saw the innocent civilians— men, women, and children—mangled, burnt, and dying after the Communist attacks.

The Da Nang deep-water piers at the mouth of the river had been built up with special docks floated into place to receive great cargo ships with tremendous amounts of military equipment of all sorts for the troops: thousands of big army trucks, bulldozers, jeeps, tanks, wrecker cars, helicopters. Ammunition of every sort rolled in in vast quantities, with all the building materials, food, and supplies needed to run a major war.

First-class jet airfields were in Da Nang now, on which U.S. jets, huge transport planes, and helicopters stood in rows, each plane separated from the others by steel partitions and sandbags to protect them from rockets or mortars.

Great crates of supplies were unloaded from planes, and night and day there was the bursting roar of jets streaming down the runways to take off for attacks, trailing long white plumes behind.

The Americans saw that South Vietnam could be built into an independent country with its good food and timber resources, water possibilities, rubber, superb beaches, and scenery. They found the Vietnamese to be an energetic, attractive, bright people. American aid in the war was colossal, and the Saigon government and the badly battered Vietnamese Army took new heart and were bolstered up.

When we first came to Da Nang nine years before in 1956, it was a sleepy, clean, pretty little fishing town on the sea. It had wide, paved, tree-shaded streets, and a population of 150,000 people. The French had been the administrators for one hundred years. When they had to leave, the raging war caused thousands of refugees from the surrounding country places to pour into Da Nang for safety. The city's population soared up into the hundreds of thousands. Now Da Nang was swarming with refugees, filled with poor little shacks and lean-tos, dirty, with piles of garbage left outside the houses along many streets. The roadways were choked with military vehicles, and thousands of motorbikes polluted the air.

In the old French residential quarter, our mission owns three old French colonial houses for our missionaries stationed in Da Nang. Flower gardens and big trees are around each home.

A small chapel at the back of our property is also used for our Vietnamese Bible school classroom. Down one side of the courtyard is a long row of small, shabby rooms which are dormitories for twenty or more Bible students when school is in session eight months of the year. Vietnamese household helpers also live in some of these rooms, and one section is for mission offices.

Three Vietnamese families also live on this property. Most of the time sixty or more of us are on this compound.

We also have our menage of pets! Our two gibbon apes, Hopalong and Chesty, were in the largest barred cage. They had many visitors all day long, many of them American military men. The gibbons would come close to the cage bars and look hard at the visitors, their black, wistful faces and cream side whiskers pushed up between the bars, their liquid eyes brooding.

One day an American friend was enjoying watching the apes. Suddenly Chesty reached out his long, black kid-gloved hand, and the next instant our friend saw that Chesty had his fountain pen inside the cage, tossing it up lightly, playing with it.

"However did he get that? Oh, please give it back!" our friend coaxed Chesty, but the gibbon wanted to play with it.

"Chi Nga, come help!" we called our house girl and Chi Nga came running. She quickly entered the cage, offering Chesty a banana. The ape exchanged the fountain pen for the banana, and the pen was unhurt.

Our friends would shout with amazement as the two gibbons would break away from the side of the cage to go leaping around on the inside bars in graceful, sweeping arcs, singing and whooping their loud, clear jungle songs.

Many Vietnamese visitors from Da Nang would cry, "O cha! We'll have to bring our families here to see these gibbons! We've never in our lives been back into the jungle mountains of our own country to see animals like these!"

Schoolchildren flocked in daily to see the pets.

In another cage, built like a little bamboo house with a conical thatched roof, we had two quaint Rhesus monkeys, like little old gnomes with sad, wrinkled faces, dressed in fur coats. They chattered excitedly at the visitors and drew back their lips with nervous grins, showing their small, white teeth. They wriggled their eyebrows up and down and set their thin, pointed pixie ears to jigging. One of them laid his ears back flat against his head, pushing his mouth out in a little circle, and made a cute mewing noise at the visitors. This meant he was pleading to get out of the cage.

So Chi Nga would open the cage and the two monkeys would leap swiftly out, one jumping into Chi Nga's arms, and the other sitting on her shoulder. The animals all love Chi Nga, as she is the one who feeds and cares for them.

Then, quick as a flash, they'd be off, up into the nearby trees, doing some of their agile acrobatic tricks and feasting on leaves and buds, or any little fruits like wild figs and wild almonds.

"My!" all the visitors, young and old, would laugh and exclaim. "We could watch them all day long; they are so comical and cute!"

Then one day, our dear gibbon Hopalong caught dysentery. We gave her the best treatment we could, but dystentery is practically fatal for these delicate forest apes. In her last suffering, she gave me one despairing, very human look and then fell forward dead!

Hoppy truly loved us, and we loved her. She'd never forget us, even when we'd been home on furlough for a year. We had her for eight years. Now the lovely flying form was still as were all the graceful, sweeping arcs through the air and the glorious swinging by her long arms. There was no more quaint running of short legs on the ground, the balancing arms, and light, graceful leaping. The great, haunting, echoing song was silent.

Chesty, our male ape, wouldn't sing for weeks after Hoppy died. He'd lay his head on his arms, with his face down, and sit quietly brooding.

I had Hoppy's little studded leather neck collar on my desk for many months, and I felt very sad and lonely without our pet. We buried Hoppy in our flower garden by our house, and her grave is still there today, years later. Chi Nga ringed it with pretty seashells, and I planted scented blue and white Vietnamese flowers on her grave.

God is tender and loving toward animals and birds. Christ told of the good shepherd who goes all night over the wild, rough mountains looking for a little lost sheep. And He said the Father sees every sparrow that falls.

Soon Chesty, now at the age of adulthood for a gibbon, eight years, had grown long eyeteeth like fangs and one day he bit Chi Nga badly! We missionaries were having our morning prayers together inside headquarters and were singing hymns around the piano. Chesty enjoyed the music, so he joined in from out in his cage, singing with his mouth opened wide and his chest filled out. In the middle of his splendid song, very high and clear, Chi Nga, who hasn't much sense of music appreciation, handed him a banana to quiet him. He was so frustrated at being interrupted in his song that he bit her finger with one of his long fangs. The doctor had to sew her finger up.

We thought then that we had better send Chesty to the fine zoological gardens in Saigon. We had a box cage made for him, and the train conductor promised to care for him on the ride down, giving him bananas and rice. A zoo attendant would meet Chesty at the Saigon station.

On the train platform, Chesty sang his fine songs for the crowds and Chi Nga, Gordon, and me as we went to see him off. Even as the train pulled out of the station, Chesty was still bravely singing!

Later on, as I would visit him in the zoo whenever we went to Saigon, he'd see me coming through the big gates. As I drew near his cage, calling to him, he'd lean far out through the bars to hold out his long, black, kid-gloved hand to me, so happy to see me, making little whimpering noises and saying deep in his throat, "Kwuk, Kwuk, Kwuk." I'd squeeze his hand tightly and he'd sing for me, for he was so glad to see me.

We missed him greatly, but he was happy in the zoo for several years. His name was on a card on the outside of his special cage: "CHESTY, THE BUSHMAN, FROM SMITHS AT DA NANG." Many people visited him and some wrote to us about him.

Then one day, when in Saigon, I went to see him and the keepers said, "Chesty has gone to Paree [Paris]." I'm afraid they meant "Paradee" [Paradise].

We were very sad without our gibbons, until another was brought to us from the Kontum District. He was a little soft

60

Stanley Smith, his wife, Ginny, and their children, Karen, Kenny, Kristen, and Kathy, pose for family photo during furlough in Wheaton, Illinois.

golden fellow who later would turn black like Hopalong and Chesty. His name was Bobo and he, too, was to become a very dear pet for us.

I greatly enjoy my flowers in the garden all year round, and our garden is like part of the house. The gravel paths are bordered with small lilies that are a blaze of pink after heavy rains. Edging the paths and on the veranda are jars spilling over with flowers: roses, begonias, small chrysanthemums, michaelmas daisies.

Over a big pergola we have great splashes of bougainvillea vines, vividly deep rose red, orange pink, and white, making an amazing color effect. Poinsettias flame their red leaf flowers from Christmas to April, and we have many shrubs of hibiscus, and brilliant colored leaves. The fragrance of jasmine and gardenia make us take slow, deep breaths of pleasure.

We liked to entertain quite a lot of military men, especially the chaplains, during the war years. They enjoyed seeing our moving pictures of Vietnam taken over the years and to hear

61

of our many experiences. Gordon had seen and learned so much about the country that he could really be useful to these men.

I greatly enjoy playing the piano or organ. Through the years I have studied Beethoven's "Moonlight Sonata" in three movements, his "Sonata Pathetique," a number of Bach's preludes and fugues, and the beautiful music of Chopin.

I also have a great love and desire to draw and paint. What a pleasure it is to paint in delicate watercolors and also in the joy and power of intense oil colors. God gives us these happy relaxations, and they are good medicine for us.

Our only sorrow is to be so far from our children, now that they are young men with families. Stanley and Ginny and their four little children are missionaries with us, so we have fellowship with them. But our oldest son, Douglas, and his wife, Ruth, and their three children have been in the U.S. Foreign Service in different countries: Marseilles, Paris, Leopoldville, Congo, and Morocco, throughout the years. Leslie, our second son, has been to Vietnam on U.S. Operations Missions at different periods, and so we have seen him from time to time.

These were great treats to us. Family loyalty is strongly woven in our lives, and we often hunger for our own dear ones. But God has asked us to represent Him here in Vietnam. "I have chosen you . . . that ye should go and bring forth fruit" (Jn 15:16). We do look to God to be especially near to all our children and grandchildren in all their needs, and He is a great source of comfort. We are overwhelmingly impressed by God's wonderful promise in Acts 2:39, "The promise is unto you, and to your *children.*"

10

29,000 Miles by Camper Coach

IT WAS TIME for us to visit America again on a year's furlough. We wanted to see as many of our groups of interested friends as possible. We believe that those who are investing their prayers and gifts in the Lord's work in Vietnam have a right to know fully how things are going. It is an important part of our missionary work to keep them informed.

How faithful and kind these groups and churches have been to us through the years! We are full of gratitude. They greatly encourage and uplift our hearts, and we could not carry on without them. Someone has said that missionaries are like a hand reaching out into the darkness, but those at home who support our work are the body back of the hand. Our relationship is vital: the body and the hand. If the body should cut us off, we would perish.

Our mission's responsibility in Vietnam is great for all of these unreached tribes and Vietnamese people, the patients with leprosy, the hundreds of orphans in our area, the islands, and our national workers. They are all a large trust laid upon us.

We must have many in the homelands sharing the pain and bearing the burdens of our brothers out here. We must work together to speed the light of the Gospel to these needy people. This is the very mission of the Christian Church. We sing:

> Oh, Zion *haste,* thy *mission* high fulfilling.
> To tell to all the world that God is Light!
>
> . . . .
>
> Behold how many thousands still are lying
> Bound in the darksome prison house of sin.

. . . .

Publish glad tidings, tidings of peace,
Tidings of Jesus, redemption and release.

Mary A. Thomson

We need many more young missionaries to help in this work in our section of Vietnam. We need more couples to evangelize among the tribes and Vietnamese, to teach in the Bible school, and to work as nurses and doctors.

By May, 1965, Stanley's family would be back from their furlough, ready to take over the leadership of the work.

Gordon and I would go by air to Chicago. Then we planned to purchase a camper coach in Elkhart, Indiana. It would be fully equipped for our speaking tour across America and into Ontario, Canada. This camper would enable us to sleep, eat, travel, and stop over at any place we had meetings. It would be our home in America for one year.

We trusted the Lord to supply all these needs: the plane fare to Chicago, and the sum for buying the camper coach. The Lord has never failed us through the years, and soon special gifts for these needs began to come in.

The thing I ask, when
God doth bid me pray,
Begins in that same act,
To come my way.*

Our God is a living God. What need then for anxiety when it stands written, "Seek ye first the kingdom of God, . . . and *all these things* shall be added unto you" (Mt 6:33).

When thou hast "Cast thy care," the heart then sings.
There shall be a performance of those things.*

Bessie Porter

The ability of God is beyond our prayers, beyond our *largest* prayers.*

J. H. Jowett

We arrived in Chicago in time to spend three days in Wheaton, Illinois, with our Stanley, Ginny, three-year-old Kenny

*Quotations taken from Mrs. Charles E. Cowman, *Streams in the Desert* (Grand Rapids: Zondervan, 1931).

and one-year-old Karen, at the home of Ginny's parents, Mr. and Mrs. Ed Scull. Soon after that they left for Vietnam again.

At Elkhart, Indiana, we picked up our mobile Mustang camper coach built on a one-ton Dodge truck chassis. It had a V-8 engine with automatic transmission, power brakes, and power steering. The whole "home on wheels" was aluminum silver with french blue. When loaded, the camper coach chassis model weighed 10,000 pounds. Big heavy-duty double tires were at the back.

First of all, three of the kind churches in Elkhart gave us a shower for our camper, with gifts of bedding, cooking utensils, towels, dishes, and curtains. Our hearts were very touched. Truly God is so good to us!

Then we were off on the splendid American highways, in our fully equipped movable home, taking meetings, and having fellowship with all our friends in the churches. We were encouraged to find a keen interest in Vietnam.

Our first travels took us into Ohio, Pennsylvania, and Washington, D.C. We visited our son, Leslie, in Washington before he left for Vietnam on another government assignment. Douglas, Ruth, and their children, Linda, Doug, Jr., and Jacqueline, were back from Leopoldville, Congo, where they'd been stationed for four years with the U.S. Information Service. They would now be in Washington, D.C. for a few years. It was comforting and a joy for us to visit our children again.

We then went for meetings into the New England states and Maine. Everywhere we stopped, the people asked us all about the camper, with a longing look in their eyes for the open road. Many said, "I wish I had a rig like that." Our camper coach was one of the first of its kind. Soon many of them were on the highways.

Gordon's brother, Stewart, and his wife, Alva, and son, Jack, drove over from St. John, New Brunswick, to meet us at Calais, Maine. The brothers don't often see each other, so our few hours together were precious. We picked wild huckleberries and had fun walking in the lovely woods.

We had a wonderful week during the summer camping in Baxter State Park, Maine.

We soon had word from Vietnam that Stan's family had arrived in Saigon just two hours after the Vietcong had set off bombs in the waiting room of the Tan-Son-Nhut Airport! The place was in a shambles. The bombs had been aimed at destroying one hundred U.S. servicemen who were at the airport on their way back to the States. None of the Americans was killed, but many were wounded.

Stanley and Ginny would be living in Da Nang at our mission headquarters, but Stan quickly made a trip by plane back to their former field in Kontum Province. He flew in an army plane from Kontum to the fort of Tan-Canh near Dak To, then went by a three-wheel Lambretta jitney the three miles to their home at Dak To. There Stanley found that their home had been looted, most of their things had been destroyed and scattered about, and a lot of graffiti was on the walls.

Guns were firing all night into Toumorong tribal settlements and forts ten miles away in the hills, and Toumorong fell to the Vietcong the next day.

Stanley packed two drums of what was left of their belongings from the Dak-To house and shipped them by plane to Da Nang. Then he returned the thirty-five miles to Kontum by Lambretta. A few days after that, Dak-To fell to the Vietcong, but it was reoccupied later by government troops.

In September, little Kathleen (Kathy) Joan Smith was born in a small maternity hospital in Da Nang. She was a strong, cheery baby.

Gordon and I had a wonderful Christmas with Douglas, Ruth, and our three grandchildren in Washington, D.C., staying with them for over a week. They were living in Georgetown and what a joy to be with them for an unforgettable happy holiday time.

Leslie was now back in Vietnam, and he wrote that he had a lonely Christmas in Saigon all by himself. He was almost thrown out of bed by a nearby bomb explosion, and he said that when the big B-52 planes were bombing the Communists, who were attacking on the outskirts of Saigon, all the windows rattled.

After New Year's, we went across country in our camper

coach, taking it easy at fifty-five miles per hour. At night we parked free of charge behind a gas station or at a truck stop or a rest plaza on the turnpikes. Only a very few times did we park in a regular trailer camp where we had to pay for the privilege. Often we'd pull into a parking place and have a siesta at noon. Despite the cold weather we were warm and cozy inside the camper.

When we stopped for speaking engagements we parked in the church parking lot or at some friend's house where we were kindly entertained.

We were in churches of more than thirty different denominations. We both spoke in the services, telling of the dark and dreadful disease of leprosy that can be cured today if compassionate hearts will help in this great ministry. We pictured the distress of the orphans and the need to save these young lives and set their feet in the paths of God. We told of the great spiritual awakening going on among the Jeh and Hrey tribes and the Vietnamese people. We sought to raise up more prayer warriors for Vietnam in this terrible time of war. We'll never forget the uplifting inspiring times of meetings with great servants of God in many of these churches.

It was while we were in Clearwater, Kansas, on January 7, 1966, that we had a cable from Stanley in Da Nang, Vietnam, saying:

> JOHN HAYWOOD SHOT IN COMMUNIST SKIRMISH WHILE TRAVELING OVER THE MOUNTAIN PASS TO HUE. HE DIED IMMEDIATELY.

This terrible news stunned us! John Haywood had come to Vietnam three years previously from Birmingham, England. He and his fiancée, Simone DuBois, were soon happily married and now Simone was expecting their first child in a few days' time. John had been entering eagerly into the work of helping our people with leprosy, and he and Simone were in charge of Happy Haven Leprosarium while Gordon and I were on furlough. John was a very promising helper and words could not express how much we all would miss him. It was a terrible experience for his young wife.

John was going up to Hue to get some more little pigs and chickens for the leprosy patients to raise at Happy Haven. The road to Hue had been fairly safe up to this time and was well traveled. But John, alone in the car, met a Vietcong ambush. The Communists shot him seven times in the chest, and there was a big gash on his forehead.

It was a terrific shock to all the missionaries and everyone's heart ached for Simone. Stanley and Dr. Harverson took charge of the funeral and burial services, and many American military men were present and lent their cars for the funeral procession. John was buried in the Vietnamese Protestant cemetery on the outskirts of Da Nang. Dr. and Mrs. Dillard, who were at the funeral, told us later in Seattle that Dr. Harverson spoke powerfully at the ceremony, "like a prophet," and many of the American military men were greatly touched. All were drawn closer to the Lord as they realized that John had been suddenly called into the presence of our Saviour who said, "I am the resurrection, and the life: he that believeth in me, though he were dead, yet shall he live: and whosoever liveth and believeth in me shall never die" (Jn 11:25-26).

Christ Himself bound up Simone's broken heart and in five day's time, after the loss of John, little Jacqueline Edith Haywood was born and brought joy and comfort to her mother.

The marvelous highways of America stretched out ahead of us for many more thousands of miles. On we went through Kansas, Oklahoma, Texas, New Mexico, Arizona, to California. After meetings in Los Angeles and San Francisco, we went on up the Pacific Coast to Portland, reaching Seattle by May 1.

After good meetings there, we had to return across the country, this time by the northern route, to Philadelphia, as we had decided to obtain our United States citizenship papers on this furlough. I was born in Ontario, Canada, and Gordon was born of British missionary parents in Buenos Aires, South America. We had been thinking of becoming American citizens for some time but had never been able to spend the required five years of unbroken residence in America. Now the

68

law was changed for missionaries, and we were only required one full year's residence in the States.

We had always been connected with an American mission board and, therefore, most of our furlough contacts were in the United States. Our three sons had always attended American schools and had already become American citizens. So we wanted to join them in also belonging to the United States of America.

All the way across country and in our camper coach at night, we studied the Constitution of the American government.

On July 4, 1966, when our full year was up and we had each successfully answered the twelve hard questions asked us by men of the U.S. Immigration and Naturalization Service, we were invited to be sworn in, in the old historical Independence Hall of Philadelphia. With 300 other "foreign immigrants" we were declared citizens of the United States of America.

Then we were booked for more meetings in Pennsylvania and in Ontario, Canada. In August we had a most wonderful two weeks camping up at my old country home of Dalrymple, Ontario, eighty miles north of Toronto, near Orillia. Douglas, Ruth, and family joined us there from Washington, D. C., renting a summer cottage by the lovely Dalrymple Lake. My sisters from Toronto, Mrs. George Blackett and Mrs. Morley Hall, and my sister and her husband, Mr. and Mrs. Arthur Wigg, from Fonthill, also came up and rented cottages near us. We had a good family reunion together and fun fishing and exploring the old home places of fond memories.

Gordon and I then drove back to Elkhart, Indiana, and left our camper coach with friends to be sold. We had traveled 29,000 miles in it without a single accident and only one flat tire. We didn't even know about that tire until someone going by us shouted out that one of our back double-wheel tires was flat! We must have driven sixty miles on it and were amazed that the other tire had held up under the heavy load.

In October we sailed from New York to Rotterdam on the *Princess Marguerita* and had a restful ten-day voyage over the Atlantic on this Dutch ship. We enjoyed meeting friends in many parts of Holland.

From Rotterdam we took a ferry across the channel to England and had a happy reunion with our relatives and friends near London, who have been such staunch supporters of our work throughout the years. Our cousin, Vernon Hedderly, originated the successful Missionary Mart at Wallington, Surrey, where he and a staff of indefatigable workers have collected all kinds of used furniture, clothing, and other things to sell for missions around the world. A periodic auction sale also brings good results. Our work has benefited many times from the donations of these missionary projects. These English friends have had a tremendous share in the progress of the Gospel in Vietnam.

Returning to Rotterdam from England, we then took a train to Basle, Switzerland, following the storybook shores of the Rhine River in Germany with its old-time castles and the Black Forest for nearly a whole day.

What a joyous time we had in Switzerland! Mr. Heini Schnieder of the World-Wide Evangelization Crusade there drove us from one end to the other of Switzerland in his car, from St. Gallen on the eastern border to Geneva on the west. We took meetings all along the way.

Back to Rotterdam again from Switzerland, we boarded the Danish freighter *Simba* on November 1, 1966, for our return trip to Vietnam. We were the only passengers on board, and the ship was bound directly for Saigon! We had two nice cabins given to us: one to sleep in, the other to work in. We had the pleasant salon of the ship to ourselves, and there was a small canvas swimming pool.

We sailed by the Mediterranean and through the Suez Canal. In the following year the canal was closed, and ships going to the Far East had to sail around the South African Cape.

After a month's very pleasant voyage, our ship arrived at Cape St. Jacques, Vietnam, now called by the Vietnamese name, Vung Tau (Valley of the Boats) at the entrance to the Saigon River. There we found that our ship would be ten days or more waiting to get up the river, as the harbor of Vung Tau was crowded with forty or fifty big ships waiting at anchor. The dock facilities at Saigon were inadequate for all this heavy traffic of unloading military supplies in time of war. Also it takes half a day for a ship to slowly navigate up the winding Saigon River, and it was now very dangerous with communist snipers and mines.

We soon found that Gordon and I could get a ride on a two-engine army plane from Vung Tau to Saigon. American military men at Vung Tau came out in their motor launch to get us off the *Simba*. We were flown to Saigon where Stanley and Ginny met us.

I went to Da Nang with them the next morning by plane. Gordon had to stay for a week in Saigon to get our baggage off the *Simba*, when the freighter finally got up to the dock. Then he was able to get everything by cargo plane to Da Nang free of charge.

We had a warm welcome back to Da Nang. The preachers came to see us from distant churches. A delegation of patients from the leprosarium brought us flowers and a gift of Vietnamese lacquerwork. It was wonderful to see the children at the orphanage, including many new ones. It was good to be back again in our field of service.

But we'll continue these great furlough trips in our memories for the rest of our lives! Often we'll relive our happy visits with our relatives, and in the churches and homes of friends. We'll travel again and again in our minds through the United States and the parts of Europe and the ocean routes out to Vietnam.

11

Battle for Da Nang

IN MAY, 1966, while Gordon and I were home on furlough, Stanley wrote us of a trip he made to the Kontum District. He went by a big Chinook helicopter to An-Khe where the ceremony for the laying the cornerstone of a new Vietnamese church was to be held. The American First Cavalry Division had made its home in this strategic area and had painted their insignia on the crest of the Hong Cong mountain. The shield was a large cement circle with a golden horse's head painted on a black background. This insignia was a bright landmark to be seen by their helicopters for miles.

The First Cavalry Division chaplain was at the cornerstone dedication of the new church and the chaplains' groups of Christian First Cavalry men would help by their offerings in building this chapel and in sustaining this work.

After An-Khe, Stanley made his way by Caribou plane to Kontum, visiting our preachers there and the church and school.

From Kontum, Stan was able to get a helicopter up to his old station of Dak To again and to visit with preacher An and the group of Jeh and Sedang Christians in that area. His house was looted, but in one place the Christians met for their services under a large nylon parachute given to them by the Americans.

Back in Kontum, Stan was able to get onto an army Caribou, a Canadian-made troop transport, flying to Dak Pek, one hundred miles north in the Kontum Province. They flew high over Dak To and then followed the road up to Dak Sut. The Communists had been fighting there, and the whole fort was destroyed as well as our fine chapel that our workers had built. Stanley could see the destruction clearly from the Caribou.

72

Just ahead lay Dak Pek and the strong special forces camp, eight miles from Laos and the Ho Chi Minh Trail. This was one of the important border-surveillance camps, guardian to 8,000 Jeh refugees at Dak Pek.

The weather was good enough to enable the Caribou plane to locate the short airstrip from 10,000 feet up. Dak Pek itself is over 3,000 feet above sea level, a valley with towering mountains on every side. Their descent took many minutes as they spiraled around and around, going down slowly to avoid enemy guns. But before long the plane was able to slam its wheels on the muddy and extremely short runway of 1,000 feet and reverse the propellers.

Stanley was glad to be back in Dak Pek after his year of absence on furlough. Pastor Tuu could hardly believe his eyes when he saw him arrive! Two chapels—for there were now 1,000 Jeh Christians in Dak Pek—were located at either end of the area. There were fifteen fortified Jeh refugee villages surrounding the American special forces and the Vietnamese and tribal strike forces camp.

There was the possibility of an all-out attack by the Vietcong at any time, so everyone spent the nights in underground bunkers. Each evening Pastor Tuu would leave his room at the back of one of the chapels and climb the hill to the nearest fort to sleep.

As Stan had flown in quite late in the afternoon, he and Tuu couldn't take time for supper, but had to get settled in the fort bunker before dark. Pastor Tuu changed into black pajamas that couldn't be seen in the night and grasped his small survival kit that the special forces men had given him. Stan, with his bag, accompanied Tuu to the bunker.

At the fort they were cordially invited to have supper with the Vietnamese government official. After a good meal of rice, spinach, dried fish, and coffee, they listened to the news on a shortwave radio. They were shocked to hear a report that a bad crisis was taking place right at that time in Da Nang between political rebels and government troops! Stanley felt very worried about his family being there without him! He and Tuu

73

talked for several hours about the work and prayed, then they turned in for the night, four feet underground.

The next day, after a hearty breakfast of rice, bean curd, and coffee, Tuu and Stan visited the refugee villages where the thousand Christians were located. Many of the adults were out in the nearby rice fields, or else searching around for any edible roots or leaves. So there were not too many in the village in the daytime. The people were half starving because the communist snipers shot at them in the rice patches or if they tried to fish in any of the streams. Stan looked forward to meeting with the Christians on Sunday in the two chapels and speaking to them.

He kept hearing about the planes bombing and strafing in Da Nang, and he became more and more concerned for his family. He prayed that he'd be able to get a plane out of Dak Pek to Da Nang after the Sunday morning services. In spite of all the terrible danger in this communist-infested area, God was working in the hearts of these primitive Jeh tribespeople in a marvelous way, and it was very important that Stanley should visit with them and encourage them in the Lord.

Stan and Tuu spent another night in the bunker, and the next morning, Sunday, they had their first service at 8:30. The chapel was packed and God was in their midst as Stanley spoke to the Jeh in Vietnamese with Tuu interpreting in the Jeh language.

After the meeting and farewells, Stan and Tuu bicycled down to the second chapel. This would soon be manned by another Vietnamese preacher, Chu, who was now learning the Jeh language. This chapel was also packed full of Jeh people dressed in their few best rags to worship God.

Halfway through the service, as Stan was preaching, he was startled when most of the congregation stood up, crying out, "*Cha oi! Xem kia!*" (Oh my! Look there!), pointing at something behind Stanley's back! Stan thought for sure that there was some viper ready to strike at him from a rafter! He turned to see a large rat, startled at all the commotion. The poor people were so excited to see fresh meat that they couldn't contain themselves, so they yelled right out and chased the rat and caught it in the middle of the service!

Again, after greetings to all the Jeh Christians and taking some of their pictures, Stan and Tuu hurried back to Tuu's living quarters to have lunch. Stan had just finished his second bowl of rice when they heard the noise of a plane engine. God had answered prayer and here was the plane! A Caribou spiraled down out of the sky, and Stan packed his things and ran down to the airstrip. It didn't matter where its destination would be, for getting out of this difficult airstrip before more heavy rains came was of the utmost importance, especially with all the trouble going on in Da Nang. The plane was heading for Nhatrang, a good place from which to get a flight to Da Nang.

With a last farewell and "May the Lord keep and bless you," the Caribou gunned its engines and they left the primitive little airstrip and began climbing steeply in tight circles to the necessary altitude of 10,000 feet to clear the peaks that threatened all around them.

At Nhatrang, Stan was told that the scheduled flight for Da Nang was about to leave but was full to capacity. The next scheduled flight was to be two days later! They would put Stan on standby, however. Stan thanked them and held onto God in faith, praying fervently. Beside him, on the bench seat, was a newspaper telling about the battle going on for Da Nang! He was terribly anxious to get home and kept asking God that he would make it.

Just an hour later, Stan had a seat on a C-123 "Provider" cargo plane. Just four hours after having lunch at Dak Pek, he was back in Da Nang! But how was he to get into town from the airport? No one from Da Nang was being allowed out there!

While Stan was trying to call his home on a phone that had long been disconnected, a friend in the U. S. government in Da Nang saw him and called out, "Your wife is anxious about you and has been going through some dangerous times. I'll drive you home!" How Stanley praised the Lord for all the answered prayers!

They made their way safely through the deserted streets and

past the several checkpoints guarded by heavily armed loyal government troops.

Stan was soon back with his family and fellow missionaries, sharing all their experiences of the past week and realizing God's goodness and care over them all! Then Ginny told of the battle for Da Nang that had taken place while Stanley was away.

On Sunday, May 15, the day Stanley was in An-Khe, the regular morning church service was held in our chapel from 9 to 10 A.M. Ginny and the children had returned to their house after the meeting. The children were playing with their toys in their bedroom which has a front window. Ginny noticed that some of the Vietnamese from our compound were standing at the front gate looking down the road, apparently at some soldiers who were trying to keep the Vietnamese people from going to market.

At about 10:30 A.M. a sound truck came to the end of the block, telling the people to get ready to fight the government troops. These were rebels! Suddenly several truckloads of Vietnamese government troops went racing by the house, loaded down with all kinds of weapons. Ginny thought, *That's strange! We never see Vietnamese troops like that in this residential end of the town.*

The next second, shots rang out! Someone had shot at the trucks! The government soldiers jumped out and began running along the outside wall of our property and down the street. Our people standing at the front gate ran into our yard.

Ginny grabbed the three children and put them in the bathroom where the shower and tub are walled in with cement and tiles which would hopefully give more protection.

By then the shooting was really going on in earnest, with rifles firing and the steady rat-tat-tat of machine guns. It was very close to the house but gradually began to move away from our property as the government troops made their way toward the rebel-held radio station about eight blocks away.

Ginny prayed with the children, asking the Lord to protect them and all the others on our property. They prayed especially for Chi Huy, their cook, for she had gone down to the market. Shortly after that she arrived back, scared to death, and out of breath! She had been at the market when the shooting started. She had run all the way home with bullets whizzing around and everybody else lying flat on the ground to protect themselves.

Dr. and Mrs. Harverson's house, near Stan and Ginny's on the compound, was hit on the tiled roof by machine-gun fire and the bullets fell with a "kerplunk" on the ceiling.

The rest of that Sunday was fairly quiet, and Ginny even had her Sunday school class at 3 o'clock. Monday and Tuesday also were quiet until Tuesday night. About 10:15 P.M. as Ginny was reaching to turn off the light, the shooting started again! Ginny grabbed the children out of bed and again put them in the walled-in bath and shower.

Ginny looked out of the window and could see the tracer bullets flying over the house. This kept up for about an hour and when it quieted down, she fixed up the childrens' beds in her bedroom in case there was more trouble in the night. She didn't sleep well as she was continually awakened by explosions in another part of the town. She was greatly concerned that Stanley should get back, as the responsibility of the children at such a time was very great.

For the next two days, Ginny kept the children as close to the house and inside as much as possible. On Friday evening, as she was preparing for bed, the shooting started again. This time she put the children on the floor by her bed with a mattress over them all, as suggested by some of the American military men who had visited them. The bullets were flying over our compound again, and Ginny could hear things dropping in the garden outside the window. They were either spent bullets or pieces of branches being knocked down by the firing. It was over in about forty-five minutes, but all that night there was gunfire in other parts of the city. Many Vietnamese civilians were killed.

About 4 A.M. the shooting started up badly again near our property, but pretty soon airplanes came and began machine-gunning a couple of blocks away. They were hitting a Buddhist pagoda there and also some points along the nearby riverfront. It lasted until 8 A.M. and then things settled down.

Ginny writes: "On the following Sunday, about 7 in the evening, Stan arrived and was I ever glad to see him! I was really praying hard that day that the Lord would bring him back, removing the many obstacles he would continue to meet. As he returned and gave us his testimony we certainly saw how the Lord answers prayer! It was a very trying week for me physically and spiritually, but the Lord was good, teaching me more of Himself and His ways."

So in this summer of 1966, the missionaries in Da Nang were going through times of much excitement and danger. A large group of rebel soldiers from Hoi An, twenty miles away, marched over to Da Nang to fire on the Saigon paratroopers at the U.S. Marine base on the outskirts of the city. They were stopped at one of the big bridges by Americans protecting the city.

For better safety, all the missionaries from the three different societies in town were moved out of Da Nang city to quarters in the big American Naval Hospital, made up of scores of Quonset huts. They stayed there for two weeks until the trouble quieted down. Stanley had to return to the city to hunt for some of their baggage, especially for the children, that had gotten mislaid on one of the trucks moving the missionaries over, and was still in Da Nang. He traveled by riverboat and Vietnamese jeep into Da Nang. He left the hospital barracks at 8 A.M. and returned at 4 P.M. with the missing suitcase, and Ginny's heart was in her mouth all day for fear he would be captured by the enemy.

12

Tet: The Vietnamese New Year

DAT (pronounced Dak) AND TIN, two of the young people in the Da Nang church, were talking together. Tin had been a Christian since childhood, as he was born in a Christian home in Da Nang. But Dat was just a new Christian, won to Christ in our chapel a few months previously. Dat's mother and sisters were strong Buddhists, but his father had no special religion. Dat received great help in his Christian life from his good friend, Tin.

"What should I do at Tet time, our Vietnamese New Year?" Dat asked Tin.

"Oh, we Christians always have a good time together. But for some new Christians it is often a hard time," answered Tin.

The Vietnamese people have two calendars: one like the Western world, which follows the sun and starts with New Year's Day on January 1. That is the solar calendar. The other calendar, which the Orientals use, follows the moon and has the New Year starting any time from mid-January to the end of February, according to the twelfth moon. This calendar is called the lunar calendar.

The lunar New Year in Vietnam is called Tet. It is a time when everyone in the country takes a big holiday. The schools have two weeks' vacation, and everyone in business or on the farm stops work for at least the first three days of the new year.

On the first day of Tet, around eleven million Vietnamese people in South Vietnam solemnly worship their ancestors and many of them also worship Buddha. Then they must all visit their relatives and friends. There are great feasts and frolics.

Tin warned Dat, "You'll have to pray for strength because

there are many temptations during Tet. The Buddhist priests will try hard to get all of your family to go to the pagoda."

"Oh, yes, I know," answered Dat. "Already they have been to our house and warned my mother not to follow the Christian way. They told her that curses will follow any family that forsakes Buddha and the worship of our ancestors. The priests know that I am now following Jesus Christ. They are strongly urging my mother and sisters to be faithful to the old ways or trouble will come. So my mother is going to make a big Tet celebration this year."

Then Dat went on to ask Tin, "What shall I do when they all worship my ancestors? Shall I eat of the food offered to them?"

"Oh, no," Tin cautioned, "the Bible tells us to *honor* our parents and grandparents. But it is a sin to *worship* them! God says, 'Thou shalt have no other gods before me.' God commands that we do not worship idols or people. So you must be firm and not partake of any of the food offered to the ancestors or the idols, Buddha, Confucius, or Mencius. God tells us that it is a great sin to worship man."

Dat said, "I'm going to make a copy of the Ten Commandments and put it up on the wall of my own little room. Also I'm going to make some other good Bible texts and put them up too." Dat, like many of the Vietnamese, was very clever at printing beautiful signs and scrolls.

"That's a good idea," said Tin. "We have some Bible texts up in our house and they help us a lot."

"But," queried Dat, "can't I eat any of the good food my mother and sisters will be making for Tet?"

"Oh, yes indeed!" exclaimed Tin. "Why, my mother and my sisters, Ai Lan and Grace, will be making loads of the same good Tet things, cakes and candied fruits and vegetables, that your mother and all the women in Vietnam will be making for Tet. You can eat *any* of the food that is not offered to the idols or to the ancestors."

"I'm sure we're going to have a good time through the big holidays and God will keep me true to Him," said Dat.

Tet comes in the springtime of the year in Vietnam, the season which the Vietnamese love the best of all. The weather in Da Nang is beautiful in these months, clear and bright after the rainy season, with the temperature around 78 degrees.

Seven days before Tet, Dat's mother, Mrs. Van, and his sisters, Spring Flower and Rose, performed what they thought was an important little ceremony for their "kitchen gods." This same rite was practiced in almost every non-Christian Vietnamese home in South Vietnam that night.

They went out to the kitchen where there were three little idols made of baked red earth sitting on a shelf. These are called the "kitchen gods." On that night these gods are supposed to ascend up to heaven and report on all the doings of the Van family throughout the past year. Their report would be given to an ancient ruler, called the Jade Emperor, who long ago had become a god. The kitchen gods would tell this emperor god of all the misdeeds of the family throughout the past year: if they had cheated, slandered, or done any evil. If the report was bad, then the Jade Emperor, for punishment, would make bad luck come to the family all through the coming year.

So Mrs. Van, Spring Flower, and Rose tried to persuade the three little kitchen gods to give a good report for them. This was done by offering a feast to the kitchen gods before they left on their journey to the skies. They placed several bananas, rice cakes, and a small bowl of tea before the idols. They smeared honey or syrup over their lips so that they'd say only nice sweet things about the family. They also gave them a bouquet of flowers, lit several red candles, and put some sheaves of white paper money beside them. Then they offered them some fancy gifts, all made from paper, that they had bought at the Da Nang marketplace. These were colored paper caps with dragonfly wings on the sides, some mandarin boots of paper, and some more paper money. There was also a well-harnessed, gay paper horse on which the kitchen gods would ride away.

Mrs. Van and the two girls set fire to the paper articles and gave a shout! Then they imagined that the spirits of the kitchen gods flew away in the flames up to the heavens!

They called out, "Tell the Emperor god good things about us!"

The spirits would be gone for seven days on their visit to the skies. While they were supposed to be away, Mrs. Van, Spring Flower, and Rose had to give the kitchen a good cleaning. They took their grass brooms and swept the ceiling and all the walls. They threw out the three old red clay figures of the kitchen gods, as their spirits had now flown away. On New Year's Eve they would be putting three new little red earthen idols up on the kitchen altar. They would buy these in the marketplace.

On that night of New Year's Eve, they believed that the three spirits would return from heaven and enter into these new little idols for the coming year. During the New Year holidays, Mrs. Van and the girls would offer them a lot of the Tet feast food, flowers, and lighted candles again. They would rejoice to have them back in their kitchen for another year.

What did Dat do about all this ritual? He watched it, but he took no part in it. He did not believe in these superstitions anymore. He realized that they were only false imaginations. He knew now that we should only worship the true God.

He said gently to his mother and sisters, "It is the Lord Jesus Christ who sees us all the time and knows all about our doings, not these little figures of clay that can't see or hear. It is He who cares for us."

His mother and sisters didn't deride or scoff at him, as some families would do, but they felt badly that he wasn't taking part in all of this with them, as he used to do. It was hard for Dat to witness to them about Christ at this time, as they were very serious and earnest in following their old-time customs of Vietnam.

Dat's mother and sisters were busy now out in the kitchen making a lot of food for the Tet celebrations. No cooking could be done during the first three to five days of the New Year. All the shops and markets would be closed. So each house had to stock up well with food beforehand.

Dat's house was filled with delicious smells! Mrs. Van and the girls cooked over the open charcoal fires in the grates on the top of their brick stove, and it was hot work. They made cookies in a homemade tin oven over the coals and put them in jars. They salted and pickled carrots, onions, cabbage, and red peppers to put on top of their bowls of rice.

Then they sliced up watermelon, sweet potatoes, and ginger root and cut thin strips of coconut and candied all of these in thick syrup. Mrs. Van made especially luscious candied pineapple slices. The Vietnamese women are very skilled in making these good things.

Dat exclaimed, "O Cha! At this New Year's time we have the best feasts of all the year!"

Mrs. Van made the two special kinds of cakes that every Vietnamese loves at Tet time. They are called *banh chung* and *banh giay* (yay-ee). She made these of green glutinous rice, soft and sticky. She put the *banh chung* into little square envelopes which the girls and Dat cut from a banana leaf, and she also rolled up the *banh giay* into long pieces of banana leaf. Later, Dat and his father would help cut the roll into slices with a taut, sharp string of bamboo. Inside the cakes there was a stuffing of dried white beans, peanuts, and little pieces of fat and lean pork. Dat and his family, like all the other Vietnamese families, would smack their lips as they ate these Tet cakes, dipping each slice into their salty fish sauce called *nuoc mam*.

Mrs. Van also made many meat and bean-paste dumplings out of rice flour. During the holidays these would only have to be steamed to be cooked.

They had lots of watermelon seeds, too, that they would crack with their teeth and eat with all the other things, as many friends and relatives would drop in to visit them during the Tet days.

"Will Tin and all his family be coming to see us?" asked Dat.

"Oh, yes," his mother replied, "and we'll all go to their house and visit them too."

"Maybe the missionaries and some other friends from the Christian church will also visit us," cried Dat excitedly.

"Yes, Tet is a friendly happy time of the year," said Dat's father.

The Van family cleaned their house inside and out and

whitewashed it freshly in rose. All the other Vietnamese families did the same, and some of the houses were colored beige or pale green or yellow.

The altar for Buddha and the ancestral tablet in each home was shined up along with all the brass altar candlesticks, the brass incense burners, the jars for the joss sticks, and the bowls for the betel nut and tea which they offer to the spirits. Fresh candles were put into the altar candle holders, and vases of fresh flowers or new artificial ones were offered to Buddha and the ancestors.

Mrs. Van had to see that there was no soiled clothing lying about. Everything had to be washed, ironed, and folded neatly. All debts must be paid before the New Year.

Dat and his sisters were pleased with their new clothes for Tet. Each member of every family—from the oldest to the youngest—should have a new set of nice clothing for the New Year.

Dat and all the family went to see the market at Da Nang during the last week before the big holiday. Everything was brightly lighted and gay. Extra stalls were put up surrounding the big marketplace, and they were full of fancy preserved fruits: mounds of dates, strips of coconut, thin slices of ginger, carrots, watermelon and lotus seeds, all crystallized in sugar. They were arranged tastefully in their varieties of color, in fancy cardboard boxes.

There were flowers in abundance, both real and artificial, at the great flower fairs: pots of chrysanthemums, big dahlias, roses, marigolds, and begonias. Dat's family, like all the other households, had to have some new pots of flowers with which to welcome the New Year.

Mr. Van brought home the favorite of all, the flowering boughs of the Mai tree. This tree blossoms at Tet time, and Dat and his sisters helped to arrange the boughs in water in a tall blue vase. They were delighted with the fairy cups like clear yellow wax blooming upon the bare branches.

"This is our most beautiful decoration of the New Year," Dat declared.

"Yes," agreed Spring Flower, "and the blossoms will stay fresh for many weeks."

As the visitors would come, Dat and the girls would place all their visiting and greeting cards for the New Year up in the Mai tree branches.

Then came New Year's Eve. Everything was ready. The altar in Dat's home was shining and the candles were lit. Mrs. Van had spread a table out before the gods, loaded down with the Tet feast food. A chicken had been killed as a sacrifice, and the blood had been taken from its throat. Mrs. Van had cooked this and then placed a little piece of the cooked blood on top of each dish of food.

Early on New Year's morning was the New Year's breakfast feast. Dat and his family dressed in their new clothes. Dat had a new sweater; the girls and Mrs. Van had new tunics. For this ceremonial day, Mr. Van, as head of the house, wore his Vietnamese-style clothes. Over white cotton trousers, he put on a black satin tunic reaching to his knees, and on his head was a tightly pleated ring turban of black silk.

Dat's mother, Spring Flower, and Rose fell on their knees with folded hands before the altar, bowing deeply. They called on the ancestors to come now and eat the food, drink the tea, and give good health and good luck to the home. They invited the ancestors to stay with them for the first three days of this Tet and enjoy all these happy feasts and celebrations. Mrs. Van and the girls set off some firecrackers to chase away all demons and evil from their home.

Then they all bowed and wished each other a "Happy New Year," and Mr. Van gave Dat and the girls each a little gift of money to spend as they wished.

Dat thought, *I'll buy some Christian tracts and booklets from the missionaries with my money and give them out to my family and relatives.*

Dat explained to his mother that he couldn't eat any of the feast food on the altar table offered to Buddha and the ancestors. He said, "I want to be a good Vietnamese, but I'm following Jesus Christ, the Son of God, now, and I want no part in worshiping man."

So Dat's mother kindly went out into the kitchen and got him a bowl of rice with pickled vegetables on it and a dish of candied fruits from the Tet food there, not offered at the altar. She also cut him some slices of the sticky rice Tet cakes that Dat liked so much.

Dat was grateful. "Thank you, Mother. I know you are sad because I'm not following the old way. But when you let me eat of this other Tet food you have made, it proves to me that you love me dearly and my heart is touched."

The family remained quietly inside their house all the first day of the New Year as Mrs. Van and the girls, like most Vietnamese families all over South Vietnam, kept tryst with their own ancestors. The streets of Da Nang were deserted on that day. No work of any kind was done. Dat spent some time reading his Bible in his room and drawing his texts and mottoes.

Then on the second day, the visiting began. All the friends kept dropping in throughout the day, and everyone was dressed in his very best. The slim women looked lovely in their elegant silk tunics of rich or delicate colors over white satin trousers. The men wore smart Western clothes. Everyone was supposed to be smiling and in fine humor to please the gods.

Dat's aunts and uncles, mostly Mrs. Van's sisters and brothers came. They weren't pleased at all about Dat following the Christian way. They made Mrs. Van and the two girls understand that if they ever believed on Christ they might be cut off as members of the family. They wouldn't be considered as relatives anymore. They would make it very hard for Dat's mother to take a stand for Christ.

Tin, with his parents and sisters, Ai Lan and Grace, also came and they, with Dat, were all happy, sure, and secure in their Christian faith. There was something so different about them because they were so peaceful and bright. Dat thought happily, "They will help attract my family to believe on Jesus, the one true God."

Ai Lan and Grace had thick black hair and were pretty, especially Ai Lan with her smooth round face, dimpled cheeks, black luminous eyes, and narrow little hands. They and Dat's sisters spoke and laughed very softly together. Their voices were soft and sweet and shy.

Dat showed Tin the colored Bible texts he had made for his own room.

"That is letting your light shine for Jesus," Tin encouraged him.

Dat told Tin, "I can't enjoy the Tet this year as I did other years because I am now a Christian. I see all this great worship of Buddha and the ancestors and I know it is not right. My aunts and uncles are warning my mother to keep to these old Vietnamese ways or she will be cut off from the family."

"God hears as we pray for your people, Dat, and He can change things," comforted Tin.

We missionaries went to visit Dat's home, too, wishing all the family a Happy New Year. We enjoyed the Tet sweetmeats and tidbits that Mrs. Van served and the green, scented tea. Spring Flower and Rose were taking some English lessons with me at that time, so we all spoke a little English to help the girls practice.

One of us had previously given the family the book of John's Gospel to read and Mr. Van now told us, "I have read the book from the Bible that you gave us. It is written in good, clear Vietnamese."

Gordon spoke earnestly, "Yes, and it reveals to us that Jesus Christ is the Son of God, our living Saviour. How do you like it?"

"Day by day, I'm thinking about this word," Mr. Van replied.

On the third day of the New Year, Mrs. Van, Rose, and Spring Flower performed another ceremony which was held in most Vietnamese homes. They burned packages of colored paper and asked all the ancestors to please leave the house and go back to their other world. The paper was "money" for the ancestors' journey and for buying food on the way. Mrs. Van and the girls also burned some presents made of paper for their ancestors. They had bought all of these at the Da Nang market. They had a little fancy "ghost" house, some small furniture, hats, long tunics, and clog shoes, all made very cleverly of colored paper.

As they burned these, they thought that all the things were then "shipped away" to the spirit world where they would be used by the ancestors.

Again they set off some firecrackers to protect the ancestors from evil. Then they burned all the remains of the incense sticks and placed the ashes in the brass urn on the altar.

Dat came over to our Christian chapel where all the Christians kept the New Year in fellowship with the true God. The teachers there explained in the meetings how Christ is not on the same level as the human Buddha or Confucius. He is the second Person of the Trinity, co-equal and co-eternal with God, the Father. They sang many hymns and Dat's heart was always especially moved with the song, "If I Gained the World, But Lost My Saviour." They prayed to God fervently, and praised Him. Then they learned more of Him through His Word.

The Christians, too, had cleaned and decorated their houses with lovely spring flowers. They also visited together and ate candied fruit and nuts and the same delicious Vietnamese foods.

They were taught clearly the truths of their faith in Christ so that there would be no backsliding into the superstitions and fears of their old religion.

They studied well a chart that we missionaries had made, explaining clearly the beliefs of Buddhism, ancestor worship, and Christianity.*

We missionaries and the Vietnamese pastors stayed with the Christians as much as possible at the Tet time. We showed movies we had taken of our previous work among the tribespeople at Banmethuot and Pleiku, as well as movies of our present work among the tribes in central Vietnam. We had lots of movies of the China Beach Orphanage and the Happy Haven Leprosarium.

Dat and Tin and all the Christians greatly enjoyed our nice, bright, Christian celebrations together during these holidays of the Vietnamese New Year.

*See Appendix. For several years I gave talks about TET to various units in the American Armed Forces at Da Nang. Their chaplains distributed hundreds of copies of this chart to interested officers and men.

13

Unstinting GI Help

IN APRIL, 1967, we had a good conference at Da Nang with our twenty-seven national pastors and ten missionaries. Dame Corrie ten Boom, that great world evangelist (knighted by the Queen of Holland and now seventy-five years of age), flew with Andrew van der Bijl ("God's Smuggler") from Holland to speak to us. The Lord blessed us all in those conference days, and we thanked Him for sending His messengers to us.

Corrie ten Boom is well known in many countries for her good Bible messages, and Andrew Van der Bijl ministers to Christians mostly in iron curtain countries. After the conference, Corrie ten Boom went on to other parts of Vietnam, while "Brother Andrew" went with Stanley to see more of our work.

Gordon had to get our preacher, Bui Bao, and his wife and some Christians back to Cu-Lao Cham Island after the conference. A marine helicopter pilot flew them the thirty miles over to the offshore island, because our boat, the *Hope,* was being repaired at the time. On cross-water flights the helicopters flew two by two for safety, so another helicopter accompanied the flight.

The marine choppers rose with a great chuff, chuff and much noisy shaking from the steel pad near Da Nang, and off they went. It was hazy, so they skimmed 200 feet above the water. Gordon sat by an open door, wondering if they would be able to land with such poor visibility.

Finally a rocky island went by the door, then another, and they could see the main island. There, on the shore, was the new small whitewashed chapel that Bui Bao had built, and a little group of Christians were standing together to meet them.

Recently the Vietnamese government had placed 1,200 refugees, fleeing from the Communists of the mainland on the island, and they were making a meager living by fishing or selling firewood.

As the helicopter swung around the lovely palm-fringed beach at treetop level, Gordon was surprised to see the village cove crowded so thickly with shacks and lean-tos! He thought the refugees would have been placed on other coves on the island. But the Vietnamese like to crowd in closely together!

The place Gordon had picked out for the pilot to land on was now only about fifty feet square. The helicopter tilted upward in front and came down almost vertically to land on this only free bit of beach available in the village.

The passengers all piled out with the huge rotors slashing the air and raising a gigantic storm of sand that scattered the villagers. Above them, the accompanying helicopter circled, for there was no place for it to land on the village beach. Both planes had machine gunners on the watch at each side door, but there were no Communists on the islands.

Gordon greeted the group of forty Christians and then got back into the helicopter and was whisked over to the mainland again in a few minutes.

He would soon return by our launch *Hope* to Cu-Lao Cham Island to take in some relief food, clothing, and medical aid to the poor refugees there. This help for the needy came to us in cartons from churches and groups of friends in the United States, Canada, and England. Also Gordon was eager to visit the new group of Christians whom we had not seen since furlough.

After these visits, Gordon flew by helicopter from Da Nang to Chu Lai, the great marine base, six miles long, just twenty-five miles opposite the island of Ly Son.

The marine chaplain at Chu Lai, Chaplain Harold Jeffers, had found out that a new church, day school, and national preacher's house were needed on the Ly Son Island, so he and his band of Christian marines took on this project as a civic action program. They did a magnificent job!

Through the untiring efforts of the chaplain and other officers and men, including some majors and colonels, they were able to "scrounge" a thousand sacks of cement and great stacks of used lumber and roofing. They loaded these materials on trucks and then on barges to be shipped across to our preacher, Mr. Huk, at Ly Son. The island Christians unloaded the construction materials and carried them up from the beach to the chapel site. They worked hard to construct their new buildings.

The marines paid for the new site out of their chapel funds. The land was a rather rocky place, but it was volcanic lava rock and fairly easy to break up. So the island Christians had to do a lot of rock breaking before they could haul the sand and the other building materials. Both men, women, and Preacher Huk, numbering thirty-five in all, worked together. They dug down deep through the rock and made a well. Then they made cement blocks by hand.

By April 14, 1967, the walls of the church were finished, the preacher's house about half finished, and the foundation for the five-room primary school was leveled. So they had a cornerstone-laying ceremony on that day.

Gordon was at Chu Lai, and around 9:30 A.M. on April 14, two helicopters took him and Chaplain Jeffers across the sea to Ly Son Island. With them were several marine officers, as well as the chief chaplain for the marines from Da Nang. A military truck on Ly Son Island met them at the little airstrip, and they drove the three miles to the site where Pastor and Mrs. Huk and the island Christians were waiting for them in their Sunday best. Later the colonel who was commanding officer of the marines at Chu Lai choppered over to be with them.

There were speeches, prayers, and Scripture reading. The cornerstone on which the date "14-4-67" had been carved, was laid in place in the front wall.

During the past years many American chaplains had taken a keen interest in our missionary work and did a great deal for us.

Chaplain Jeffers was outstanding in his zeal to see a proper church and school erected on the island. He made trips to the Philippines to purchase some supplies for the buildings. He

US marines load food and clothing at Crescent Beach
Orphanage.

ordered a four by five foot stained glass window to be made
there for the new church, depicting "Christ and the Fishermen,"
but in Oriental style.

They purchased a pump organ and sent one of the Christian
young men to Da Nang, where I began to give him music lessons so that someday he could play the organ at Ly Son. A
large church bell was erected on a separate pedestal.

The following month Gordon visited Ly Son Island again.
He flew down from Da Nang in a giant C-53 helicopter to Chu
Lai in twenty minutes. Then he expected to go over to the
island from there, on the usual medical chopper flight that the
marines had organized, but on that day the flight had been
canceled.

Marine Chaplain Robinson was now taking Chaplain Jeffers'
place, whose year of service in Vietnam was finished. Chaplain
Robinson looked around for a means of crossing with Gordon
over to Ly Son Island. The American navy at Chu Lai kindly
said they could go on one of their "Swift Boats" which have
regular patrols in that area.

They were soon skimming along at twenty knots, leaving a tremendous wake on the calm sea behind them. The officers and men on board were kindness itself, sharing their lunch with Gordon and Chaplain Robinson.

In an hour's time they were offshore in front of the church and soon called a sampan out to take the men off the Swift Boat. The chaplain took over a number of damaged cases of corned beef, some of which was spoiled, but a lot were still good. These were given to the Christians while they worked on the church, as they had to leave their fishing and gardening to do so.

Gordon said, "I have never seen Christians working so hard to build their own chapel, school, and preacher's house. They hired a special Vietnamese mason and carpenter to guide them in building, but the Christians did most of the work themselves."

Gordon brought back six of the island boys with him to enter the new Christian high school established on the Christian and Missionary Alliance compound in Da Nang.

These boys would be supported in the high school by the marine chaplain and his men in Chu Lai. These marine Christians saw that they had the power to give these poor people on Ly Son Island a chance. They were helping them to have their first church and school, and they were excited in getting these nine lads off to Christian high school. Christianity isn't dull! How fascinating and delightful it is to be able to share with and help others!

Gordon and the schoolboys were picked up by the patrol boat again. The boys were thrilled with the good apples the officers gave them, the first they had ever eaten. It was also the first time these boys had ever been off the island, and they were excited at the sights and sounds of the huge base at Chu Lai.

The chaplain invited Gordon and the boys to lunch in the officers' mess, and shortly afterward they were able to return to Da Nang by helicopter. This was a big cargo chopper with no seats, so they stood up or sat on their bags. The island boys kept jumping from window to window to see the sights below along the beautiful coastline with islands, beaches, and shipping.

Our China Beach Orphanage was growing fast! The Vietnamese district officials from the Dai An area, forty miles west of Da Nang, asked us to take in forty Vietnamese children, most of whose fathers had been killed in the war and many of their mothers also. The air force gave us a C-123 cargo plane, and Gordon and a chaplain went with the plane pilot to bring in the children.

Then the Vietnamese authorities from another war-torn district came and asked us to take in one hundred children from their area. The officials were looking after their papers, such as birth certificates, and release from relatives. When these children were brought in by the air force men, we had 264 children in the orphanage.

These were all precious children with great potentialities. We appealed for friends in America and England to help sponsor them and love them into the Kingdom of God. We asked the prayers of many prayer helpers that each child might turn out to be a worthy Christian, living for our Lord in Vietnam.

A number of groups in the American armed forces showed a deep concern for these children. Doctors and dentists gave them free treatments. The chaplains urged their men to become interested, and the result was splendid! The men brought the orphans packages of food, clothing, toys, candies, games, and school supplies. One group contributed twenty-four large loaves of fresh bread every day. Others spent their spare hours wiring the buildings for electricity. Offerings were taken from time to time in the military chapels to help defray the orphanage expenses.

All these helpful gifts made us dizzy with elation! Practically every day a car or truck would come into our compound to unload surplus food, damaged tins of canned food, construction materials of all kinds, broken bags of cement, twisted steel and dunnage lumber from the naval docks; used iron beds, mattresses, and bedding. Right to the last day of the war, the GI's gave us this generous, selfless help unstintingly!

Dr. Stuart Harverson also received valuable help from the

American armed forces for his work among the Hrey tribes in Ha Bak and Son Ha areas. Dozens of times they gave him the use of a helicopter to take in his Hrey workers with supplies of medicines, clothing, food, and blankets. The special forces guarding that area also gave school supplies and food, and tin roofing for their huts when the thatched roofs would have been burned by raiding Communists.

The armed forces also helped the doctor and his Hrey workers to get supplies in by helicopter for the Hrey workers in Gia-Vut and Minh-Long. All the roads were closed by then into Bato and all the other Hrey tribal centers. If the Americans hadn't helped by plane, we couldn't have reached these thousands of Christian Hrey tribespeople.

The United States First Cavalry Division, completely airborne with 500 helicopters, had moved into AnKhe, one of the big centers in the Kontum District. They created a tremendous base of operations there for the high plateau tribal country. AnKhe had been a dusty Vietnamese and Bahnar tribal village, almost lost in the windswept expanse of a vast upland valley. The French once had a big garrison there that fought bitterly against the Vietminh. Now great battles were again being fought for this area since 1965, and AnKhe had become a raw boomtown. Several thousand Vietnamese from the coast moved up to work at the First Cavalry base, and so the group of Christians in our AnKhe church grew to over one hundred. With much sacrifice on their part and with help from the American men, the Christians now had a new church building.

Andrew Van der Bijl, Stanley Smith, and Gordon went to the dedication of this chapel at AnKhe. Because the coastal roads and the No. 14 Highway from Quinhon to AnKhe were now closed in the war, the missionaries were flown south from Da Nang in an American cargo plane to Quinhon on the coast where they boarded a huge C-130 cargo plane filled with marines for AnKhe. There were one hundred men squatting on the floor of the plane, crammed in like sardines. Because the air-cooling system was not working, fumes from the turbo-prop engines filled the plane, nearly suffocating them for half an hour. Finally they opened a hatch in the roof, while still airborne, and they were able to breathe again.

They landed, but not at AnKhe. The weather was bad there, so they had gone on to Pleiku. The missionaries slept in the airport waiting room on the cement floor in their sleeping bags. The next morning, Sunday, they were able to fly into AnKhe by noon.

Then they learned that a few hours before the Communists had lobbed a hundred mortar shells into the First Cavalry base and a number of American men had been wounded and killed.

Except for a bit of C rations, the missionaries had not had a meal since breakfast the day before: But by 2 P.M. Sunday, they arrived at the AnKhe chapel and got food and drink. The heat was almost unendurable there in April.

At 9 A.M. Monday they all gathered for the dedication service. One chaplain of the First Cavalry attended. The Vietnamese district chief was there with his escort of twelve soldiers. The Roman Catholic priest was also invited, and he said later that he had never heard such a fine sermon as the one Brother Andrew preached that morning, through Stanley as an interpreter.

That afternoon Gordon got on a plane to Saigon, while Stan and Andrew stayed on for two more days of meetings at AnKhe before going on to visit Kontum. Gordon's ride was in a big C-130 cargo plane again and it took five hours with numerous stops to fly the 300 miles to Saigon. They'd had no food or water, and it was suffocatingly hot, up to 100 degrees. Arriving at the C. & M.A. Mission home in Saigon at 10:30 P.M., Gordon raided their icebox before turning in.

During the past weeks he had been traveling a great deal by cargo plane and a variety of helicopters. With the noise and heat and long waits at the military airports, it was a bit tiring at times. But Gordon felt that if the American servicemen could stand it to help save Vietnam, why couldn't a Vietnam missionary?

At this time Dr. and Mrs. Harverson left for a six-month furlough in England.

Mary Henderson, who was looking after the mission bookkeeping, also taught English classes to twenty or so Vietnamese and Chinese in her home. She held a meeting each Monday evening in English for her language students, and a number of them were saved.

Stanley and Ginny and their children now returned to work at Kontum. They couldn't go back to their nice home they had built at Dak To as it was practically destroyed, and the Communists were very dangerous in that area. A big air force C-130 Hercules plane carried Stan and Ginny's Land Rover and household goods with their family up to Kontum.

Our son Leslie was now in government work in the highlands of Vietnam, and we only saw him once or twice a year. He was in the psychological warfare program, dropping by plane over communist-held tribal territories wordless, illustrated leaflets and posters to the tribespeople who did not understand the Vietnamese language. He went with tribal soldiers into various mountain areas on foot to visit some of the tribal villages. The risks were great.

They made tapes in the different tribal languages, and then they used loudspeakers from the planes to talk to the jungle mountain people. Leslie was intensely interested in doing this kind of work because he knows the tribal country and people well, and he did not want to see them fall into the hands of the Communists.

After January 1, 1968, we and our national church would be leaving the Worldwide Evangelization Crusade to become associated with the United World Mission, with headquarters in St. Petersburg, Florida, under Dr. Sidney Correll as president. During the nine years of working under W.E.C. we found that there were a few minor differences between us in the principles and practices of missionary work, especially in the realm of appealing for finances and field organization.

So a joint statement was drawn up that: "In love and spiritual fellowship we recognized that the differences in policies and practices of the two organizations—our Society in Viet-Nam, named Co-Doc Truyen-Giao Hoi, and the W.E.C., had decided to separate with mutual regret."

There were no changes in the programs of our national

churches, orphanages, leprosy work, and Bible school. Mrs. Simone Haywood and Dr. and Mrs. Harverson continued to work with us as members of W.E.C., loaned to our field organization.

The blessing of God that we had had all these years under the W.E.C. now continued under the United World Mission.

We were so busy with so many projects that life was quite a whirl. But it was wonderful to be able to serve the Lord and see His work advance despite the difficulties of war.

We often showed our missionary movies and spoke to groups of the armed forces. One Sunday afternoon, a dozen chaplains with delegations from their units—air force, marine, seabees, and army—came to hold a big meeting at the China Beach Orphanage. We had a wonderful time together and warm fellowship in the Lord.

Dr. and Mrs. Stuart Harverson wrote to us from England at this time of the sorrowful news that their son with Missionary Aviation Fellowship in New Guinea had been killed. They wrote:

> A few weeks ago we received a cable that our son, John, was missing for over a week in the highlands of New Guinea. He was flying with some tribal Christians. Extensive search was made, but nothing was found of the missing party.
>
> We may never know what happened to that plane, but we know that God was there, and we have no will but His.
>
> Twelve long years of preparation for the mission field and twelve short months of service! Yet we dare to believe that God, in his perfect wisdom, ordained it all. David always set his troubles to music, and he gave us the 23rd Psalm:
>
> "Yea, though I walk through the valley of the shadow of death, I will fear no evil, for thou art with me; thy rod and thy staff they comfort me. . . . Surely goodness and mercy shall follow me all the days of my life: and I will dwell in the house of the LORD for ever."

Dr. and Mrs. Harverson soon returned to their field in Vietnam to continue their great work among the Hrey tribespeople. There were several thousand Christians and a Hrey orphanage now of sixty children.

14

Perilous Times

BECAUSE OF THE DANGERS of travel in wartime, we women missionaries were confined mostly to Da Nang in those days. So what was my own special missionary work when at home in Da Nang?

Our Bible school is usually in session every year with twenty students for eight months, and for years I've taught in it, three hours a day, in the Vietnamese language. My subjects have been: The Gospel of John; 1 Peter; Epistle to the Ephesians; Study of the Universe and God's Plan through the Ages; Studies on the Holy Spirit; Studies on Prayer; Studies of Christian Books translated into Vietnamese, such as *Mimosa* by Amy Wilson Carmichael, *Pastor Hsi,* by Mrs. Howard Taylor, *The Man God Uses* by Dr. Oswald J. Smith, and other books.

Outside of the Bible school teaching hours five days a week, a typical week for me was as follows:

Sunday: Our Sunday morning Vietnamese service in Da Nang is held in our Bible school chapel at 9 A.M. I played the organ and about every two months I gave a sermon talk in the Vietnamese language.

At 11 A.M. for nearly ten years we attended the American military chapel a few blocks from our Da Nang home, and I often played the electric foot-keyboard organ there, which I greatly enjoyed; the instrument was a wonderful treat to me.

On Sunday afternoon I prepared my flannelgraph message for the evening Gospel service in our Da Nang chapel. We use colorful flannelgraphs and backgrounds a great deal in our witnessing for the Lord, and I have several trunks full of them that we've used over the years.

Before giving the story in the evening service we always had much lively Gospel singing of choruses and hymns.

Monday: For several years, each weekday morning the missionaries living in Da Nang gathered at our house for an hour of Bible reading and prayer from 7:30 to 8:30 A.M.

On Monday evenings I sometimes gave a flannelgraph talk at Mary Henderson's meeting in her home, with her students who were learning English.

Tuesday: I taught music lessons to five of the boys at the new C. & M.A. Christian High School, three of them orphans from our China Beach Orphanage and two of them from the Ly Son Island group.

Wednesday: A prayer meeting was held in our chapel. Our Vietnamese preacher, Mr. Giang, led the hour of bright testimonies from old and young and saw that everyone got a chance to pray. Even six-year-olds and grannies were expected to take part. I took part in this meeting, and it was a warmhearted time of blessing for us all.

Thursday: This was my day for inviting four or five of our American friends here in Da Nang for dinner at night. Chaplains, officers, and civilian engineers came for fellowship with us. Many of them were helping us in our work, especially at the orphanage and leprosarium. It was a pleasure to get to know these men, and they seemed to appreciate for a change a home-cooked meal with nice linen, pretty dishes from our relatives in England, with candles and flowers. After dinner we had singing at the piano, and sometimes a few games together, like Scrabble, Chinese checkers, or anagrams.

Friday: Quite often I showed my flannelgraph stories to the leprosy patients from Da Nang who came to our skin clinic held on our compound.

Often there were patients, too, from our leprosarium, staying at the clinic for special treatment. We had good times together, and in one year of my teaching there, I have listed forty patients who came to accept the Lord through the flannelgraph Bible messages.

Saturday: For two hours in the morning on this day I worked with my Vietnamese translator. He took the messages in English that I was to give and put them into good Vietnamese for flannelgraph talks, sermons, and studies from good books. In this way I was confident that the messages I was giving were in good Vietnamese idiom.

On Saturday evening we went over to the orphanage at China Beach, and I held a meeting for over two hundred children and the staff. Sometimes we had a swim and picnic supper on the beach beforehand. Then I just about wore myself out teaching the children choruses and motion songs. After the sing-song I gave a flannelgraph story. The meeting always lasted two hours, and I was ready to drop with fatigue afterward. But we had joyous times. Usually before leaving for home, I gave organ lessons to two of the orphan boys.

Now and then on Saturday evenings, Gordon and I stayed to listen to the children in their different dormitories, where they live from twenty to thirty in a room, having their evening prayers around a long table with their housemother. They read the Bible lesson responsively, and then each child led in prayer. It was touching to hear them.

By early September every year, I'd have written out a big Christmas play, sometimes original, and my Vietnamese translator would put it into Vietnamese. When hundreds of copies of it were mimeographed, the young people in our Da Nang chapel, along with our Bible school students, the orphans, and special patients in the leprosarium, all began practicing it, each group for their own Christmas program. I always had the huge task of overseeing the orphanage and Da Nang chapel groups in their practicing each week from September to Christmas.

We are exceedingly happy in this busy life. There is much joy in feeding our "sheep and lambs." It is a great and high calling, a captivating adventure.

Stanley wrote from Kontum that he had been to Dak Pek by helicopter, and he weathered out a rocket attack while staying overnight with the Green Berets in their fortified camp.

An enemy mortar round landed fifteen feet from the house of our Katu preacher, Mr. Trien. No damage was done except for a dozen holes in the tin roof. Everybody was living underground now at Dak Pek for safekeeping.

Intelligence reports said that Kontum was due to be mortared, so Ginny and the children were flown by helicopter an hour and a half over the mountains to Da Nang. It was Thanksgiving Day in 1967, and they arrived just in time to go with Gordon and me to a lovely American Thanksgiving dinner at the 37th Signals Battalion in the Da Nang air base. The tables and walls of the mess hall were gaily decorated for the occasion with turkeys, pilgrims, pumpkins, and the Mayflower sailing ship.

Dak To, Stan and Ginny's old station in the Kontum District, was being hit badly by the Communists in those days, but the American troops there got a great Thanksgiving Day prize: the Hill 875! For twelve days, units of the 173rd Airborne Brigade had been trying to take the hill, but the fighting had been fierce and bloody. Over 1,000 North Vietnamese had been killed, and the victory had cost the Americans 136 killed and 150 wounded on the slopes of the hill.

Soon after the victory, helicopters whirled in on the smoking peak to bring the conquering troops the turkey dinners that cooks had been keeping warm for them! It was an extra special feast for the troops because it was their first hot meal in twelve days! They ate their dinner on paper plates and tin mess trays amid the rubble of battle: bomb craters, burned bamboo and other jungle woods, and empty shell casings.

Stanley had been at Dak To while some of the bombing and shooting was going on. He watched the buses leave to go to Kontum on a Sunday morning. About 11 A.M. one was dragged back. It had been hit by a claymore mine, and some of the passengers had been killed, others wounded.

Stan and his Land Rover full of workers had to return to Kontum that afternoon, so they followed a convoy down. Halfway there, the convoy stopped in dense jungle at the very place that the bus had been mined that morning. Rifle fire was heard. The convoy started up again, and they made it back safely to Kontum.

Then a battle came that night to Kontum, and Stan made a

tape of it. He squeezed under his low bed for he had no time to run out to his dugout. Later we listened to the tape and heard the fight just as Stanley heard it from under his bed!

The rattle of machine-gun fire came in spurts. Then, whoosh! Whoosh! Bang! Wham! Bang! Mortar shells exploded 200 yards from Stan's house. They were terribly loud and realistic on the tape. Stanley's voice came muffled and in grunts because of his tight quarters. The Communists were less than a mile away from the city! It was very dangerous! At midnight, with only a flashlight and all alone, Stan felt pretty insecure under the bed. But he got the whole sound of it on the tape.

A number of Americans were killed and wounded in that attack, and some were officers whom Stanley, Ginny, and the children had visited. The special forces camp at Kontum, just 200 yards from Stan's house, was badly hit. The Communists were doing accurate shooting, especially on the military camps, otherwise their mortars would likely have hit our church, school, parsonage, and Stan and Ginny's rented house nearby.

Two days later, Stan flew over to Da Nang for a committee meeting and thankfully joined Ginny and their children. How we humbly praised God for His protection.

The war was certainly swirling around many of the missionaries, but because our side had command of the air and control of the towns and cities we were usually comparatively safe and could keep on with the work.

Gordon tried to visit Happy Haven Leprosarium at Cam Hai, three miles south of the Marble Mountains on the outskirts of Da Nang. But the area was being more and more infiltrated by the Vietcong. Our Vietnamese workers and nurses had been able to carry on there and make trips along the beach in our old truck without much trouble, but we missionaries were warned not to go.

Then the marine chaplain and colonel in charge of the area suggested that Gordon visit the leprosarium to take in a doctor and dentist for the patients. They wanted to establish a weekly medical project for the people with leprosy, under marine protection. Gordon thought this would be a wonderful idea. Every night hundreds of the villagers from the area flocked into our leprosarium for protection from the Communists. The people built little lean-tos and shacks and slept in these overnight. Our two superintendents out there, Mr. Huan and Mr. Tue, were very busy helping these refugees with medical assistance.

Gordon drove to the Marble Mountains on the outskirts of Da Nang with our Vietnamese leader, Mr. Lich, and the leprosarium supervisor, Tue. They left their car in front of the marine sentry. The colonel arrived with a major in a jeep, and two huge amphibious troop carriers called Amtracs lumbered up with a lot of armed marines perched on top of each.

They started down the road toward the leprosarium, the colonel, major, Gordon and Mr. Lich in the jeep between the Amtracs, expecting to go two miles to a new marine outpost and then to turn off to the beach to go another mile before turning into the leprosarium. Gordon suggested that they go by the beach all the way, because the road was frequently mined. However, they said the road had been cleared of mines that day and cars had already gone on it as far as the marine camp and so it should be safe.

On the edge of enemy territory, they left the Marble Mountains and lumbered down the dusty road, the vehicles keeping 200 yards distance from each other. All the houses in the area had been destroyed by the Communists and there was no sign of life. Everyone was on the alert!

About a mile and a half down the road, they heard a big explosion over a rise ahead, and they came up to a cloud of dust and smoke. When it cleared, they could see the huge Amtrac lurched over into the ditch. It had hit a mine!

Gordon saw marines going over to look at something on the ground about fifty feet away, and he thought they were examining some electric detonator. But it was the driver of the Amtrac, who had been hurled out of the cockpit and had a broken arm! A couple of other men had also been thrown off. It was a miracle that no one was killed, or the Amtrac burned, for it had a lot of gasoline in tanks underneath.

Everyone was out with rifles and machine guns at the ready.

They radioed for a tank retriever to come and pull them out and to send medical help for the injured.

The colonel said he could not continue the trip, so he had his jeep driver drive the party back to Marble Mountains again. They were keenly disappointed at not reaching the leprosarium, only another mile away, but they were thankful to God that it had not been worse. Next time they would take the beach road that our truck followed.

Our station among the Cua tribe, Tra Bong, was always under fire. Mr. Quang, our Cua tribal preacher, had carried on bravely through the years at Tra Bong in spite of repeated attacks by the Vietcong.

At this time we placed Mr. and Mrs. Hap there again to help Quang. They and Quang had been the first evangelists in this area nine years before. Mr. Hap was now seventy-three years old, but he wanted to return to Tra Bong and help the church through these terrifying days of distress and hunger.

Tra Bong was now cut off from the outside world except by helicopter and Caribou cargo plane. The one road into this backcountry town was under Communist attack. The plane trips in were dangerous and infrequent in the rainy season. Quang came into Da Nang at that time for a committee meeting, and what he had to tell us was heartrending.

The Communists had killed all his brothers, two of whom had been fine Christians. One had been helping the Wycliffe translators, Miss Eva Burton and Miss Jackie Maiers, to learn the Cua language, and put into writing and translate the Gospel of Mark and the Book of Acts into Cua. He had gone up to Kontum with the girls to help in the translators' workshop there. Returning to Da Nang, he went on to Tam Ky by bus and was caught by the Communists there. They took him back into the mountains and tortured him for one year because he'd been "working for the Americans." Then he died. The Communists scalp the Cuas, then show them to their relatives, and kick and beat them to death! The poor tribespeople desperately fear the Communists!

They had caught two young boys at that time and bound

105

them in nylon rope. They told the boys that if Quang continued to work for the Americans, they would kill him. They said that they hated Quang intensely for his work for God in this Cua center.

The boys were able to undo their ropes and swim underwater across the river to safety again. They gave the warning to Quang. But Quang just committed it all to the Lord, trusting in Him, and went on serving Him faithfully. He had many tests of his faith. At that time his little boy was wounded badly by a grenade which went off near him. Quang and his wife and five children slept in an underground bunker every night. In the rainy months the bunker became filled with mud and water. Only God helped them survive the cold, hunger, and suffering.

The 3,000 Cua tribespeople who had been living at Tra Bong as refugees, guarded by the special forces and Vietnamese government soldiers, had had their bamboo houses burned three times by the dreadful communist terrorists! The Cuas could not enter the forest for materials to rebuild because the Vietcong would kill them. The people had hardly anything to eat and no clothing to wear. At night they'd sleep on the porches of the Vietnamese villagers for shelter. The children slept naked, as they had no blankets. They huddled around little fires during the rainy, cold nights.

The special forces at Tra Bong gave what help they could, but because of the heavy rains the planes could not bring in supplies regularly. Our mission wanted to ship in tons of relief food and clothing but there was little air transportation available. It hurt us not to be able to do more than send a few packages of clothing with Quang from time to time.

The Cua and Vietnamese Christians in Tra Bong told us they were not afraid to die. One hundred twenty-five Christians met in the little chapel every Sunday, and over Tra Bong there was always the incessant roar of guns and the fear of attack.

15

Visitors

THE PRESIDENT of United World Mission and his wife, Dr. and Mrs. Sidney Correll, from St. Petersburg, Florida, visited us, and we had a wonderful ten days together.

Helen Correll wrote a Vietnam Diary while she was with us, and I would like to quote some from it here:

> Gordon came down to Saigon to meet our Pan American plane. The next day we left Saigon for Da Nang on an Air America plane. We flew over mountains with very little visibility and we came in for a landing at Quinhon. The American captain of the plane told us that there was quite a storm between Quinhon and Da Nang. Visibility was only ¾ of a mile.
>
> "I'll get you there," he told us, "but it may be rough."
>
> The sign "Fasten Seatbelts" was on all the time. Rain was deluging the windows of the D.C.3. The Vietnamese passengers were getting sicker by the minute. Sidney and I were having a wonderful visit with Gordon on the plane.
>
> It was then time to land at Da Nang, but we kept on flying—15 minutes, 30, 45 minutes went by—one hour! We joked a bit, saying that maybe the pilot had missed Da Nang, and we must now be up near Hanoi!
>
> It was a great relief to land at last! The airfield had been closed, and many planes had been kept aloft until the weather cleared a bit. We found that we had skirted the tail of a typhoon on the way up the coast. We were saddened to learn that a huge C-130 cargo plane with 23 servicemen and personnel aboard was lost in the same storm when it crashed into a mountain near Da Nang!
>
> We spent an entire day in Conference with the Vietnamese

preachers. We felt humble in their presence for we were indeed among men "who had hazarded their lives for the Gospel." What firebrands for God! Most of them had been preaching for ten years among the tribal and backcountry Vietnamese but now had been chased out by the Communists—their churches and houses burned, and they must now set up new churches in refugee centers. Some had been converted to Christ from Buddhist homes and other from Confucianist homes that practiced ancestor worship. They were gentle, quiet-spoken men, who were slow to speak for themselves.

These men have built churches and have seen these churches and all the villages wiped out, have had many of their members killed because they were Christians! They tell stories that would rend your heart. Some came down from the Demilitarized Zone and traveled through dangerous territory to meet us. One young man arrived two days later than the others. The storm had washed out all the bridges, and he had to wait for the water to recede. He worked at Bato among the Hrey tribespeople, and the Communists were thick in that area. Thirty of these pastors were at the Conference. They are doing a great work of evangelism among these tribespeople and back country Vietnamese who had never heard the Gospel before.

While the Sidney Corrells were with us, we were able to share in the dedication of the Ly Son Island church.

We waited at the great helicopter pad at the Marine Air Group near the Marble Mountains, and this was the first helicopter ride for Dr. and Mrs. Correll and for me!

It was a big bird, a cargo 53! There were no seats among the cargo, so we sat on the floor with the marines. Flying offshore, we arrived at the Chu Lai base, nearly one hundred miles to the south in a very short time. Here we were met by Marine Chaplain James Robinson, who had arranged a ride for us out to the island.

We boarded a Sikorsky 34 helicopter and were given life jackets to put on, for fear of having to come down into the ocean. The helicopters seldom fly alone, so another copter went along for protection.

When we reached the island fifteen minutes later, they circled the church so that we could photograph it from the air. Then they flew us to the beach nearby, and I was surprised to find how gently they slowed down their descent, and we softly sank on the wheels on the sand. But the big rotor blades made a wild, swirling sandstorm!

The Ly Son Island people, smiling and welcoming us, came crowding down, then were scattered by the storm made by the rotors. The people carried our luggage, and as we walked the narrow trail up to the church, some of the girls walked behind Helen and me, gently pinching our arms and stockings. They had never seen stockings before, and they laughed and giggled at what looked like our loose skin. They had never seen a white woman until I came here to this island with Gordon five years previously. Now here was Helen, too, and they were delighted to look us over.

In front of the church was an archway of bamboo, leaves, and flowers with a sign in Vietnamese telling about the dedication of the chapel that day.

The service of dedication began as a crowd stood outside on the front steps and banks, and Gordon prayed the dedication prayer. Then the doors were opened wide to the strains of the new little organ playing "Open the Gates of the Temple," and the people poured inside and sat down. How nice everything looked with the colored glass window of "Christ and the Fishermen," the new pews and new organ! It was a tremendous day for all these Christians who had worked so hard to build their church. We acclaimed the marines at Chu Lai for their dedication in providing funds and materials for the new church, school, and preacher's house. We praised the Lord for all that had happened here during the five short years since the Gospel first came to Ly Son Island.

When we returned to Chu Lai at 3 P.M., a Huey, the Rolls-Royce among helicopters, was called to take us to Da Nang. Dr. Correll sat in the second pilot's seat, which had a helmet, earphones, and mike, so that he could talk to the pilot. Helen, Gordon, Mr. Lich, and I sat on the one seat that goes across the helicopter. They strapped us in with seat belts. The side doors were wide open, and when the pilot banked steeply, we were looking down over the edge of nothing! That was a scary thrill, hard to beat!

We could see through the bubble in front of the pilot's seat. We had one gunner aboard and a "gun ship" helicopter was flying near us for protection. It was very exciting! Helen wrote: "If you want to know what it is like to fly on a magic carpet, that was *it!* The movements were smooth and light as a butterfly." But as for *me,* I felt very shaky and fluttery.

Suddenly, looking ahead of us, near the beach, we saw smoke and bursts of flame! As we came closer, we could see a spotter plane flying over the land and dropping smoke bombs. Then a Phantom fighter jet came zooming in, dropping bombs along the targets. The jet flew out in a great circle around us and came whining in again. Fortunately no Migs get down this far from Hanoi, as they would be spotted many miles away by the great American radar system on top of Monkey Mountain at Da Nang, and would be soon met by our fighter planes far up the coast of North Vietnam. United States planes were the only ones in the air here. But we could have been fired at by communist missiles from the ground! Helen said she wasn't frightened at all but was terribly excited! I myself felt very shivery. If only the doors had been shut, I'd have felt better, but we were hanging up there, high in the sky in a quivering bulb, under wide, whirling rotors. And we were having a ring-side seat at an actual air strike! It was amazing! A strong, solid Vietcong area was being penetrated! We were told that all the civilians had been warned in the area, and they were now either in deep underground bunkers or had gotten out of the vicinity into refugee camps.

Dr. Correll had his movie camera and took pictures. These can be seen today in his moving picture called, "The Other Viet-Nam," shown in many churches in America.

Soon after witnessing the air attack on the Vietcong, we were flying over our leprosarium; then we passed the Marble Mountains, and the pilot choppered us down the beach, close over our China Beach Orphanage. Sidney got good shots of it from the air.

110

Then, as a last gesture of VIP treatment, the pilot flew us low over the city of Da Nang and up the Da Nang River. We were swooping so closely to the hundreds of sampans on the river that we could look right into the low doors of their little riverboat houses! I was really scared as we skittered low over the big American-built bridge on the river, twin to the "De Lattre de Tasigny" French bridge beside it. I was sitting next to frail, little Mr. Lich by the door on our side and I clung to his arm, but it was like a slender stick and wasn't much support. Gordon, on the other side, was sitting halfway out of the chopper, with one foot on the skid below and hanging on tightly against the rush of the ninety-mile wind! He was enjoying every minute of it!

I was thankful indeed as we came settling slowly down onto the marine pad at Marble Mountain again.

What an intensely thrilling day we'd had! And we said a big thank you to all the marine officers and men who made the day possible!

Stanley, Ginny, and children, by this time, were back at Kontum again, and so Dr. and Mrs. Correll with Gordon and I visited there with them and six Vietnamese preachers. We flew there, and Sidney got pictures of the Kontum church and school, Stan and Ginny's dugout by their bedroom door, and pictures of the brave workers, both men and women.

As in all our days, little did we know of the terrors that lay ahead!

16

A Dark Tet to Remember: 1968!

"Everywhere, everywhere, Christmas." Bring out all the Christmas things! First of all I had to put on my little seasonal apron with small Christmas trees on it and wreaths of colored sequins and tiny jingling bells. I can do the Christmas decorating better and the last-minute work on the costumes for the Christmas play if I wear a pretty Christmas apron.

We were telling the Christmas story beautifully and dramatically this year by a new Christmas play, "Ye Shall Find the Child," an hour and a half long. It had a wonderful message.

For more than one hundred of our orphans this was to be their very first Christmas. Some of the thirty-five orphans in the cast had only been in the orphanage for a few months.

Every gesture, every inflection of the voice, had to be drilled into the children through the week after week of practicing since September. It is excellent training in public speaking for our orphans, Bible school students, and the other young people, and we were very proud of them.

We gave the program first on December 15 in our own Da Nang chapel. Then we put it on in one of the new schoolrooms being built at that time at our China Beach Orphanage. We gave it next to the American military men at the 1st Corps Chapel near our Da Nang property. On Christmas Eve we presented the play at the Chapel of the Flags; and finally, on Christmas Day, to the marines at MAG 16 Helicopter Base near the Marble Mountains. In each place the children and students did superbly, and for each presentation we had our own colored spotlights, footlights, painted backgrounds, big curtains, and beautiful costumes.

The American military men thanked the children warmly for their lovely portrayal of the Christmas story and told how

112

it lifted up the hearts of the GIs here in Vietnam at Christmastime.

During Christmas week, the orphans were invited, in groups of fifty, to Christmas dinners at various bases of the armed forces, and all were most generous with their gifts of toys, candies, oranges, and apples for the children, and some gave splendid offerings from their chapel funds.

Gordon and I were invited to the U.S. hospital ship, the *Sanctuary*, anchored in Da Nang Bay, to show some of the pictures to the doctors and nurses of our missionary work in Vietnam. We were taken out to the big ship by the ship's officers' launch and we had a delightful dinner with the ship's captain, executive officer and chaplain, in the captain's private suite. He had pretty Christmas decorations and candles from home.

Then we visited around the wards, especially with the wounded Vietnamese soldiers on board, admired all the gay Christmas decorations over the whole ship, and had good fellowship with the American doctors and nurses on board. We stayed overnight in a ship's cabin and had a good rest. After breakfast, we saw some helicopters, loaded with wounded from the battlefields, land on the ship's rear deck. The bloodstained casualties of war were quickly rushed on their stretchers into the operating rooms.

We had celebrations during Christmas week with our leprosy clinic patients in Da Nang, with a service explaining the meaning of Christmas, the coming of our Saviour to everyone who will receive Him.

The leprosy patients at the Happy Haven had a Christmas service with many Vietnamese government officials attending with us. There were gifts of clothing, candy, and toys for all the children of the patients.

That evening we entertained twelve of the Vietnamese government officials at our home for dinner, and Mr. and Mrs. Lich entertained eleven more of the party at their home for a Vietnamese dinner.

Soon after the New Year, January 1, 1968, Gordon had to return to America for meetings with our new board, the United

World Mission, and returned to Vietnam by England and Holland. In Holland he interviewed two girls who were preparing to come to Vietnam for two years: Miss Mimi du Fosse, a physiotherapist for the leprosy patients, and Miss Nelly Heyboer, a registered nurse, especially for the leprosarium and clinic; also a young man for practical missionary work, Yohan Compagnien. They would be coming out to Vietnam in the spring of that year.

It was now the end of January, the beginning of Tet, the Vietnamese lunar New Year of 1968. Both the Communists and Allies had announced that they would observe a cease-fire for the holidays.

But the Vietcong and the North Vietnamese treacherously took advantage of these cease-fire promises to unleash a massive offensive against hundreds of South Vietnamese cities and towns! *That was a dark Tet to remember!*

Stanley and Ginny and their children were able to leave Kontum just before that city was violently struck by the enemy. Everyone there had had word that the attack was imminent, so Stanley brought his family to Da Nang just in time.

Our two most northerly provinces of South Vietnam, Quang Tri and Hue, were directly threatened by the Communists. The imperial city of Hue was held for twenty-six days by the North Vietnam Army. It was a time of dreadful terror! Five thousand innocent civilians in Hue were shot to death or buried alive! Three German doctors and some nurses helping in the Hue hospital were taken prisoners.

In Saigon it was an awful nightmare! Just before the Tet holidays of that year, 1968, the Vietcong commanders sent their men into these two cities of Saigon and Hue on buses, in taxis, on motor scooters. Some were concealed in trucks loaded with the beautiful flowers for the Tet celebrations. They hid ammunition under the flowers planted in large clay flowerpots. The Vietcong blended into the local population, as at that time all the relatives of the city people were flocking "home for Tet," as is the yearly custom. So the communist soldiers, dressed as civilians, pretended to be joining their families, going home to keep tryst with their ancestors on the first three days of the Tet.

They had pocket money to buy Tet firecrackers "to chase off the demons."

In Saigon alone 3,000 elite Red troops mingled unobtrusively with the thousands of countryside people pouring in. No one noticed when, at times, the Communists even "tested their rifles," because of all the firecrackers being exploded to welcome the New Year! Half of the South Vietnamese Army was on the carefree, careless leave at Tet, the big joyous holidays of the New Year.

Even when huge red banners suddenly appeared in some Saigon streets, commemorating the old historic battle of Dong Da, the United States Command Intelligence was not familiar with this story or they could have taken warning! It told of how a former Vietnamese hero, Nguyen Van Hue, won his famous victory over the Chinese in 1788 by launching his troops into battle *during Tet!* No Vietnamese told the American intelligence about the warning banners and the historical episode. Perhaps no one even thought of the banners as a warning. Everyone was unprepared for the terrible offensive.

Just after midnight on the first day of Tet, devastating blows hit Saigon and Hue! Thick columns of smoke rose up from burning homes. Streets were covered with corpses. Day after day the blood-drenched battle raged for the control of South Vietnam. The communist troops holed up in the shanty towns and labyrinthine back alleys of Saigon and in the swarming Chinese city of Cholon. In one night they attacked eight police stations there! Government troops counterattacked with tanks and machine guns. Only three of Saigon's nine districts were considered secure and had the blue color. All the other six districts had the bright red signs of danger.

The great Tan Son Nhut Airport was badly attacked by Vietcong and North Vietnamese units, as was the residence of President Thieu and many other headquarters places, the radio station, and of course, the American Embassy! If they could seize that great new embassy building, even for a brief time, it would be a shattering blow to the U.S. prestige!

But the three-inch teakwood doors of the embassy held. U.S. Marines arrived in great numbers. The attack was on in one sustained roar! The Vietcong wore civilian clothes but they had identifying red armbands and neckbands. Explosions rocketed the main building. Glass was shattered. There were deafening fusillades of automatic-weapon fire.

In one house on the embassy compound, one of the two American officers sleeping there, Colonel Jacobson, whom we had met previously, could only find a coat hanger with which to fight! Then a young marine bravely sprinted across the grounds and tossed him a .45 caliber pistol through an upstairs window, followed by two clips of ammunition!

If the Vietcong had been reinforced, they might have gotten the embassy. But no help came for them! It was five hours of agonizing tension, and the nerves of the Americans holding the important buildings were raw.

But the battle for the embassy was won! The compound became peaceful again, and even some of the flower beds were left, blazing their colors in the morning sun.

In the ancient, imperial city of Hue, the combat was even more savage! Hundreds of heavily armed communist soldiers got inside the old walled fortress known as "the Citadel." This is a three and one-third square-mile area which until a few years previously was the residence of His Majesty Bao Dai, and before him, all the other Vietnamese emperors. Now the communist soldiers held sway there!

One thousand U.S. Marines in Hue fought in bitter house-to-house fighting and gained control of the southern end of the city. Clouded skies and mist hampered the air coverage.

The Communists had proudly hoisted their red and blue flag over the province headquarters, but the leathernecks stormed through, hauled down the communist flag, and replaced it with the Stars and Stripes!

A special school for tribal students in Hue was shelled by the Communists at that time. Any survivors among the tribes' boys were captured by the enemy and taken into the mountains. Some of Dr. Harverson's Hrey children were among these students; the fine Christian son of Trien, our Katu evangelist in the Kontum area, was in this school; and some Cua children from Quang's group of Cuas at Tra Bong. No word has been heard of any of these since!

What about us missionaries in Da Nang? Fortunately for us, Da Nang was well defended, and it was the only city in Vietnam where the Tet offensive was successfully repulsed!

The Reverend Louis Myers, a Southern Baptist missionary in Da Nang, was the one chosen to relay to us how the American military were planning to take care of all of us missionaries here at that time. Mr. Myers met at the American consul's, with an American security group and the head colonel of the 1st Corps. They explained to Mr. Myers how we'd be cared for if Da Nang became more dangerous. They said that "Da Nang was the safest place in Vietnam during those one and one-half weeks of the Tet Offensive!" A few Communists infiltrated the city, but they were all ferreted out. If mortar shell attacks came, the security plans were all ready to take us missionaries and families over to the 1st Corps Headquarters buildings. Military police would come to our houses in their cars to get us. We would then be taken out on navy boats to one of the big American warships of the Seventh Fleet offshore.

They told us that they'd never let Da Nang become another Hue!

We had to have our suitcases packed, ready to leave at a moment's notice. Stan, Ginny, and I hardly dared to go out to the orphanage for fear the military police might come while we'd be away!

Our headquarters house is directly opposite a big police station and we feared that if the Communists got into the city, they'd take control of our house and machine gun the police center from there! So every night, Stanley came with his car across our compound to get me. Strict curfew was on and if we had walked out in the garden at night, we could have been shot at by the vigilant Vietnamese guards, thinking we were Communists. I'd take my two packed suitcases and hat and coat with me, and I'd sleep in a "safe corner" in Stan and Ginny's rooms with the children.

One night we received word that all of us missionaries must go over to the big hotel of CORDS, the American Aid headquarters in Da Nang the Americans called "the Alamo." So we all got into Stan's car with our suitcases, mosquito nets, and some bedding and drove to "the Alamo" two blocks away.

It was crowded with missionaries and social workers who had come down from Hue. They told us of their dreadful experiences in that city. Great sections of the city had been destroyed, and the two big bridges linking the two parts of the city were shattered by the Communists. The missionaries had seen many dead bodies on the streets outside their houses! Seven Christian Service workers on loan to the World Relief Commission had hidden in a cement bunker inside an old French house there for nearly a week and had lived on American C rations.

We were each given a camp cot in "the Alamo" and were put in nice apartments on all five floors. Two other missionary families were with Stan, Ginny, the children and me in one apartment. Stan and Woody Stemple, a C. & M.A. missionary, put up all our camp beds and mosquito nets. Marines guarded the hallways and rooms. Seventy Filipino soldiers guarded the broad stairways. We had a peaceful night and all returned to our homes the next morning.

But dreadful news came to us over our morning radio! Banmethuot, the jungle town among the Raday tribespeople where Gordon and I had lived and pioneered from 1934 to 1955, had been savagely attacked! Six of our dear colleagues of the C. & M.A. had been cruelly massacred! Carolyn Griswold, a charming young lady, was secretary for the mission there for several years and had also been doing outstanding work among the Raday young people; her father, Mr. Griswold, who had come out to join his daughter after his wife had died in Florida, was working as treasurer for the Banmethuot Leprosarium. Ruth (Stebbins) and Ed Thompson had been missionaries in our old field of Kratie in Cambodia. Then that country had been closed to missionaries for some years, and Ruth and Ed had come over to Banmethuot to work among the Mnong Preh tribe at Dak Song, sixty kilometers from Banmethuot. Ruth Wilting was one of the fine missionary nurses at the leprosarium. Bob Zeimer was our valiant colleague, about whose coming to Banmethuot we had written in our book, *Farther into the Night.* He did a wonderful work for God at Banmethuot. Mrs. Marie Zeimer was badly wounded in the attack, but would get better.

Hank Blood of Wycliffe Translators, who was putting the tribal Mnong-Rolum language into writing, was captured by the Communists, as was Miss Betty Olsen, a young nurse from Chicago recently arrived at Banmethuot for the leprosarium work. They were all our colleagues and dear friends.

Bombs had been placed in the three mission houses there, and the houses were blown to pieces. Gordon had built those two-story villas in 1950. But bricks, cement, and wood could be replaced. It would not be easy to find those who would measure up to the six wonderful missionaries whose lives had been so cruelly snuffed out by the Communists' bullets and grenades!

Our hearts ached over the two who had been captured and marched off barefooted into the rough jungle mountains. Word came later that they had died. About the three missionaries captured five years before by the Communists from the Banmethuot Leprosarium, no one has heard definitely yet, if they are living or gone on to glory. Heaven is inexhaustible happiness, and there are boundless rewards for the martyrs for Christ.

When Ginny Smith heard the radio news that morning, she turned very white and had a nervous attack with pains in her back. It was a terrible strain to be here at this dangerous time with three little children. Their furlough was almost due again, so we decided that Ginny and the children would leave soon to go back to her parents' home in Wheaton Illinois, Stanley would follow them in a few weeks' time.

Oliver and Joyce Trebilco, who were now working under the Bethany Fellowship Mission of Minneapolis and cooperating with Wycliffe in putting the Hrey tribal language into writing, came to our house to tell us something of the dreadful Communist Tet offensive on Kontum. The Trebilcos had been up at Kontum attending a big Wycliffe workshop for the translating of the many different tribal languages in Vietnam. They were advised to leave the city when Stanley's family left, but they continued on in the work. All of the Wycliffe Vietnam workers were in their houses in the Kontum workshop colony when they saw the situation was becoming very dangerous. They decided to leave then, but there were no American planes available to take them. Their colony of workshop houses was right in the direct crossfire line between the communist attackers and the special forces camp.

The Wycliffe missionaries and the Trebilcos stayed for a number of days inside an American military camp, in bunkers of cement and sandbags. They lived on military C rations because the Kontum market was completely destroyed by the enemy. It was a very perilous time for them!

Then American planes were finally able to fly all the missionaries out to Nha Trang. There the Wycliffe workers were able to quickly buy a big house and make a new center for their workshop.

Oliver told us how half of Kontum had been destroyed. The roof of the house Stan and Ginny were renting was shattered. A big shell had pierced it and fallen on the bed where little Karen and Kathy had slept. The whole Wycliffe workshop colony was destroyed after the missionaries had left just in time!

Our Vietnamese preacher, Mr. Luong, and his family, in the Kontum parsonage, crawled into their sandbagged bunker deep under their beds during one awful attack. They had locked their doors well. Then the communist soldiers came, pounding on the doors, demanding entrance. They threw grenades at the house, bashed in doors and windows, sprayed the rooms with machine-gun bullets. Luong and his wife and seven children were all hiding low and quiet in the bunker under their beds. The tiny children, one and two years old, didn't utter a sound. So they all came through safely! Luong said, "We were trembling but praying to God. We lost all our books and Bible studies that we treasured. They were shot to pieces. Our cupboards, typewriter, dishes and clothing were also all ruined."

Stanley went up to Kontum from Saigon to visit all the preachers there, after he saw Ginny and the children fly off from Saigon to America.

Our Cam Lo station at the Demilitarized Zone had been hit ferociously. The church and parsonage had been practically destroyed, and it was a miracle that the Pastor Toi and his family came through safely in their tiny underground bunker. The bunker was built of cement, but it had no sandbags on top of it or around it.

Minh, our half-French orphan boy, went up to visit at Cam Lo at Tet time and while he was there, God led Mr. Toi to ask Minh and some other church young people to fill up seventy-five bags with sand and to reinforce the bunker with the sandbags. Soon after that, the awful attack came! The communist soldiers came pouring in to Cam Lo, "shooting, with their bullets coming thickly like rain!"

Some of the frightened Christian neighbors crowded into the little bunker with Mr. and Mrs. Toi and their seven children. Seventeen people were in the tiny bunker, all terribly crushed together.

The church and the house were destroyed by mortars and the shells sent the sandbags flying! If they hadn't had the sanbags, the bunker would have been destroyed and all would have been killed. The bunker became full of the smoke of gunpowder, and the smallest children fainted from the acrid smell and the crowding.

For four hours they all stayed in the bunker. Then they came out and saw their church and house all in ruins. All of their dishes were smashed in little pieces.

Many Communists were dead on the ground not far away, and one American GI was also lying there dead, with a number of South Vietnamese.

After that, the Communists sent in mortar shells from a distance, and Toi and his family had to live in the little bunker for twenty days. The seventy Christians had all left the area by now. If they hadn't fled they would have been killed as their houses were laid flat.

During this time it rained continually and was very windy and cold. They had only a little rice and sugar for food. The market was destroyed and, anyhow, they didn't dare to go out to search for food. They lived on rice gruel and sugar water.

They all became thin like skeletons. But they trusted in the Lord continually and He brought them through!

In the Mekong Delta far away in the southern part of South Vietnam, all of the cities had been hit very hard. The hospitals were jammed. They said the mattresses became soaked like sponges, full of the blood of the wounded.

It was a terrifying offensive! Because half of the South Vietnam Army was on leave at the time of the Tet attack, troops had to come out of the rural areas to defend the cities. This left the rural places open to the Vietcong, as it took several months to get order restored again in the cities.

Television brought the war vividly into American homes. Thailand, Malaysia, Indonesia, and Australia, the neighboring countries of Vietnam, became worried and concerned.

In the big communist drive for a week and a half, the Communists lost 31,000 men; South Vietnamese also were killed by the thousands; 920 Americans were killed, and 4,560 men were wounded.

The Communists failed in their main objectives of the offensive, although they caused much suffering, bloodshed, and material damage. They slowed down the civic action and relief programs of the government for several months, as the many troops who were engaged in this work in the country districts had to come in to defend the cities.

The Communists had expected the population to rise up and welcome them; they had expected the South Vietnam government to fall; they expected the South Vietnam Army to defect to them in large numbers. They expected to occupy many cities and important towns. In all of these, they signally failed, and they lost tens of thousands of soldiers, killed and wounded.

Everyone was proud of the South Vietnam Army which defended the cities well, along with the Americans. It was the greatest victory for the American-South Vietnam Allies up to that time. The Communists did not fully recover from their losses for a long time. There grew out of the Tet offensive a new atmosphere of discipline and alertness as the people realized that they were fighting for their very existence against the Communists.

17

Hallelujah, What a Saviour!

RIGHT AFTER the vicious Tet offensive had died down, we began training some of the orphans in their coming Easter program. They would learn to sing in Vietnamese, John Peterson's lovely cantata, "Hallelujah, What a Saviour!"

In the tonal Vietnamese language it is impossible to sing in four parts and have all the words make sense. The word meanings depend on the accents. A word spoken with a rising sound means one thing; a falling tone means something else; a level tone means something else again. A question tone changes the meaning again.

In translating the words of the hymn music into Vietnamese we must use words whose tones will follow the melody as much as possible in order to make sense. But in the other three parts of the harmony—alto, tenor, and bass—the same words do not follow the tones and are therefore quite uinintelligible. They are singing four different words at the same time. They may be singing entirely different meanings or words with no sense at all.

But the orphans learned the cantata melody well, and on Easter Sunday night they sang it up at the front of the new chapel at the orphanage. The girls were all dressed in their white *ao dais*, the Vietnamese costume with white silk tunics over long white satin trousers and white sandals. The boys were in Western dark trousers with white shirts.

A beautiful big picture of Christ in the garden with Mary, at the Saviour's empty tomb was hung as a background to the choir. Tall white Easter lilies surrounded them. They were flown in from Dalat by a relative of Mr. Lich's, who grows these beautiful flowers there in the mountains. Many American men of the armed forces attended the Easter cantata and received much blessing.

A friend from the Wheaton Bible Church in Wheaton, Illinois, wrote about a meeting at which Ginny Smith spoke. She had just arrived home on furlough. The letter read: "The high point of our evening was a message from Ginny Smith, recently returned from Vietnam, where she and her husband, Stanley, have been doing such a fine work. When she finished speaking, the atmosphere was charged with the presence of the Lord. All of our hearts were deeply moved."

Before Stanley left Vietnam to join Ginny and the children on furlough, he visited the Kontum District again. He was thrilled to spend Easter Sunday morning at Dak Pek where nearly 1,000 Jeh tribal Christians gathered for a service in spite of the danger of a possible mortar or rocket round landing in their midst.

Fifteen or more Jeh villages from the mountains of this area were settled at the Dak Pek center for protection. So some of these Christians had formerly heard the Gospel at their old villages of Dak Ro-Ta, Dak Gle, and Plei Bom. More and more were believing on Christ, and now there were 3,000 Christians. They didn't believe just to get some outside help, as it was impossible to get rice, fish, clothing, or medicine to them. The roads were cut and the few planes could only bring in enough food for the military. So the Jeh people were believing on Christ only for their soul's salvation. They were living on leaves, roots, a few pumpkins, and some salt at that time. There was no rice, fish, or meat. Many were dying from starvation, especially newly born babies, as the mothers could not feed them.

Many of the Jeh men had been captured by the Communists and some were killed; others were imprisoned deep in the forests. A few were able to escape and bring news of the others to the church.

One who was captured was Mr. Ngo, father of A-Yen, one of the young Jeh at the China Beach Orphanage. Ngo had been a co-worker with our evangelist, Mr. Tuu, in that area. He had his Gospel of Mark with him that had been translated into the Jeh language by the Wycliffe translators, Pat Cohen and Dwight Gradin. As Ngo was reading it, his North Vietnamese communist captors asked him, "What is that book?" Ngo told them that it was the Gospel of Mark, God's Word. They instantly destroyed it as well as all of Ngo's Christian literature that he had in Vietnamese.

But Ngo could still pray. He shut his eyes and prayed in the Jeh language. The Communists asked him,

"To whom are you talking? What are you saying?"

Ngo answered, "I'm talking to the Lord Jesus Christ. He is my Father and my Saviour."

They mocked and laughed at Ngo and the other Jeh Christians. But the Jeh prayed on. They sang the hymns in Jeh that were translated by Pat Cohen and Dwight Gradin and then were taught them by their preachers, Trien, Tuu, An, and Chu: "Jesus Loves Me," "O, Happy Day," "Trust and Obey." Later we heard that Ngo was killed by the Communists.

After leaving Dak Pek, Stanley was flown by helicopter to Mang Buk, where he stayed at a special forces camp high in the mountains northeast of Kontum. He was seeking to open up work there. Thirty-five hundred unreached Sedang tribesmen were there, protected by twelve Americans and a group of Vietnamese special forces. Stanley was putting two Vietnamese evangelists in this Mang Buk center. It was a difficult, desolate place, reached only by helicopter. During bad weather, sometimes forty days would go by without an aircraft being able to land with supplies.

From Mang Buk, Stanley choppered back to Kontum and then flew on to Xuan Phuoc behind Quinhon, among the Hroy and Cham-Bahnar tribes.

The air force squeezed Stanley into a Caribou transport plane and they arrived at the jungle refugee settlement just at dark. Not knowing where he could locate Pastor Tin, the Vietnamese evangelist there, Stan spent the night in an underground concrete bunker with the special forces. Early the next morning, Mr. Tin was able to find Stanley because he had heard of his flying in. It was Sunday and Stanley was able to meet with the entire group of tribal Christians.

Formerly this mission station was at Phuoc Lanh among the the Cham-Bahnars, who are closely related to the Hroy tribespeople. Phuoc Lanh was now occupied by the Communists and several thousand Hroy and Cham-Bahnar tribespeople had fled to Xuan Phuoc and La Hai. They had to leave their church building at Phuoc Lanh, all their rice fields, bamboo huts, and possessions to go to this new refugee settlement.

There were 240 Christians in this new group, and they showed their love for Christ by helping to build a new church. They went out into the forest nearby and cut down some trees at the risk of being shot by the Communists hiding there. So the Christians were able to supply the wooden frame and the bamboo slats to weave into walls for the church.

Stanley was able to get help from an American chaplain and the group of American soldiers in that area. They gave the tin roof for the chapel.

The Vietnamese in the C. & M.A. church at Tuy Hoa, a town on the seacoast, heard of these tribal refugees praying for a new church and they sent $100.00 toward the building of it. Even the orphans at China Beach sent some money, $12.00, to help build the church. This gift was from their own personal gifts given to them by their American sponsors.

Mr. Tin had many wonderful testimonies of how God had spared his life from mines exploding on the road, and from communist sniper bullets shot from the bushes as he rode along on his motorcycle!

We praised God for this pioneer work among a new tribe of people, being carried on by another faithful Vietnamese missionary working under conditions that were dangerous and difficult.

Soon after these visits that greatly encouraged the workers and tribespeople, Stanley left for Saigon to return to America.

He was in the Saigon C. & M.A. mission home waiting for his plane, and on the very morning he was to leave, at 3 o'clock some giant communist 120 mm. mortar shells landed right in the mission compound! The explosions were like thunder and the flying shrapnel and debris were terrifying. The shells were evidently aimed at the large combat-police complex across the street from the mission home. They were exploding all around, and one shell killed a refugee and wounded his wife and child right in front of the mission home.

Miraculously, the incoming rounds missed the top of the mission building by mere inches, sparing the lives of many missionary families staying there!

Stanley got under his bed with a second mattress over him and he cried to the Lord to have mercy, especially on the women and children in the home.

God heard the prayers of His missionaries that early morning. The only damage was to three parked mission cars in the yard, which were put out of commission for awhile.

Stan felt a great sense of relief as his Air Vietnam jet lifted off the runway of the Saigon Tan-Son-Nhut Airport. This airport had just been rocketed shortly before Stan's takeoff!

After stopovers in Hong Kong and San Francisco, Stan's jet finally arrived at Chicago's O'Hare Field, where the reunion with his family was precious!

At this time, in May, 1968, we joyfully welcomed two missionaries from Holland, Mimi du Fosse and Nelly Hayboer. We were sorry that they were only coming out for two years, but they began to study the Vietnamese language and work at their ministry of healing at the orphanage, leprosarium, and clinic.

First of all, they took in a little five-year-old Vietnamese orphan boy with club feet. His name was Chinh, meaning "important." His little club feet were so badly twisted that a half-dozen American orthopedic surgeons at the U.S. Naval Hospital spent some time examining, photographing, and x-raying them. The doctors soon did a first operation and little Chinh was happy in his plaster casts, playing in a box under the shade of two huge tropical trees in our yard, in 100 degree weather.

After a number of other operations by the American doctors, Chinh's legs and feet are straight today; and he runs and jumps with the rest of the children.

Then it was the day of dedication of the new chapel and

school, May 18, 1968, a festive day at the China Beach Orphanage! The carpenters and masons had put their last finishing touches to the lovely new building. Flowers had been planted in the long flower planters at each side of the front entrance. The cement base for the flagpole was just hard enough to walk on. The huge yellow Vietnamese flag with the three red stripes waved out in the breeze from the ocean, for we are right on the beach. The flag was a gift from the Vietnamese commanding officer in this area, General Lam.

Just before three o'clock, two trucks brought the brass band of the First Marine Division and they installed their instruments near the altar rail at one side of our lovely new chapel.

Gordon stood at the entrance, welcoming the distinguished guests, and the band started to play a medley of hymns.

An American marine general, the mayor of Da Nang, the U.S. Admiral's Chief of Staff, other high officers, and many chaplains attended this service of dedication. Some doctors and nurses from the German hospital ship *Helgoland* came. Other important personages and Vietnamese Christians arrived. These guests of honor all sat in the center of the church.

As our 235 boys and girls, dressed in white and blue, filed quietly into the large auditorium, our hearts were deeply moved. The older boys and girls sat up in the choir loft. The others sat in the side pews of the church.

I was seated up front at the little pump organ, and tears were streaming down my cheeks as my heart overflowed with emotion, to realize that the orphan children now had such a fine church and school and all of this love and honor was being shown to them!

When the mayor of Da Nang arrived and was seated, the service began. An older boy brought a tasseled satin Vietnamese flag, also donated by the Vietnamese commander, General Lam, from its stand and stood out front holding it, while the children all marched up to the front and sang their own national anthem, accompanied by the Marine Band. It was magnificent! The children's voices and the band filled the church with resounding music and the audience had shining, wet eyes, as they were moved by the patriotic song for Vietnam:

> Vietnam! Vietnam!
> The name familiar since childhood!
> How we cherish the name of Vietnam.
> Our beautiful fatherland!

There were several speeches and messages from the Bible, the band played a number of hymns, and there were four songs by the children, in their various age groups. Some were action songs. The youngest group filled the large platform and one of the very smallest boys, newly arrived at the orphanage, clowned it up in the front row. He hadn't been to many practices and didn't know the song, but he was having fun with all the "Daddies" in the audience and wasn't one bit bashful!

Refreshments were served afterward, down by the school on the beach. Several military units had brought gallons of Kool-Aid and cookies, and the marines had brought a large two-layer iced cake, beautifully decorated. They brought plenty of paper cups, but no one thought to bring paper plates or plastic forks with which to eat the cake! We couldn't very well use the children's chopsticks, so everyone ate iced cake out of a paper cup with his fingers, the mayor and general included. The orphans had a great feast, and no one went away thirsty.

The school, downstairs under the big chapel, is made of concrete and has ten classrooms. Each room has a brass plaque on the wall, telling which unit of the armed forces helped build it. The cool breezes coming in from the sea make the classrooms pleasant for study.

Everyone who enters the chapel upstairs, exclaims at the simple beauty of it. The four windows in front, in the vestibule, have special hand-painted imitation "stained glass" pictures of "Christ and the Children," "Christ with His Disciples," "Christ in Gethsemane," and "Christ on the Cross." Also in the vestibule are two marble plaques, one in Vietnamese and the other in English, stating that nearly all of the money and materials for the school and chapel were donated by the various units in the U.S. Armed Forces.

Inside the door, as one enters the church auditorium, on another marble plaque, is the touching verse adapted from the old hymn, "I Think When I Read That Sweet Story of Old":

> But thousands and thousands
>   Who wander and fall,
> Never heard of the heavenly home;
> We want them to know
>   There is room for them all,
> And that Jesus has bid them to come.

The church has two round windows at each end with imitation stained glass windows. A large three-and-one-half-foot brass cross was made from melted-down artillery casings, and it weighs fifty pounds. We had it molded in Da Nang at a small foundry, following a design Gordon made out of cardboard. It hangs against a pleated red cloth screen behind the communion table.

We had a special wrought-iron altar rail made in Da Nang with crosses every three feet. When Communion is served, each participant is reminded of the death of our Lord as he kneels before the cross. The leather kneeling pad is red to match the screen.

There are no windows in the walls to distract the worshipers. Ventilation is provided by openings above the walls, and the warm air goes out the opening in the ridge vent. The plywood walls are painted with "helicopter green" paint that had been discarded, and the ceiling rafters are painted white. These two-by-twelve-inch rafters came from the naval docks where they had been used to shore up cargo in the holds of ships. We hauled them away in our truck, and we could take as many as we needed.

Light enters through a number of green plastic skylights in the roof. It is spacious and cool and the acoustics are excellent. It is possible to seat many hundreds of children in the chapel, using the choir loft and a rear balcony.

How we praise God for making this vision come true! Hallelujah, what a Saviour!

18

A Little Girl in a Red Dress

To SAVE THE LIFE of a little nine-year-old Vietnamese girl in our China Beach Orphanage who had a very bad heart condition, Gordon spent three weeks in America.

Little Trai (her name means "Fruit") had heart trouble that made her face puff up and her feet and legs swell. She would become very weak, with a deathly pallor. Her heart was badly affected after rheumatic fever.

I saw her one day huddling on a deck chair on a veranda of the orphanage and thought, *This poor little girl looks as if she can't live very long in this condition.*

The Dutch girls and Gordon took her to the American hospital ship, *Repose,* out in Da Nang Bay, and the doctor said she had a largely swollen heart with leaking valves. Later, we also took her to the German hospital ship *Helgoland* in the Da Nang River in the center of the town, and she stayed in a hospital bed there for a number of weeks. Both ships' doctors said that Trai must go to America for special treatment and operation if her life was to be saved.

The *USAID* Public Health officer wired a cardiologist in Los Angeles about Trai, and he wired back that he was willing to try to perform the delicate operation on the little girl. She would go to the University of California Hospital in Los Angeles, to the Department of Pediatrics and Cardiology. They would give her intensive tests and treatments, free of charge.

USAID arranged with the U.S. Air Force for a medical evacuation plane to take Trai free of charge. She would fly with wounded American soldiers on stretchers on a flight from Saigon to the Travis Military Air Base outside San Francisco.

Gordon got all of Trai's passport and visa papers through with the Vietnamese government. He also had to get his own papers in order so that he could leave the country. He still didn't have permission from Washington to fly free of charge to help little Trai, so an American doctor and a major from Da Nang went with Trai. She didn't want to lie down on one of the stretchers in the Medevac plane, like a wounded soldier, so the doctor and major propped her up between them on pillows and she was happy in their care. They watched her pulse all the way and it wasn't too bad, but as they neared America, her heart beat terribly fast. They soon got her flown right to the Los Angeles hospital where she was resting when Gordon arrived.

Two days after Trai had left Da Nang, authorization came for Gordon to fly on a Continental Airways plane. Gordon had all of his necessary papers ready, so he left immediately. He was on an empty 707 Jet going back to Oakland, California, and Gordon was the only passenger with seven stewardesses! He was soon in Los Angeles, and he stayed with Trai in the hospital a lot, talking with her in Vietnamese.

After ten days in the hospital, Trai was released. They couldn't do the operation on her yet because they would have to wait until she was older, likely in her teens, before they could perform the operation. In the meantime they had given her some treatment and medicine and she could return to Vietnam. But she would have to go back to America again, for she needed to be under a special heart surgeon's care. So they said it would be best if Trai could be adopted in the United States so that she would be near her heart specialist and a good hospital all her life.

Trai was now like an entirely new little girl. Gone were the puffy face, the listless eyes, and weakness of body. It was a miraculous change to a sparkling, slant-eyed, almost healthy little moppet, who romped around like other children.

Carrying dolls and a large, white poodle and some pretty clothing given her by kind American friends, Gordon and Trai drove with some old friends of ours from Gordon's boyhood days, the Cliff Smiths. They were going to their home at

Redondo Beach and Trai kept exclaiming at the eight-lane freeway swarming with cars! Of course she had never seen such roads or cars in all her life! Later when they took her for some special rides, she jumped up and down and cried, "Faster! Faster!"—as if seventy-five miles an hour wasn't fast enough.

Mrs. Ruth Smith and her two little sons, kindly took Trai to Disneyland where they spent six hours, and Trai didn't seem tired at all. She was alert, quick, and intelligent and Disneyland was indeed a fairyland to her!

She loved to visit big stores and was especially pleased with a red dress, matching purse, and red shoes they bought her.

"She picked out the red dress herself," said Ruth Smith, "and these were the first pair of shoes ever bought for her. And to think that they were red!—the favorite color of the frail brown-skinned little girl."

Gordon and Trai waited in Redondo Beach at the home of the Smiths for a week to try to get a free trip back to Vietnam, but this was not possible owing to the heavy traffic reserved for the military. So Gordon had to pay their way back to Da Nang on a commercial flight. But it was worth the $800.00 to bring little Trai back to life with a future ahead of her. She had to take special medicine daily.

As they left Los Angeles after eating as guests of the Smiths in the lovely round restaurant, high up, overlooking the airport, they were all proud of Trai. She was in her pretty new red dress, with her little red shoes and purse, and a little round white hat (the first hat she ever had), and tiny white gloves. "And she knew just what she wanted to eat," said Ruth Smith. "Watermelon!"

They changed planes at Honolulu and at Manila, and each set of stewardesses went out of their way to kindly entertain Trai.

When Gordon and Trai stepped off the Air America plane at Da Nang, the Dutch girls and I were there to greet them. We were surprised to see Trai so well, sweet, and triumphant, the little girl in the red dress! That little dress was to be the envy of every little girl in the China Beach Orphanage!

We soon began to try to find a home for Trai in America,

for we knew that she'd have to be there under a doctor's special care for the rest of her life. A fine couple in Minneapolis, Mr. and Mrs. Peter Kramer, opened widely and lovingly their arms to her. Already in their hospitable home they had adopted several other orphans from Korea.

Trai is there with them today, and her American name is Sarah. She is doing well in school and soon learned to speak English fluently and is greatly loved by all. When she grows a few more inches, the doctors will be able to put in a new plastic mitral-valve in her heart!

Then American doctors in Da Nang began bringing to us a number of other Vietnamese heart patients, saying they must go to America for special open-heart surgery. We became increasingly involved in getting these children to America. Gordon carried on this program for over three years.

Cardiologists found that many children in Vietnam had heart defects and that these diseases, which had to have open-heart surgery, could not be treated in any hospitals in Vietnam. Soon

Children play near chapel at China Beach Orphanage. Many received medical help free of charge through the kindness of people in America.

Gordon Smith and Trai return from heart surgery in the United States.

134

cardiologists in all parts of South Vietnam looked to Gordon to help them when they found children who needed to be operated upon in the United States.

The Ministry of Health in Vietnam made a contract with our mission to facilitate the sending of these children out of the country. A hospital in Minneapolis, Minnesota, the Metropolitan Medical Center, consented to take all the children we would send to them for open-heart surgery. There the Vietnamese patients received a wonderful welcome, loving care, and the best of surgical skill for heart cases to be found anywhere.

Open-heart surgery is very risky and some of the children, sent later on, either died in America or on their return to Vietnam. When their hearts were opened they were found to be in worse condition than previous tests had shown. But many were healed and are living a normal life today since their defects were fixed. All of them would have died young if they had not been operated upon.

Open-heart surgery is very expensive, running into thousands of dollars for each case. Airline fares are also expensive, and it is a long way from Vietnam to mid-America. But thanks to the overwhelming kindness of people in America, our patients were sent and treated absolutely free of charge! Heart surgeons donated their skills, hospitals donated their care and treatments, and even gave free room and board to the Vietnamese nurses who accompanied the children.

Pan American Airways, with special permission, is able to donate free transportation from Saigon to Los Angeles and return at the request of the Vietnam government. Western Airlines kindly gives contributions from their charitable funds so that we can purchase return tickets to Minneapolis. The Americans all go out of their way to help make the children comfortable on the long journey, meeting them at stopovers with wheelchairs when it is necessary.

Our friends, the Cliff Smiths of Redondo Beach, California, have been meeting the children and taking them to their home overnight, seeing them on the plane the next day as they travel either to Minneapolis, or on the return from the hospital, westward to Vietnam.

Through the military MARS telephone system, Gordon could sit at his desk in Da Nang and talk to Cliff Smith in his home about details for the children's trip.

The only expense for the whole project is an honorarium for the Vietnamese nurse who takes off six or seven weeks from her work to accompany the children and stays as interpreter with them while they are in the hospital. These few hundred dollars for the nurse were easily raised among the U.S. Armed Forces in Da Nang. Chaplains were glad to use some of their chapel offerings for such a cause. Twice the men of the 1st Marine Motor Transport Battalion contributed generously to this fund. When it comes to helping some needy child, we found out that there is no one like the American fighting man to share eagerly and generously from his pocket, especially the marines.

Gordon's particular job was to do all the paper work for these patients' trips, spending days in Saigon "walking" the papers through many government offices in order to obtain passports in three or four days instead of as many months.

For the first heart patients going to America, Gordon went with them himself to Minneapolis. Then Vietnamese nurses began to take his place and would take four or five boys and girls at a time.

This service is being cared for especially today by a group of concerned citizens of Minneapolis who have founded PACT, meaning "Partners Aiding Children Today." They have a Vietnamese representative in Saigon today who handles all the details of the paper work and the sending of the heart patients to Minneapolis. This has lifted the burden from Gordon, who can now give full time to his regular missionary work.

19

A New "Happy Haven"

ON JULY 10, 1968, the Vietcong came into the Happy Haven Leprosarium at Cam Hai and captured Mr. Huan (pronounced "Hwoong"), our supervisor and preacher there, and Mr. Tue (pronounced "Tway"), our preacher and medical technician.

These were fine Vietnamese workers and our hearts were filled with alarm and great distress! The wives and children of the two men were heartbroken!

The Communists had been getting bolder around our leprosarium, and before this tragedy happened we had wanted for a long time to move the patients to a safer place. But none of the Vietnamese villages would have the people with leprosy near them.

Mr. Tue had just come into Da Nang and told us about the Communists daring to come into the leprosarium recently and of their holding a meeting there. One Sunday afternoon a crowd of them, carrying aloft their communist flag, marched in. They went to the leprosarium chapel and hoisted their flag on top of it! The flag had a blue and yellow background with a red star in the center. Then they pushed open the chapel door and entered. There were twenty singers in their group, and their instruments were mandolins and banjos. A lot of children from twelve to thirteen years were among their followers and many youths of around twenty years. The leaders who spoke at the meeting were about forty years of age. All of these followers were strangers. None were *North* Vietnamese. The northern people of Vietnam have a different way of pronouncing their words from the southerners. The letter *y* in the north is pronounced as a *z*, and instead of the *ng* sound used in the

137

south, they use *n*. There are other very noticeable differences, so that a southerner knows a northerner immediately when he speaks, and vice-versa.

A number of Communists with guns stood around the church where the others were meeting. The Vietcong ordered all of our leprosy patients to attend the gathering. They warned that if they refused they would be seized and taken off to the mountains. We know that the Communists would soon kill them as they wouldn't run the risk of catching leprosy! So all the patients crowded into the meeting, some sitting, some standing.

Mr. Huan was off at a church in a neighboring village. Mr Tue was down on the seashore at the time, buying some fish and shrimps. Some patients escaped and ran to tell him that the Communists were in the leprosarium. Tue returned and saw the communists' flag up on the church and the Communists holding the meeting! He would not attend, and the wives and children of the two preachers didn't attend.

The meeting was two hours long. They sang and talked. Tue told some of the patients to be sure to listen to everything and tell him all the important things that were said. The Communists told the patients that Tue and Huan were not really preachers working under a missionary society but were American government workers. They accused Tue and Huan of forbidding the patients to attend the communist meeting.

They said that the leprosarium leaders forbade the people to listen to Radio Hanoi and other communist broadcasts. They ordered them to only listen to Saigon broadcasts. (This was not true. The leaders had only told the patients to turn down their radios so that the others could sleep. They were free to listen to any program they wished.)

The Communists accused Tue and Huan of telling the patients to follow the Americans and never to follow the Communists. They said if they could catch Tue and Huan actually saying these things, they would seize the two workers and shoot them right there in the leprosarium.

There were many refugees from the country all around who came into the leprosarium for protection from the Communists. They also drove in their buffaloes, cows, and pigs. The Communists spoke to these refugee people too, and assured them that the Vietcong were winning all the battles, so they had better follow them and not the Americans!

The children of the neighbors all around our leprosarium were not true to us. Mr. Tue and Mr. Huan had been helping the people by letting them all pour into our leprosarium at night, even bringing in their livestock and building little shanties on our property. Our workers gave them medicine and any treatments that they needed. But the children and many of the villagers showed no gratitude to our leaders or to the patients.

The Communists paid the children money for everything they could tell them about our workers or patients. They greatly desired to get American weapons, radios, documents, money, and food. The children hid some weapons and grenades inside our leprosarium in some of the houses belonging to the patients. They had stolen these from the Americans. Mr. Huan saw this and quietly and secretly got rid of all of them. The children told the Communists that Huan had taken all this war material they had gathered and had given it back to the Americans.

Some of the U.S. Marines in their camp nearby lost a radio. They asked Tue if he knew where it was. Tue answered, "I'll try to find it." The children had stolen the radio and given it to the Communists. So things were getting more and more dangerous.

On the night of July 10, Huan and Tue, with their wives and children, were gathered for the weekly prayer meeting with the leprosy patients. While over twenty of them were on their knees praying, one hundred Communists with guns, dressed in their black pajamas, came into the leprosarium. They surrounded the chapel.

The Communists called for Huan and Tue to come outside into the grove of pine trees. The leaders came out and a group of Communists surrounded each of the men. They put guns in their faces and made them answer questions. Then they tied Tue and Huan's hands behind their backs, grabbed some clothing in the house nearby, women's dresses from a box sent from America, and bound up their eyes tightly.

139

Mrs. Huan and Mrs. Tue ran to the communist leaders, crying and pleading with them to let the men go! The Communists pushed back the women with their guns. There were one hundred men guarding the two captives.

They made Tue and Huan take off their shoes and told them to run! They must hurry to get away before the Americans found out about the capture! So the two leaders had to run off barefooted with the Communists. It was now late at night.

When the patients brought the news to us early the next morning, Gordon knew that we must evacuate the leprosarium quickly now, or more from our staff there would be captured or killed.

For months Gordon had been trying to get the land at Hoa Van, a beautiful crescent beach across Da Nang Bay, for a new leprosarium site. Now Gordon immediately took the news of the capture of our valiant preachers to the top Vietnamese general in Da Nang, General Lam. The general assured Gordon that it would be all right if he would move our leprosarium over to this secluded beach at the foot of the mountain pass going north to Hue.

The general realized that because of all the communist activity, the leprosarium was now untenable. The Vietcong had threatened to take more of our people if they did not cooperate with the Communists and give them food and medicines.

They were shooting mortars near and into Da Nang from our leprosarium area now, so they had to be rooted out! They knew that the Americans wouldn't return fire into a leprosy hospital for fear of shooting innocent sick people. So the Communists felt secure in our haven!

They shot at the marines and mined the roads. Not many months before, they had blown up with a mine the Amtrac trying to get to our leprosarium with help for our patients, and three marines had been wounded.

The Communists had Chinese AK-47 assault rifles and their fire was often heard coming from the clumps of pine and eucalyptus trees around and even from inside the leprosarium.

Then the Vietcong boldly ordered one of the heads of our Vietnamese staff out there, since the two preachers were gone, to "tell Mr. Gordon Smith that no white man, military or civilian, would be permitted to go any more inside the leprosarium. If they violated this order they would be killed!"

Even recently, an American platoon of tanks, loaded with infantrymen, was patroling around the leprosy colony. Suddenly they were hit by rifle fire from the trees nearby. The American commander cried, "Let's face it! You don't open with *rifles* against a platoon of *tanks!*"

But the tree line was like a solid wall of fire with rifle attack! So the Americans opened fire from their tanks and killed twenty or more Vietcong. Then they spotted Vietcong running into the leprosarium. The Vietcong knew that the Americans wouldn't shoot into the leprosy colony, so they retreated in there. The patients were panicky now and wanted to leave the leprosarium at once.

Gordon talked it over with the American marine general who said that he was sorry but they could not maintain security in the area because of our leprosarium. He suggested that we move our patients elsewhere and they would help us with the operations.

We had been given a fine place now, on the basis of a refugee settlement, the Crescent Beach, to which we could move the patients. But how were we to get them with all their belongings there? They dared not move out of the leprosarium at this dangerous time without strong protection.

So the American marines made arrangements. A platoon of the 1st Tank Battalion, First Marine Regiment, would assist the leprosy patients in relocating. They quickly set up an operation to haul away all the patients and as many of the fine cement tiles on the buildings and as many as possible of the doors and windows in only one day.

"Move the village!" was the order. And the marines moved in.

At dawn, nine huge amphibious tractors (Amtracs) and seven tanks, lumbered down the three miles of beach from their Marble Mountain base. Gordon and our son Leslie, visiting us at that time, and Mr. Lich, swung into line with the procession, in their Land Rover. It was rough going, even in lowest gear, through the deep ruts made by the Amtracs in the sand.

The seven tanks circled around the leprosarium, providing necessary cover against the Vietcong.

The nine Amtracs paused at the gates of the Happy Haven Leprosarium. There, on each big gate post, were the marble plaques inscribed in English and in Vietnamese:

WHERE LEPERS ARE CLEANSED AND THE POOR HAVE THE GOSPEL PREACHED UNTO THEM

The first Amtrac had to push the gates over in order to let the big vehicles enter the property. As the cement posts toppled, Gordon and Mr. Lich salvaged the heavy marble plaques, to be placed on the gates of our new site later on at Crescent Beach.

Fifty of the strongest leprosy patients began removing the fine, rose-colored tiles from two of the eleven buildings on that early morning. It was hard work! Their mutilated hands and feet, with no sensation in them, were injured by the heavy cement tiles and nails. They also dismantled many doors and windows. They stacked everything into the cavernous interiors of the Amtracs. The leprosarium staff, too, helped the patients in all the work.

Leslie and Gordon walked up the lovely tree-lined road to the hospital site. The forests of Australian pines and the eucalyptus trees we had planted had grown gracefully tall and the leprosarium was a lovely spot! It was very sad to be tearing it all down now. Gordon and Mr. Lich and other members of the staff remembered the hard years of building up this leprosarium and serving here. Now the two courageous preachers were captured. How the men's hearts went out to them and to their families!

But hundreds of patients had been helped to find new life, and most of them had found Jesus Christ as their own personal Saviour. They knew that the Lord would replace the bricks, wood, and cement, enabling them to build again another Happy

142

Haven on the new site, twelve miles away, across Da Nang Bay.

The U.S. Marines kept busy detonating booby traps by the fences, set there by the Vietcong. The marines feared leprosy and so didn't help with the dismantling work. One young marine was literally shaking with fear and was anxious to get out of the leprosarium. Gordon tried to assure him that leprosy wouldn't be that contagious for him! He probably couldn't catch it unless he had long, close contact with it.

The marines even found a Vietcong "school" hidden in a refugee shack in the pines! There were primers, sheet metal tools, workbenches, a few dud rounds, and empty 105 mm shell casings.

A Vietnamese army interpreter with the marines, made all the refugees in the leprosarium form into two groups: those with proper cards of identification, and the other group for those with lost or misplaced credentials.

They found a "Chieu Hoi" in the refugee group. This meant that the man had once been a Vietcong. He had operated from this area of the leprosy colony. But he had surrendered and returned to the government of Vietnam under the "open arms" program. Now he was masked to protect his identity. A stocking, with holes in it for eyes, was put over his head. He pointed out to the U.S. Marines several refugees who were Vietcong! These had been given some medicines from our leprosarium which had been given to the enemy!

The patients each carried their loads of poor personal belongings in two baskets slung from a long flat pole on the shoulder. They loaded everything into the maws of the Amtracs. Finally, in early afternoon, the patients gave up. They were too tired to do anymore.

Gordon, Leslie, Mr. Lich, and all the patients and staff looked for the last time at the place which had been truly a haven for our unwanted and distressed people.

But now it wasn't a happy place anymore. They all looked ahead now to the new Happy Haven; to the big task of rebuilding a new hospital, a new chapel, a new school, and new homes for our suffering people.

The marines were reluctant indeed to see such a fine medical center abandoned! Perhaps, someday, when peace would come to Vietnam again, we could reestablish this place as a medical training center. This land, given to us by the Vietnam government, would still belong to our mission.

The tanks remained in the leprosarium area until the marines had screened all the refugees there. Then they transported the people to the city of Hoi An refugee settlement, eight miles south, on the coast.

The Amtracs procession with our three trucks and Land Rover departed by way of the beach again to the Marble Mountains marine headquarters. Arriving there, the Amtracs lined up, lowered their ramps, and the patients unloaded all the goods in big piles. From these, our trucks would transport all the salvaged materials to our new large, secondhand boat, *Hope II* at the Da Nang River dock. This boat was our only means of access to our new site of Crescent Beach across the bay.

Later on, freight trains would be running from Da Nang to Hue, on the railway cut from the side of the mountains within one-fourth of a mile from our leprosarium. We could then use the train for getting some things to the leprosarium.

The patients were ecstatic over their new homesite! It is situated in an abandoned valley where no one had lived for twenty-five years. There is good land, a river, spring water from the mountainsides, and fishing.

We erected a sturdy flagpole on the beach, with a yellow and red Vietnamese flag flying on top and a large Red Cross flag underneath. Tracks of wild boar and deer were on the sandy beach.

The sun sweeps the majestic mountain slopes that rise high above the crescent curve of beach. The views are overwhelming and exalting. The sea ebbs and flows along the two miles of shore, like the sound in a curled shell held to your ears. From the soft, beige sand, we look across the bay to Da Nang six miles away. In the distance are the Marble Mountains twelve miles away. Eddies of fresh perfume come down the moun-

144

tain slopes and sweet, pure breezes come in from the sea. Our new Happy Haven is an endlessly fascinating place.

Each day, after the patients landed there, *Hope II,* towing a heavily loaded aluminum barge behind it, hauled over tons of lumber, cement, the tile roofing, and American army tents for the patients to live in while building their little huts. There were 210 adults with leprosy and their forty-four children.

The U.S. Navy gave us all the lumber we needed at that time. This was dunnage lumber used to shore up cargo on the American ships. The Vietnamese government gave us a small amount of cement and roofing like they gave to all refugees. Some gifts of money were coming in from kind friends to help in this resettlement project.

The rebuilding of this new Happy Haven village, right from the start again, was a tremendous undertaking. But we looked in faith to God. Plans had to be made for all the new buildings, and roads and bridges had to be built. Thousands of coconut palms would be planted on the beach, and groves of banana plants. We needed a wharf for our boat.

All would be undertaken in perfect confidence in our loving heavenly Father. Our eyes were upon Him who had already seen us through forty years of crises in Vietnam, victorious and rejoicing in His unfailing provision.

20

Orphans Camp Out Under Fire

ONE HUNDRED AND TWO of the older children among the 260 orphans at the China Beach Orphanage, Da Nang, had planned for days before that year's Tet, 1969, for a three-day camp-out on Crescent Beach. This is where we were now establishing our new Happy Haven Leprosarium.

So on February 19 we took the children over on our white, sixty-foot boat, the *Hope II*. It had two red crosses painted on the bow and a Red Cross flag at the mast. We had to make two trips to accommodate the crowd of boys and girls and all the equipment and baggage.

Gordon accompanied the boat on both trips to watch that the youngsters did not fall overboard. I went on the second trip. It was a warm, quiet day at 82 degrees and the sea was a dreamy, smooth turquoise. The towering mountains encircling the great Bay of Da Nang were pale as they were wrapped in haze. There were many American freighters and warships and units of the Seventh Fleet at anchor in the bay. The white U.S. hospital ship *Repose* was moving out to sea as we passed by.

After a seventy-minute ride, Hoa Van, which we named "Crescent Beach," was before us, a golden arc of two miles. There at one end, in a sheltered cove, the Happy Haven Leprosarium with its 210 adult patients and forty-four children was taking shape with many small wooden houses with tin roofs.

We landed the orphans half a mile down the beach from the leprosarium, using a large aluminum assault boat that the Americans had given to us, to get them on shore. The *Hope II*, with its five-foot draft, had to anchor in deep water.

The children soon put their tents up on a grassy bank above the shore, near a stream. Their tents were made from sheets given to us by an American military hospital. In order to cover the indelible bloodstains on them, we had dyed them a dark green. The sheets could be used again on the orphans' beds after this tenting trip and a good washing. The inevitable loudspeaker soon was blaring out orders and music, without which a Vietnamese outing would be incomplete.

The mountains loomed up from the valley, thousands of feet high, with a long, deep scar of the newly widened and asphalted main Highway No. 1, leading up to the famous Pass of the Clouds and on down the other side, the forty miles farther to the city of Hue.

The day previously, Gordon had phoned the U.S. Harbor Security Patrol, informing them of our camp and asking them to kindly get in touch with the marine base on top of the pass. Gordon then drove up the road from Da Nang to visit the captain of marines in his mountain fort. The message had reached the marines shortly before, but it had been garbled on the way. Instead of our bringing a hundred "orphans," the marines said they were told we were bringing a hundred ARVINS (Army of the Republic of Vietnam).

Gordon told them that there would be lights and bonfires below on the beach, and the marines assured him they would not be shooting at us. Since we were the only ones with permission to use the Crescent Beach, any strangers would be suspects. So far, no strangers had come around the area.

Gordon was told there were supposed to be several thousand communist troops in the surrounding mountains. For weeks the artillery and warships had been shelling the steep slopes and valleys above the highway and over on the other side of the mountains. We could see the shells exploding among the rocks and trees only a half mile away from our beach site.

We felt comparatively safe down in our pleasant valley as not only the marines and Vietnamese soldiers looked down on it, but there were some Vietnamese soldiers guarding the railroad and tunnels just a half mile from us on a nearby hill. The

147

The orphans have a three-day camp-out on Crescent Beach during Tet 1969.

wide, soft, sandy beach had been uninhabited for many years until we came.

Soon the children were splashing and playing in the clear blue green water. Gordon and I were to sleep on the boat, in the front cabin, and we had our bedding with us. Our little galley cupboards were well stocked with food, water, plastic dishes, and cooking utensils. We had a two-burner stove with bottled gas.

A young man, Stephen Brodowsky, who had just finished two years service as a medical corpsman on the hospital ship, *Sanctuary,* had been staying with us for two months to help us in the practical missionary work before he took off on a trip around the world, mostly on foot. He came on this trip with us and contributed much to its success.

Our son Leslie would have been with us, but he was away at the time, taking a planeload of food and clothing to Christian refugees of the Jeh tribe, across the mountains at the special forces camp at Dak Pek. There were 3,000 Jeh believers in three churches in that area.

Steven and Gordon soon joined in swimming with the children, but I stayed on board to get "settled in." It was hard for me to get off the boat down into the assault craft. I had to climb down a ladder into it, and then when the beach was reached by poling, I had to climb up the ladder again and walk down a jiggly plank onto the shore, while the boat wallowed in the light surf. I looked forward to the day when we could build a good pier where the *Hope II* could dock properly.

I sat in a comfortable camp chair on the deck and reveled in the soothing, peaceful, soul-refreshing sea. A gentle breeze caressed me, and the anchored boat lay bobbing softly on the smooth water. The mountains and the sea were like a delicate watercolor painting of pale, misty blues and greens. The scent from the sea, from the distant kelp on the rocks, and from the mountains all around us, was pleasant. We had our supper on a folding table on deck in the serenity of the sunset.

Gordon and Steve then went over to the big bonfire, and the leaders had the children present their program of skits and songs. Soon artillery shells, from our side, began bursting up on the mountainsides, a mile or two from us. But none of the children paid much attention. These young people had been bred among the alarms of war.

Then the big cruiser *Newport News* started bombarding the mountains, near and far. Every two or three minutes the great ship's guns, standing off only one mile away, would shake the earth with their blasts. The shells whirred over our heads, landing above the highway, high up in the hills, bursting into clouds of white or black smoke, sometimes showing gleaming fires in the dark. But the children were still unconcerned.

As the two men sat with the circle of boys and girls around their blazing campfire, watching the children perform their little dialogues and sing their happy songs, they thought how fantastic it all was! Overhead, at times, a stream of fiery red balls would streak silently by, as these tracer shells disappeared at tremendous speed into the forests. The children took little notice of either the noise of the guns or the burst of the shells a few moments later, which rumbled like thunder, reverberating from peaks and valleys all around them.

All night long the cruiser kept up the shelling every few minutes, so sleep for us was quite fitful. By dawn the warship had disappeared and everything was calm. We could only hope that the Communists up in their hideouts in the mountains had been checked in their determination to launch a major attack on Da Nang during Tet, 1969!

On the second day, Gordon who had strained his back hauling on the boat anchor rope, found that his hip was aching dreadfully. He had been suffering somewhat for several days. Now, after swimming and the other exercise with the children, he was completely immobilized and could hardly move in his bed. While Gordon had to stay on board, Steve helped me get onto the shore in the assault boat, and we visited the camp. It was great to see how well organized everything was under their leaders, with the boys gathering wood and building fires, and the girls doing the cooking and housekeeping. The Vietnamese flag flew in a central place, and each group had its own embroidered ensign.

Steve and I walked along the shore to visit Happy Haven. Little spring birds flitted and twittered and sang in the thickets. There was no other sound now in the morning. The ocean was a glassy turquoise blue again and very still.

The leprosy patients had built thirty of the one hundred little wooden huts needed in a circle on their new site. These huts were made with the dunnage lumber. Leslie and Steve had been getting up early many mornings to haul this wood from the navy docks. The roofs of the huts were of corrugated iron. Each little home was neat and clean with the yards well swept. A stream from the mountains wound past the big circle of houses and each family had a number of ducks enjoying the water. There were fences across, to keep the ducks in their owner's front yard. They all had little vegetable gardens growing from American seeds given to them by the China Beach USO. Onions, garlic, carrots, cucumbers, peppermint, watermelons, and squash were flourishing in the good soil. One bigger garden had forty pumpkins growing huge among their leaves and vines.

We visited with the afflicted people. Some had lost all their toes and fingers and walked on feet that were like pounding rods. Their legs had no feeling at all from the knees down. Many had claw hands, and Mimi and Nelly, the Dutch nurses, would soon be giving them the warm wax treatment to soften the hands, and then the physiotherapy treatment to straighten the fingers. Some patients had eyes sunken like stones in their pale faces, with eyebrows and lashes gone. There were forty-four little children in these families, but only one or two had the disease. They were receiving Dapsone pills as precaution against leprosy.

After visiting all the new huts and the tents of the settlement, Steve and I were very hot and tired. We reached the chapel around noon. Mr. Lich, the Vietnamese director of the leprosarium since Tue and Huan had been captured, met us there. He rang the chapel bell for the people to come to the meeting that Steve, Mr. Lich, and I would hold for them.

Soon over one hundred men, women, and children gathered, and we told the illustrated story of "Snowflake," a little wayward sheep who became lost. There were many Bible verses with the story and when we came to the invitation for any in the audience who hadn't yet received Christ as their Good Shepherd, to come forward, five patients quickly came to the front without any pressure. They were four women and one man, all quite badly disfigured in faces, hands, and feet. They accepted Christ and His eternal life for their souls, and someday they will have new, glorious bodies in heaven.

Mr. Lich and two of the other leprosarium leaders had caught a rock lobster which they said they would cook and bring later on to Gordon, lying prostrate in his bunk.

Steve and I walked back to the boat barefooted in the water all the way, to keep cool. We climbed up the plank and down into the assault boat and were soon back on *Hope II*. We had our lunch ready by 2 P.M. I spent another wonderful afternoon resting and studying in my comfortable chair in the shade on deck, right at the water's edge. Again I reveled in the perfect atmosphere, contemplating the mountain slopes like a huge mosaic of varied greens, and the languid turquoise sea.

Mr. Lich and the other workers came with the lobster all

cooked nicely and ready for our supper. Again, Steve and I ate out on deck, but poor Gordon was still in bed suffering with his back and unable to move.

That night only Steve went over to the children's camp and bonfire. I stayed with Gordon, sitting on deck reading with a bright pressure lamp, listening to the light dipping sounds of water around the boat. The new moon of the Vietnamese lunar New Year lay on its back up in the sky.

Soon the gunfire and thunderous explosions started again from the unseen warship which seemed so close in the dark. The tracer shells—white, red, and green—from one of the Vietnamese military camps in the mountains, streamed swiftly, silently, and steadily across the peaks. I could see the children skipping around their bonfire and hear them singing. Some fires caused by the shellings broke out in rings on the mountainsides. The atmosphere was eerie!

Once I nearly jumped out of my skin when a grinning face peered up at me from the water at my side of the boat! "Thank God for your light, Ba! He gave me lots of fish here!" It was one of the leprosy patients, paddling in his bamboo basket coracle, catching fish in the light of my pressure lamp! He held up silvery fish, each a foot long, for me to see. He had about a dozen of them. What a feast he'd have the next morning!

Our night was almost sleepless again, with the warship booming continuously very close by and the resounding roars as the shells hit faraway mountains where "Charley" was hiding. Would "the world be falling in" on these communist battalions, or would they be hidden so deeply in networks of tunnels and mountain caves that the shells didn't touch them?

Rich, red beams of the rising sun shone in a pathway over the ocean, and the children were up saluting their flag. After breakfast there was orderly packing up, and two assault boatloads brought the little campers clambering back on board with their gear. Their leaders were really tired. They had taken the children up the jungle streams and hiked until everyone had had his fill!

This time we took them back all in one trip, putting some

152

down in the hold for ballast. It was quite a load with 112 people, but the boat could have taken much more in the way of weight. Strict warning was given again about sitting still, and we were on our way back.

A little wind was blowing now offshore and the sea was a bit choppy. Soon there were drooping heads and upset tummies and longings for us to get across the bay into the calmness of the Da Nang River.

We drew up at our dock where our truck and car were waiting for us to take the children back in relays, safely to their China Beach Orphanage home.

It was so good to take time off with the children to have a little fun, even with war all around us night and day. These boys and girls have lost their parents and homes in the war, but they have found peace because unselfish friends in the homeland have seen to it that they have this happy Christian home, the China Beach Orphanage.

Two nights after returning from the camping trip, on February 23, we really went through the "after Tet offensive" in Da Nang! At 2:30 A.M. I was awakened by an awful racket of bombs and grenades going off not far away and I thought: *The Communists have gotten into Da Nang and are fighting through the streets!*

Gordon, almost better from his backache by now, woke up, as did Leslie, who had just returned the day before from Dak Pek. Through Leslie's open window, we saw a great red glare and volumes of smoke going up about half a mile away in east Da Nang, across the river.

We knew then that it was the big Vietnamese Army ammunition dump that was blowing up. It had been hit by Vietcong rockets! For twelve hours, without a stop, the ammunition kept blowing up. Sometimes several big bombshells went off together, and our whole house shook! Our windowpanes cracked and two of our lampshades and several lightbulbs came shattering down on tables and floors. Dust rained from our wooden ceiling all over our house, and all our furniture and floors were covered with grime. Chi Nga and I were rushing around sweeping rugs, wiping the furniture, and washing floors. After the explosions were all over we would have to have a regular spring housecleaning.

Leslie brought in a fragment of bomb that fell in our garden. It was a jagged bit of steel, still hot. Our leprosy clinic roof was pierced by another piece, but no one was injured. Then a chunk went through the roof of our storeroom, causing a short circuit and fire, which our worker, Tri, soon put out.

Fortunately the ammunition did not go off all at once. This might have killed thousands of people. Instead, the bombs and shells popped off individually and sometimes by the score, hundreds of thousands of them.

At the same time that the ammunition dump was blowing up, the Marble Mountain area was badly rocketed, as was the MAG 16 Camp.

Stephen and Yohan Campagnien, the young Dutchmen who was also helping us in the practical work, came running over from their rooms on the compound, to our house and we all had breakfast together amid the din of bursting shells.

Strict curfew was in force, but our truck with red crosses painted on it was permitted to cross the river to the orphanage. Leslie, Stephen, and Yohan drove over and they found all the 260 orphans, the staff and Mimi and Nelly, all meeting together peacefully in the big chapel for their Sunday morning service. The chapel had been shaken a number of times, they said, with the violent blasts, but the children were all calm and happy.

Helicopters shuttled between the shattered Vietnamese villages near the exploding dump and the city hospital. Soon the dead and dying numbered in the hundreds. Mimi, Nelly, Dr. Harverson, and Stephen, who had helped in surgery on the *Sanctuary,* were all called to the hospital to help.

A few Communists were caught in the city, and troops and tanks were standing on alert everywhere. But the expected invasion of the city by the Communists did not take place. Soon the streets were crammed again with vehicles, and life went on as usual.

21

Preacher Huan Escapes

LOOKING OUT THE WINDOW one morning, I saw two men on a motorcycle whiz by. Could that be Huan? I couldn't believe my eyes! But the one on the back of the motorcycle looked like Pastor Huan—returned from the dead! Yes! It was he!

All of us on our mission property in Da Nang came running to crowd around him! We had the same feeling that the disciples of old must have experienced when Peter was delivered from prison and appeared to them. We'd had no word of him or Tue since they were taken by the Vietcong from the leprosarium over six months ago!

First thing, Huan burst into tears and told us that Preacher Tue was dead! He hadn't been able to stand the hard captivity any longer and had tried to escape, but the Communists shot him!

Huan was swollen up with beri-beri and was pale with anemia. He said, "I've gone through a terrible time! I'm happy to be free, but I'm so sad that Tue couldn't escape also!"

We took him immediately by car over to the orphanage where his wife and children were staying. They wept with joy and relief as they fell into each other's arms. The dark night of waiting was over and all the suffering! But oh, the awful sorrow for poor Mrs. Tue and her four children! They knew dear Tue was now in heaven where happiness is boundless and inexhaustible, but how they missed him during these years here on earth!

After some weeks, Huan felt strong enough to tell us the details of his captivity and escape. We well remembered the night when Huan and Tue were called out of their prayer meeting with the patients at the leprosarium by a group of one hundred Communists with guns. The chief had put his gun in Huan's face, asking, "Why are you making it hard for the Communists here at the leprosarium? Why are you helping the Americans to catch us? Why don't you give us food and medicine?"

Huan answered, "We cannot give you food and medicine. We only have enough for the patients. Also, if we gave these things to you, the Americans and the Vietnam government soldiers would catch us."

The Vietcong continued asking, "Why did you help the American marines two days ago to hunt for a house with some Vietcong in it near the leprosarium?"

"Why didn't you help us Vietcong to get into the leprosarium and be disguised as patients?"

Twice the Americans had caught the Vietcong doing this.

The Communists marched Tue and Huan off in their bare feet, their hands tied behind their backs, and with their eyes bandaged, into the night. The preachers were filled with horror at being caught by the Communists! They could hear their wives and children crying and pleading for them.

Huan said they were taken to a Vietcong headquarters, underground, about three miles from the leprosarium. It was strongly reinforced with sandbags. They had to wait there for ten days until higher officers in the Vietcong army would order them taken up to the high mountains.

The underground hideout was small and dark. It was full of bugs and mosquitoes. The men were given only a little rice and some salt and a little water, twice a day. They had nothing else to eat.

Every time the American marines came scouting near their hideout, the Vietcong made the prisoners each go into corridors off the main underground cell. There they had to lie down on the ground, and the Vietcong staked out their hands and feet and gagged them with cloth in their mouths, so they couldn't call out to the Americans. They put booby traps with grenades on top of the cell roofs, so that if the prisoners tried to escape, they would be blown up.

After ten days in this painful hiding place, the orders came that Tue and Huan were now to leave Cam Hai and be marched away up into the high hills. Their hands were tied behind their backs; they had no shoes and no underclothing. They just had one shirt and one pair of trousers each, and it was very cold up in the hills.

Huan thinks they went southwest of Da Nang, over near the Laotian border. He didn't know exactly. Any time they passed a backcountry Vietnamese village, the Communists called out all the civilians—old men, women, and children—and made them curse and scorn Tue and Huan, and mock them cruelly. The old men had to take swords and pretend to cut off the prisoners' heads. Women and children had to throw stones at them, hitting them painfully.

Then they began climbing the mountain trails. They went by night now, with no light, and with their hands always tied behind their backs. In the daytime they were all hidden in underground holes so that they couldn't be spotted by American search planes.

Their feet became bloody and torn from the rocks, brush, and briars. For ten long, hard, exhausting nights they climbed. Bloodsuckers stuck to them in packets, drinking their blood avidly. The lower branches and leaves were covered with the creatures. Blood ran down the prisoners' legs, and they couldn't use their hands to get the leaches off. When they became so full of blood that they fell off, ulcers would form on the skin in three days' time and often became infected. There was no medicine to heal them and no bandages!

Sometimes it rained in torrents. The paths became streams and the prisoners splattered upward in their bare feet in the water, mud, rain, mist, and fog! They were tramping up in the clouds, in the chain of forested mountains, sometimes cut by deep ravines. Along with bloodsuckers, there were mosquitoes, and vicious-biting insects.

They became very dirty and longed for soap! The Vietcong wouldn't let the prisoners bathe in the rivers. They forced them to drink water at any dirty stream. They had to drink, as they became very dehydrated, and so they drank any water they came to.

Their only food was half of a small can of cold cooked rice, twice a day. Sometimes the rice was uncooked. The guards wouldn't light any fires for fear the American scouting planes would see the fire or smoke.

After ten days of great suffering, they reached the jungle Vietcong trail which linked with the Ho Chi Minh roads. They were now in Vietcong country, 4,000 to 5,000 feet high up in the mountains. The Communists now untied their hands, as the prisoners wouldn't be able to find their way back from here. There were many North Vietnamese troops up in these mountains, and they were on the move for attacks. On their backs they carried guns, rockets, missiles, and grenades, dwarfing their small, scrawny frames.

By now, Tue was becoming worn out. The suffering on the mountain trails, the loneliness, and despair broke his spirit. For over a month he'd borne the pain of it all, and now he didn't have the strength to bear it any longer! He tried to make an escape, but the Communists were soon after him and shot him in the back. Huan saw the bloody clothes they brought back! We know that the living Saviour was right at Tue's side with outstretched arms to carry him straight into the bosom of our heavenly Father. Tue was a wonderful young pastor and servant of God.

Up at the Vietcong camp, they put Huan into a tiny bamboo hut with some other prisoners. There were captured men from Da Nang, Hoi An, and Tam Ky. It was rainy weather and extremely cold. The prisoners had no blankets and no fire. They all had to go into the forest with guards and cut down branches to make their beds. They slept on these branches and tried to cover themselves with the leaves. Huan doubled his sore feet up under him. The frigid winds of the mountaintop were like needles sticking into him.

The next morning, Huan saw that five prisoners had died in the night from the cold and rain, with having no food, only a few rags for clothing, and no medicine. The Communists made Huan dig the graves for the five men.

For nearly six months Huan was up in the high mountains with ten South Vietnamese prisoners. There were no Christians among them, and Huan was not allowed to talk about Christ to them.

They had to work very hard, digging the campground, cutting wood for the Communists, and planting rice. One night in the forest, Huan with the other prisoners and guards met a tiger. Its orange eyes shone out brilliantly. Another time, a tiger came right up to their camp. Three times while Huan was there, the Vietcong killed tigers. They ate the tiger meat, which is very strong-smelling, tough, and gristly. The Communists killed leopards, too, and ate them. They ate rats, nests of birds, monkeys, the lovely gibbon apes, and any meat they could find. There were very few deer left.

Huan and the other prisoners got none of the meat. They just had their two small handfuls of rice each day. They had to work all the time. Patches of rice fields up there grew the dry mountain rice, and Huan was forced to work in them and in the gardens. All of these were hidden in narrow valleys for fear of American planes sighting them.

Because he just got rice, Huan became ill with beri-beri and began swelling up. He was very anemic too. He gathered and ate any leaves that were scented like herbs, and they helped him.

By now his shirt and trousers were hanging in dirty scraps and rags. So he and the other prisoners were given the black calico Vietcong pajamas. Huan was in his bare feet continually, and he had no way of cutting his toenails. Finally they fell off because he was in water and mud so much and the bushes and thorns prickled and tore at his feet.

After one month in this Vietcong camp, the Communists took Huan to another hideout to make him help carry provisions for them. At this place, he and the other prisoners had to first cut down bamboo to help build the houses for this headquarters for the Vietcong.

One night, while there, one of the prisoners, a man from Hoi An, twenty-seven years old, tried to run away when the guards weren't looking. Huan knew this prisoner as he had been caught at Cam Hai about the same time as Huan and Tue. Many soldiers followed him, found his tracks, captured him, and brought him back. They put his feet in stocks, and he wasn't given any food for five days, just a little water to drink.

Because this one man had tried to run away and now was put in stocks, all the other prisoners were punished in the same way. They, too, had to have their feet in stocks, night and day for five days. The holes of the stocks were very small, and Huan said they couldn't move their legs. Those were five days and nights of unspeakable torture, but Huan said he had Almighty God to see him through with patience and courage. He pitied the other prisoners who knew not Christ, the Saviour.

The prisoners grew long beards after every two or three weeks. They used fire to burn off their own beards.

Then the Vietcong told all the prisoners that they would be going down to the lowlands to get food and supplies. Huan found out that they were going down to the Thanh My and Thuong Duc areas. He knew Thanh My, as our mission had had a church there for years among the far-back Vietnamese settlers on the Thanh My River and among the Katu tribespeople in the surrounding tribal villages.

Before they left, Huan and two other prisoners, at night, had to hull rice in a mortar made from a tree trunk, each man lifting and lowering in rhythm a heavy pillar of wood on the rice. Huan has a frail little body of about eighty-five pounds, but he had to ply the heavy pestle vigorously.

Then Huan and the other prisoners, with their guards, walked down to the market at Thanh My. It was exciting to get to a place in the wilderness that he knew! There were backwoods Vietnamese there who were forced by communist terrorists to trade fish, clothes, and medicine from Da Nang, selling all of this to the Vietcong.

The guards made Huan and the other prisoners carry grain, fish, salt, corn, and betel nut up the mountain trail to the camp. Their bamboo tribal back baskets were heavily loaded, and their shoulders were sawed by the liana of the shoulder straps.

Suddenly, one day, Huan saw two American marines who were prisoners of the Vietcong. Their hands were tied behind their backs. They were wearing Vietcong sandals made from pieces of automobile tires and rubber thongs, and they had on the black Vietcong cotton clothes. Their hair and beards were long. Their guards made the Americans carry big, heavy cans of rock salt on their backs. The white men were very sad and wouldn't speak. The Vietcong had their guns pointed at the white prisoners' backs. They went one way and Huan's group went another.

Huan saw the Thanh My River, recognizing it from being there on former preaching trips. He didn't see any of the old Katu villages we used to visit. We knew that the Communists had killed four of the Christian Katu chiefs there, and the villagers had been forced to follow the Communists far back into the mountains and become their slaves.

Huan, the other prisoners, and the guards got back up into the Vietcong mountain territory with the food and provisions. There were many North Vietnamese troops who had just arrived at the camp. These wore different clothes, khaki-colored uniforms, and their hair was cut short. They looked healthier. They wore military hats with the communist star. On their chest pockets was the sickle and hammer insignia. They were the same height as the South Vietnam men, about five feet tall, but like the southerners, they were strong and wiry.

In the month of August and all the fall months, it rained heavily in the mountains day and night. Huan and other prisoners caught dysentery frrom drinking dirty water, eating hard, uncooked rice, or from other sources of germs. He had no medicine. The cold and wet meant much suffering for them. Huan looked for firewood, and they were able to light a small fire underground. The guards let the sick ones with stomach cramps get near the fire. They longed for a sunrise and the warmth of the sun.

The Vietcong guards now said, "We must continue on our way very quickly, up into more jungle mountains to another Vietcong headquarters."

One very sick prisoner couldn't keep up with them. He had fever and was vomiting; he was shaking with chills and had no medicine. So the Communists tied his hands to a tree and left him. When they returned to get him, they found him dead. Huan had to help bury him right there near the trail.

They went to the other Vietcong headquarters in these mountains and were there for five days. Then they were sent down to buy more food at another Vietcong market on the Thanh My River. While there, the American Phantom jets came bombing. The Vietcong had a network of tunnels to which they could run and make a fast fadeout. The prisoners and guards waited in this secret hideout until it was dark. Then they came out and went to every bamboo hut in the village. The people were well subdued and gave the Communists all the supplies they could carry. Then the procession returned hurriedly up into the mountains.

At 10 P.M. the terrifying American planes came bombing as the group climbed up the mountain trail. Huan fell down with his heavy basket of food on his back. The branch of a tree pierced his side. The blood flowed, and a sick feeling beat all through him. He moaned in his helplessness. The planes roared overhead, but the Americans couldn't see them under the dense forest trees.

After the planes went, the guides put Huan into a hammock and made the other prisoners carry him to the top of the mountain. The Communists talked of how they hated the Americans and they told the South Vietnam prisoners to hate them too.

They had no medicine or bandages for Huan's wound, but they put on plaques of tobacco leaves. Huan longed for penicillin but later he got other leaves from the forest and chewed the leaves with salt and put this on his side. The leaves have chlorophyll in them and somehow the wound healed.

He had to stay three more weeks in the mountain base waiting for the cut to heal. He prayed all the time, and he said he felt the Lord Jesus very near to him, comforting him. He thought a lot about his wife and children, and he tried to plan how he could escape. His thoughts were often on eternity and of all the everlasting happiness and glory God has prepared for

His children in heaven. There would be no more pain and suffering, no more sorrow and heartache and bondage.

He longed exceedingly to taste some meat or fish or some *nuoc mam,* the fish sauce that the Vietnamese people love. He could smell the fish and *nuoc mam* that the Vietcong were eating and how his mouth watered! He humbly asked his captors for some fish bones to grind up, fry, and eat. Huan told me, "I had the No. 1 priority on this delicacy." The other prisoners didn't take any of it, as they saw he was so wasted away, and he needed the calcium from the bones.

"I ground the bones into powder between stones, and it helped me," Huan said.

Then after a few days, the Vietcong's sow in the camp gave birth to seven little pigs. One died and the Vietcong gave the little dead one to Huan. He cooked it with his handful of rice and "the feast" strengthened him greatly.

The captors became a little more friendly and talked a bit to Huan now. They questioned him about his work at the leprosarium. They asked,

"When the Vietcong captured you, were you sad? Do you hate us? Are you angry at us?"

Huan remained silent.

After three weeks in the mountaintop base, Huan's wound had healed and he had to carry food again for the Vietcong. They went down to the Vietcong village once more, near Thanh My, where we used to have a church. There they bought a lot of salt and carried it up to the tops of the high mountains to some Katu or tribal villages up there. They would exchange the salt for dried corn, chickens, and pigs. The tribespeople had many animals but were starving for salt.

On this mountaintop, Huan saw a Vietcong hospital made of bamboo and thatched grass shacks. There were many wounded Vietcong soldiers there and much suffering. They had very little medicine or food. They had Vietcong doctors, instruments, and nurses (some of them girls), both from the south and the north.

Up there, he saw many tribespeople working for the Communists. They were planting rice fields, corn, pumpkins, sweet potatoes, manioc, onions, tobacco. They had chickens, pigs, cows, and water buffaloes. The Communists paid the tribespeople some money, and so they had bowls from which to eat, chopsticks, and big pans. They had their tribal gongs, drums, and jars, and they made their sour rice wine up there and drank it from long bamboo stems stuck in the jars. Many of the aboriginal mountain folk had ivory plugs in their earlobes, made from pure ivory of elephant tusks. The Pkoh tribe in this area own tamed elephants, so these may have been Pkoh tribespeople. Or they could have sold ivory to their neighbors, the Katu. Some of the tribespeople had long stretched earlobes, and many wore brass arm rings from wrist to elbow. They smoked long bamboo pipes and had their front teeth sawed off at the gums. The Pkoh tribespeople had all been captured by the Communists eight years before and the whole Katu tribe, except for about sixty people, were also now slaves of the Vietcong. These tribespeople Huan saw on the mountaintop didn't wear their own handwoven tribal loincloths, wraparound skirts, and blouses. They were all dressed in the Vietcong black pajamas.

From where they were sleeping, Huan could hear trucks, tanks, and tracked vehicles rumbling in the night. So he is quite certain that they were near the Ho Chi Minh Trail.

Huan again passed by where the Vietcong hospital had been, but now it was completely destroyed by American planes. From the air it was just a cluster of bamboo and grass shacks. Huan saw many dead, and a number of Vietcong bamboo huts were smouldering.

Back at the Vietcong headquarters, the prisoners rested a little, then they had to go down again to a Vietcong village near Thuong Duc, a three-day exhausting march, to get more food.

There were ten South Vietnamese prisoners and two Vietcong guards. One of the prisoners was by now a good friend of Huan's. He was a Mr. Xuan (pronounced "Swoong") from a village near the Da Nang Airport. He was a former village chief, about fifty years old. He had been captured nine months before Huan.

Huan asked his friend secretly, "Where are we going?"

The man said, "We are going down near Thuong Duc. Perhaps we can escape from there, down the river to Da Nang."

Mr. Xuan was a rich man and he thought a lot about his wife, children, and all his family. He longed to get back to them.

By this time, the Vietcong guards believed they had subdued the ten prisoners into obedience to their side. They had been through six months of brainwashing and on all the marches down the mountain trails to get food, the prisoners had behaved well. So during the nights on this trip the guards didn't tie the prisoners up.

As they reached the river at midnight, Huan and Mr. Xuan talked secretly together. Xuan whispered, "Let us escape tonight to Da Nang!" Huan agreed.

When the guards and all the prisoners were sound asleep, Huan and Xuan crept softly away in their black pajamas and bare feet.

They looked for the Dai An River, and Mr. Xuan, who knew the district well, was able to find it in the night. The river was at high flood season, but Mr. Xuan was an excellent swimmer. Huan was a poor swimmer, but he would try it.

They hid their black pajamas in some bushes, and Xuan helped Huan swim halfway across the river. In the middle, there were desperately strong rapids. Huan feared them and was too weak and gaunt to try to breast them. So both the men had to return! They put on their dry pajamas again and crept back to the camp. The Vietcong guards were still sleeping soundly.

Huan whispered to Xuan, "You go and I will stay! When you get back to Da Nang, go to see Mr. and Mrs. Gordon Smith. Tell them I tried to escape, but I am too weak! I cannot cross the river."

So Mr. Xuan crept off by himself. He was able to swim across the raging river, escape into the Dai An District, where he was soon safe with the South Vietnamese troops. They helped him get back to Da Nang to his own loved ones. He didn't come to tell us the news as he had to lie very low for months. Today he is a village chief again near Hoi An.

Around 5 o'clock the next morning the Vietcong guards realized Xuan had escaped! They questioned Huan, "Did you know that he was escaping? Do you know where he went?" Huan answered very innocently, "I'm sorry. I don't know where he is! I was sleeping!" Huan had fallen asleep soon after Xuan left.

The Vietcong guards were very angry and tied up all the prisoners tightly. They told the Vietcong control officers in the area about the escape, and these officers searched for Xuan. But he was out of their reach by then.

When the Vietcong guards could not find Xuan, they hurried with the nine prisoners up the hard three-day march to the top of the mountains where the headquarters was hidden. They put all the prisoners in stocks for four days and nights with hardly any rice or water.

Huan lost hope! It was dreadful suffering, and he greatly missed Xuan. He kept praying continually: "O God, help me! Open the way for me to escape from this torture!"

After three more weeks at the headquarters, the Vietcong told Huan that he and the other prisoners were to go down again to the river village to get more food. They made the long, hard, three-day hike again.

Near the Thuong Duc section, American planes came into the valley, strafing and dropping bombs. They flew low over Huan and the other prisoners, and the Americans thought because of their black pajamas they were all Vietcong. They killed one of the Vietcong guards. The prisoners were in great terror! They got down into bunkers underground, but bombs fell near their hiding place. They crawled out of this bunker and ran to another one. After they left the first bunker, the planes bombed it four or five times! But the second bunker was concealed deeply in a hillside and they didn't bomb it.

When the planes stopped bombing, Huan crawled out of his hiding place and looked for his prisoner friends and the Vietcong guard. The American bombs had killed the second guard too!

Now Huan was "wise as a serpent." He took the dead guards' guns and he led the eight prisoners back up the mountains to the headquarters! He feared to stay down in the lowlands at that time, as the Americans and the South Vietnamese were attacking strongly all the black-clad Vietcong they could see.

Because Huan returned to the headquarters with all the prisoners, acting like a Vietcong guard, the Communists now believed that he was on their side. They welcomed him back. Even the other prisoners didn't know that Huan was just pretending to be on the Vietcong side. They thought that he had really turned Communist!

After ten days the prisoners had to return again to the Thuong Duc section for food. They had one Vietcong guard and he let Huan help lead the eight prisoners. They trusted Huan, and he had freedom to go to a number of places. They thought that if he had wished to escape he would have tried to do so when the two guards were killed and would have taken all the eight prisoners with him. But this whole area and the mountains on this side of the river were under strong Vietcong control, and Huan knew that he and the prisoners would soon have been caught.

They arrived at Thuong Duc, and the prisoners were given their first feast of meat in six months. The American planes, in strafing the riverside villages, had killed many cows and buffaloes. So the officers of the Vietcong control in this area ordered the villagers to give some of the meat to the guard and the nine prisoners. Also their baskets would be filled with meat for the Vietcong headquarters up in the mountains. If the Vietnamese villagers had refused to give the meat, the Vietcong would have killed them.

By 1 A.M. the guard and eight prisoners were all sleeping heavily after their good feast of meat. Now Huan changed rapidly and quietly from his black pajamas into an old khaki military uniform of North Vietnam which he had recently stolen from the chief guard's house at the headquarters up on the mountaintop while the guard was asleep.

Huan, now looking like a North Vietnamese soldier, with insignias, crept away from the sleeping prisoners and guard and joined a group of North Vietnam soldiers that he knew was going by ferry to Dai Loc, the big South Vietnamese military center in the area. Huan changed his voice and talked in the North Vietnam dialect. He is an excellent actor, so the North Vietnamese didn't recognize him in the dark of night as a southerner. He followed near the end of the line of the North Vietnam troops and went safely by ferry boat across the wild rapids in the river to Dai Loc.

Huan heard some North Vietnamese say, "We shall go this certain way when we leave the ferry boat," so Huan crept away in the opposite direction when they got off the boat.

He decided to hide near the Dai Loc District government compound. He dug in the sand on the riverbank, took off his North Vietnam khaki uniform, rolled it up tightly, and buried it deeply in the sand. He was only in underpants now and could pass as a country peasant. He lay down in the sand and waited for dawn.

At 7 o'clock he saw many farmers from the Dai Loc District going with their water buffaloes and oxen to work in their rice fields. He walked along with them into a refugee camp nearby.

When he got into the camp, he went to the chief and said,

Pastor Huan, *second from left,* ministered to Hroy congregation and orphans at Tuy Hoa, after his escape.

168

"The Lord Jesus Christ has helped me to escape! Could you show me a Christian family here?" Huan knew there were many Christian refugees who had fled from the Vietcong at Thuong Duc. The United World Mission had forty or more of the orphans from there in the China Beach Orphanage.

Huan was taken to a C. & M.A. refugee, and this man kindly gave him trousers and a shirt. He took Huan to the C. & M.A. preacher, Mr. Bich, in the camp.

Huan lived with him, hiding from the Communists for awhile, and the pastor gave him food. How happy and thankful Huan was! Then Mr. Bich brought Huan the forty miles into Da Nang on the back of his Honda!

What a joyous reunion it was at the China Beach Orphanage with Huan and his wife and family! His wife had given birth to a baby boy while he was away and now the baby was two months old. It was such unspeakable joy that they all wept and wept! They greatly praised and thanked the Lord. Also they sorrowed with Mrs. Tue and her family because Tue had been killed!

Huan and his family lived on our mission property for a few days, taking some medicine. After that, Gordon introduced him to Chaplain Nelson on the *Sanctuary*, the U.S. hospital ship. Huan was received into the hospital there for over a month. Many American doctors examined him and treated his beri-beri. Every morning Chaplain Nelson helped Huan greatly by praying with him.

Huan was on the hospital ship for Christmas, and Dr. Billy Graham, visiting the American troops in Vietnam, came aboard the ship. He shook hands with Huan and prayed for him. Huan will never forget that!

Mr. Miller, one of the Wycliffe translators, and Gordon showed movies of their missionary work to the patients, spoke to them, and to all the Americans and Vietnamese on board.

Huan never forgets the wonderful food he received on the ship, and the treats, like American ice cream and candy. How he appreciated the good medicine and care! After his *Sanctuary* treatment, he was able to begin work again as a pastor. He asked the committee to send him to a pioneer refugee center on the edge of Da Nang city called Hoa Khanh, to begin work there from scratch. There was no church, no house, no Christians. But Huan and his wife served there for two years and built a chapel, parsonage, school, and started a sewing class! He led 150 Vietnamese to the Lord and they are fine Christians there today.

We missionaries from Da Nang often visited him there, and Huan especially enjoyed having the Reverend Hank Jones of Campus Crusade preach there. Stanley and Ginny, back from furlough, also were there in the crusade meetings.

The American chaplains in that area helped greatly in getting the material for the church and the other buildings. The nearby Force Logistics Center helped, as did the Construction No. 8 Battalion, through their earnest chaplains.

While at the Hoa Kanh church, Huan had two kidney stone attacks, and during one of the bad spells he was cared for on the German hospital ship *Helgoland*. For the other attack, he was in the German Malteser hospital in Da Nang. He also had an operation for a dangerous stomach ulcer on the *Helgoland*.

He is in good health now and today is down at Tuy Hoa on the coast near Quinhon, caring for the Hroy tribal church of around 900 Christians in all of that area. He is beginning an orphanage there to care for the many Hroy tribal orphans.

22

Miracle in a Tiny Girl's Tragic Life

THREE-AND-A-HALF-YEAR-OLD Cong, of some village near Da Nang, should have been dead. That is, if a unit of the U.S. Marines hadn't cared. They found this sick, little brown Vietnamese doll lying on the ground, blind, whimpering amid the ruins of her home and parents. The Communists had just burned down her village, killed her parents and the other villagers, and even had cut little Cong deeply across the top of her head. She should have died. The Vietcong wanted her to, desiring no witnesses.

"They killed my father first. Then they hit my mother and she soon died," said little Cong in her voice weak with fright.

The marines took her for their little mascot. As she was blind, no one around wanted her. She had been abandoned to die there on the ground. The marines carried her into our orphanage. She was just skin and bones and very ill. She had suffered terribly with glaucoma because of malnutrition, and one eye was completely destroyed. The other eye was almost gone.

Our two nurses from Holland, Mimi de Fosse and Nelly Heyboer, took charge of her, feeding her well and taking her to the nearby American Naval Hospital for treatment. She responded well, soon gaining weight and brightness and becoming a lovable, talkative, very charming little girl. The eye doctors at the hospital said that Cong might see again in the one eye if she could have a corneal transplant. But they gave her only a slight chance for the eye to be healed.

We also took her out to the two American hospital ships that came into Da Nang Bay to care for the sick and wounded American GIs, the *Sanctuary* and the *Repose*. The eye doctors

171

on these ships told us to try to get Cong to America for a corneal transplant on the one eye before it deteriorated much longer with the glaucoma. This corneal operation can't be done in Vietnam, as the Vietnamese won't give an eye from their dead for a transplant. They fear to enter the next world without an eye, as they think they would then be blind forever.

The American doctors on the hospital ships and also an eye specialist we wrote to in Pennsylvania, Dr. Strausse, all recommended that we take Cong to San Francisco, California, to Dr. Max Fine in the Mt. Zion Hospital there, as he is world-famous for doing corneal transplants. They said, "He is not only the best doctor in U.S.A. for this work, but likely in the whole world!"

The U.S. Marine Air Group in Da Nang sponsored Cong. Their chaplain, Bruce Schumacher, at the MAG 16 Marble Mountain Headquarters Helicopter Base, began to collect offerings among these marines and their friends and churches in America, to pay the living expenses for Cong and me in America. Chaplain Schumacher wrote to Dr. Fine, asking if he could do the expensive operation free of charge, and Dr. Fine kindly answered, "Yes, I will do it."

Obtaining a passport for a Vietnamese to leave this country sometimes took many months, and in medical cases permission had to be obtained from the Minister of Health. But it took Gordon only two or three days to "walk" the papers through the many offices and obtain Cong's passport and visa to enter the United States. An enlarged photo of Cong helped a lot too, and Gordon's being able to speak Vietnamese was useful. Also the fact that we have been here in Vietnam for forty years seemed to impress the various officials concerned.

Gordon asked the manager of Pan American Airways if he could possibly obtain free tickets for Cong and me, as her escort, to the States and back and he was most sympathetic. They are swamped, he said, with such requests and permission had to be obtained from the Civil Aeronautics Board as well, with the request coming from the Minister of Health of the government of Vietnam. In a few days, the head office of P.A.A. cabled their willingness to give Cong and me free return

172

tickets, but they didn't want much publicity about it or they'd be overwhelmed with needy cases like this.

So on April 9, 1969, Gordon, Cong, and I took off on an Air America plane from Da Nang to Saigon. An extra stewardess was put on their plane to San Francisco to help little blind Cong and me and also another little three-year-old Vietnamese girl, Thuy, whom I was also escorting to America for adoption. The stewardesses were kind and helpful, amusing the children with toys and dolls. Cong loved to play with all the little salt and pepper holders and tiny plastic cups that we had on our food trays. These kept her amused for hours, as she felt them with her quick, light little fingers.

Our jet reached San Francisco in twenty-two hours from Saigon. We left Saigon on Wednesday, April 9, and we arrived in San Francisco on Wednesday, April 9, losing one day enroute.

Friends of ours, Dr. and Mrs. Ulyss Mitchell, came on board to greet us. Also there were about a dozen news and television reporters there to meet little blind Cong. Some came on the plane, taking our pictures before we got off. Thuy, the little adopted child, was met by her new "grandma" to take her to Miami, Florida.

Cong was very quiet and good when the reporters interviewed us in a special room at the airport. She had on her red corduroy overalls, white woolen shirt, and little pink sweater, all clothing from boxes sent to us by friends in America for the orphans. We were nearly frozen in cold San Francisco in April after our hot weather in Vietnam.

The reporters took scores of pictures and the head man of Pan American Airways was there, very kind and friendly. Later we saw ourselves on television in the hospital, although little Cong was too blind to really see anything. Immediately Cong began hugging everybody and going to them lovingly. She was in a warm, joyous mood.

Ulyss and Viola Mitchell drove Cong and me directly to the Mount Zion Hospital where Cong was given a bed in the blue-carpeted pediatrics ward, where she was surrounded by kind, bright nurses. I was asked to stay in her room for two weeks or so, to help keep her company, talking Vietnamese to her. The friendly nurses soon learned some Vietnamese words like *nuoc* for water and *com* for rice.

On April 12, Cong went into the operating room and was nearly four hours on the table. Afterward, Dr. Fine came into our room, unsmiling and shaking his head.

"Her eye," he said, "the best one, is very bad! There was no lens in it. The eye had been perforated by the glaucoma. There is only fair hope for this eye. It is not good!"

Then six days later, Dr. Fine put Cong to sleep to observe her eye. He found the transplant was taking nicely. "She will be able to see with glasses," he assured me. I asked him if Cong would just see light and dim shadows, but he said confidently, "She will see a *lot* with glasses from that one good eye. The glasses will give her the lens she hasn't got." That was thrilling, encouraging news!

More than twenty-five phone calls in our hospital room came to me from people asking to adopt Cong. The calls were from Philadelphia, Palm Beach, North and South Carolina, New York, Buffalo, Rochester, Ohio, Detroit, Iowa, and many places in California. They had seen Cong's picture in the paper and they wanted this petite, black-haired, almond-eyed girl. So Cong could have many homes in the U.S.A.!

Beautiful toys were sent to Cong, including a soft Raggedy Ann doll. She received money to buy her some warm house slippers. One stewardess from the plane from Saigon came to the hospital to see Cong and brought her a cuddly toy puppy that played "Brahm's Lullaby," and a little toy xylophone.

Wonderful friends who read about her in the papers and saw her pictures, sent lovely clothes, such as pretty underwear, dresses, a little hat, shoes, T-shirts, socks, gloves, a purse, pajamas, a teddy bear, a jewel box that played music, and lollypops! How kind everyone was! They wrote Cong charming little letters from all over the U.S., and numerous "get well cards." The American people showed beautiful kindness.

It was a tremendous uplift and comfort to my heart, and the hearts of our colleagues in Vietnam, to see their great response toward a poor little blind war orphan from Vietnam. We were greatly moved. Cong would never forget America and all this love and kindness!

Cong's name in this instance translated from Vietnamese means "peacock," but the marines called her Julie. Soon Cong could say her name in English, "Julie Peacock." She loved ice cream and cottage cheese, calling them "keem" and "chee." She also enjoyed the American cereals, Rice Krispies and Wheaties, calling them "white bread," as they resembled in texture the crisp paper-thin rice wafers the Vietnamese make and which are called *banh trang* (white bread).

As I stayed with her in her hospital room, sleeping in a bed right beside Cong's, I'd hear her talking, especially in the night, to herself.

One night she cried out in Vietnamese, "Oh, the village is burning! Burning! The Communists have set it on fire! The houses are burning! Burning!" She then cried out, "Where is my father? Where is my mother? Where is Yen, my sister? Oh, I am sad! I'm very sad!" She was far away in memory with her loved ones and was living again the terrorist attack of the Communists on her village and home.

Sometimes she'd sing in Vietnamese the little songs she's learned already at our China Beach Orphanage: "Don't be afraid! Believe on Him." "Jesus loves me, this I know." She'd even sing these for Dr. Max Fine and he'd join in with her.

After three weeks in the hospital, Cong and I were able to move out to the well-known and pleasant missionary receiving home, the Home of Peace in Oakland. I had to take Cong back to Doctor Fine and his colleague, Dr. Picetti, three times a week for another month, for examinations, eyedrops, and fresh bandages. Friends drove us from the Home of Peace in Oakland to the San Francisco hospital.

Then the stitches were removed and Cong wore an eye shield with a small lens in it for awhile and she began to see things! Sometimes we'd be able to go over to San Francisco by bus and streetcar, and these were great experiences for Cong! She'd want to stay on the bus and go riding all day long. The kind bus drivers would have to carry her off for me.

Millions saw her on nationwide TV, as the TV men came

175

right into the Home of Peace with their equipment and took pictures of little Julie Peacock playing with her toys. She had a doll that said, when Cong pulled her wire, "I like ice cream!" Cong would repeat it in a dainty, bell-like voice, "I like ih-ceem! I like ih-ceem!" Her little greetings of "Hello" and "Good-bye!" covered the land.

One day in our room at Home of Peace, I was writing at a small table and Cong was playing with some cardboard boxes and her toys. She was talking to her big doll given her by the San Francisco telephone girls, and I quickly jotted down everything she was saying, translating from her Vietnamese. She sounded like a little Vietnamese mother talking to her baby, and she had no thought of me sitting nearby. She must have remembered her mother talking to her like this, as she'd never played with other little girls who had dolls.

She scolded the doll:

"You've dirtied your *ao* and *quan* (your coat and trousers)! Do you hear me? I'm angry! Very angry! I'll hit you now." She slapped the doll lightly. Then she crooned, clasping the big doll in her arms, "Oh-o-o-o poor baby! Poor little baby!" She petted and sniffed at the baby's cheeks.

"Now you've dirtied your hands and your mouth! Where is the soap heh? m-? m-? a-a-m, m-?

"I'm very angry!" She shook the baby. Then she pretended to wash the hands and face.

"Now you're clean!" She "scrubbed up" the floor around her.

"And you've lost your shoes, eh? You've also lost your inside shirt. Hm?" She shook the doll again, warning, "Don't you dare dirty your clothes or face again! If you do, I'll catch you! Heh? Heh? I'll catch you, like today! Do you hear me?"

She stood the doll up and put her face next to the doll's face. She shook the doll again and tapped it lightly on the cheeks. "I'm angry! Do you hear me? Heh? Heh?

"Lie down now! Oh-ah! You don't listen to me, Baby! Now can you stay there? Huh? Huh? Do you hear? Sleep now. Sh! Sh! Sh!"

Later on, Cong herself got inside the big cardboard box. I

was startled as she suddenly gave a loud wail. It was the heathen cry of mourning for the dead! She chanted:

"Oh, Mama—oi, oi! I am sad. I am *very* lonely and sad. I have no one to put me to sleep! I have no one to help me! Your little baby here has no one to help her!

"O, O, O, oi! Oh Mama! Oh Mama! Oh, don't die, Mama! Oh, my mama is dead already! I'm just a little child, all alone here. *Cha oi! Cha oi!* My mama is dead already!"

She called on the dead, as the Vietnamese people do, in a long, plaintive cry, and with a quivering, tearful voice, she said, "There is no one to help care for me; I'm just a little baby!"

She rocked in the cardboard box saying, "Oh, tch! Tch! Tch! Ai-ee-ee-ya!"

She got out of the box and stood over it crying, "My mother is dead and buried already! I, her child, want my home! O, o, o, a-a, I'm very sad! There is no one to care for me, a little child!"

Many times she mourned, "O, o, o-a-oi! Mama! Mama! Today you died! O Mama! Oi, oi, a, a, a, oi!"

She still stood over the box, mourning, "My mama is buried in this box. Oh, Mama, oi! Amen!" (She had learned "Amen" through the prayers in the China Beach Orphanage.) "There is no one to care for this little child! O, tch, tch! I saw Mama laid in this box and put down into the earth!"

Then she called on God as she'd learned to do at China Beach. "For God so loved the world that He gave." That is all she remembered of the verse. Then she closed with "Amen. A—men!"

She now said to her doll, lying where she'd laid her on the mat, "Little child, sing about Jesus! Stand up and sing! 'For God so loved the world that He gave, One!' "

I wrote down what she said, word for word, and my heart was very touched as this little orphan girl of three and a half years opened up pictures to me of the great sorrows in her little life. She had lost her mother, the biggest tragedy which could befall any child.

While in the Bay area of San Francisco and Oakland, I was

able to take a number of meetings in churches and Bible colleges while friends at the Home of Peace looked after Cong. Then Cong and I flew down to Los Angeles for the month of June, as I could now put the drops in Cong's eyes myself. We stayed with our old friends the Cliff Smiths and took many meetings in churches there.

We visited some of the homes of leading members of the famous International Orphans, Inc., who were helping us at that time in building a four-story building at our China Beach Orphanage in Da Nang, in memory of General Hocmuth, who had recently been killed by the Communists at Hue.

Tiny, happy Julie Peacock was fondly welcomed by these precious, warmly interested I.O.I. friends. We also were invited to many churches, and Cong would come with me up to the platform in her new clothes, L.A. style, and she'd smile at the audience. Cong could sing now, showing her two rows of small, perfect teeth. And Cong could laugh! She would talk to the people using her new English words, and this was her little speech: "Hi! Marines! Dr. Max Fine! San Francisco, Julie Peacock. Bye-bye!" The audiences fell in love with her.

It was as if little Cong felt she had an important mission to accomplish, and she did it charmingly. She turned people's attention to another side of Vietnam: the generosity and tenderness of the U.S. Marines, the worthwhileness of bringing the unwanted and needy little ones into places like our China Beach Orphanage, the kindness of so many in America who helped toward restoring Cong's sight, the testimony to the goodness of our Lord in making it all possible.

For one week, while we were in Los Angeles, I was able to leave Cong in Mrs. Ruth Smith's care, and I flew to Washington, D.C., to visit our oldest son, Douglas, his wife, Ruth, and our three grandchildren, Linda, Douglas, Jr., and Jacqueline. It was a very happy time.

A few months before, Douglas had had a very serious operation for a perforated ulcer of the stomach. There was danger of peritonitis, and he gave us all a terrible scare! But he had had the best of care in the George Washington University Hospital and in a month's time he was back at work again in the State Department. As I visited them in June, Douglas was in the best of health.

Stanley and Ginny and their four little K's, Kenny, Karen, Kathleen, and Kristen, who were soon to return to Vietnam, also came to visit with us all in Washington. They were holding meetings not far away at that time and were able to spend a day and night with us. We had a precious family reunion.

I was also able to meet our son Leslie back in Los Angeles when he arrived there with two little Vietnamese boys from Da Nang who had to have urgent open-heart surgery in the University of Missouri Hospital.

The Cliff Smiths, Cong, and I met them at the Los Angeles airport. I had to weep as we saw Leslie pushing the wheelchair from the plane, with the two little Vietnamese boys in it, huddled up in sharp pain. They were dressed in a few odd bits of clothing from boxes sent by friends in America. They had had a bad time on the trip, for the boys were very ill and had heart pain, and the stewardesses had to give them oxygen. Leslie gave up his seat to them so that they could lie down, and he didn't get much sleep from Saigon to Los Angeles.

We had a good visit together around the boys' beds, as they stayed the night in a hotel near the airport, leaving the next day at noon for Columbia, Missouri.

Leslie phoned me several times and was so happy to report that the two boys, one of whom was given only a 30 percent chance of recovery, had been operated upon successfully. Leslie brought the boys back to Vietnam one month after I returned with Cong.

On July 1, Cong and I went back to San Francisco and Dr. Max Fine had Cong fitted with strong glasses, and her lovely, dark eye now could see a lot! She ran lovingly into everyone's arms and was a real charmer.

While in San Francisco, Dr. and Mrs. Matzger met me at the Mt. Zion Hospital and asked me if I would take back to Vietnam a little two-year-old Vietnamese girl called Vinh. Dr. Matzger had brought the child to America a year before for open-heart surgery. The operation was successful and little Vinh had stayed with the Matzgers in their home. Now Vinh

Cong, wearing glasses and now able to see, is welcomed back by the other orphans.

was ready to return to her parents in Dong Ha, a town near the Demilitarized Zone, one hundred miles north of Da Nang.

On Thursday, July 3, Cong, Vinh, and I left San Francisco. Our friends, the Ulyss Mitchells, Mrs. Ruth Smith and her sons, Todd and Bill, and Dr. and Mrs. Matzger were all there to see us off.

At the airport, Cong ran from one big window to another, looking at the huge glistening and gleaming jets. She hadn't been able to see them when we arrived in Los Angeles three months before! Now with her new eye and glasses she could see, and she shouted with excitement and delight! The people in the waiting rooms were touched at the miracle in this little child's tragic life!

When we got on the Pan American Clipper, Vinh cried heartbrokenly for her dearly loved American "parents" and Cong cried for her "Mummy" Ruth Smith, who had looked after her so lovingly. A stewardess brought a bottle of milk for Vinh and, after drinking it thirstily, she fell asleep. Cong, too, settled down into her comfortable seat and didn't cry anymore.

As the plane was full going to Honolulu, we could only have one seat each. So I sat in the middle seat with the children lying on each side of me, with their little feet in my lap. We traveled like that all the way to Saigon. Cong and Vinh slept most of the way, just sitting up to eat the delicious meals.

With help from several stewardesses we changed planes at Honolulu. We didn't have daylight until after Wake Island, so it was night most of the way.

We arrived at Saigon on a Saturday morning. On our trip back we had gained a whole day. Gordon and two press reporters were at the plane steps to meet us. After a number of photos, the A.P. reporter kindly drove us to the C. & M. A. mission home in his car.

The heat of Vietnam in July was, of course, overwhelming! We soon had the children sitting under a lukewarm shower, and they didn't need to wear much clothing. The long trip, change of time, and the great heat, made them just want to lie on their beds under the ceiling fan and sleep most of the time.

The next day, Sunday, we dressed the children in their prettiest American clothes and took them to the International Protestant Church in Saigon, which has services in English. The children sat quietly through the service and were warmly greeted by many of our friends afterward.

After lunch, we were driven to the airport and got on an Air America two-engine plane for Da Nang. Again little Vinh slept all the way, lying down in the seat, but Cong was too thrilled about getting back to Da Nang and to all her old friends there to go to sleep.

The three Dutch missionaries, Mimi, Nelly, and Yohan, met us at the plane. Cong was very excited to really *see* these, her former nurses, for the first time! All the people on the mission property gave us a warm welcome. We put two mattresses down on our living room floor for the two little girls, where it was cooler for them in the 94 degrees for sleeping.

The Vietnamese children on our compound came in and stood staring at Cong! They couldn't get over the miracle of her being able to see now, and of her wearing glasses! Little Vinh played with her toys in her small traveling box from

181

America and kept looking at the colored photos of her temporary foster-parents, Dr. and Mrs. Matzger, which they had put into her box for her. She repeated softly, "Mummy," "Daddy" over and over. Everyone at our house fell in love with this sweet little girl sitting so quietly and looking so trustingly at us with her big, beautiful brown eyes.

We took the children to the Marine Air Group 16, who had helped finance their little mascot Cong's way in America. She charmed the commanding officer and Chaplain Bruce Schumacher with her bright, warm ways and loving hugs. The marines often visited Cong from then on at China Beach Orphanage.

The next morning, a marine arrived from Dong Ha to take little Vinh back to her own parents. Her father is a policeman in Dong Ha. We all felt sad saying good-bye to her as she went off in a plane. But we have kept in touch with Vinh and her family up to the present day.

When we arrived at the China Beach Orphanage with Cong, she was immediately surrounded by scores of children eager to see if she could really "see" them. Now they wouldn't have to watch that she didn't fall off the veranda or bump into a wall. Cong looked like a little princess doll in her pretty clothes from America, and when we unloaded all her toys and dolls, everyone gasped! She unselfishly shared many of her nice things with the other children in the small tots' room, and then she settled down well into the pleasant routine of the orphanage life.

23

"Despise Not One of These"

THE GOOD FRIENDS at International Orphans Incorporated in Los Angeles, California, worked hard, especially under the warm inspiration of Four-Star General Lewis Walt to raise a substantial sum of money for an imposing building at our China Beach Orphanage, to the memory of General Bruno Hocmuth of the U.S. Marines. He was a man who loved our little children and he was killed in action in Vietnam. He gave his life so that these little ones might grow up in freedom from Communist oppression. We believe it will not have been in vain.

The building is four stories high, overlooking the superb My Khe Beach on the South China Sea. It is built of concrete, strongly reenforced with steel bars, making it solid enough to withstand mighty typhoon winds.

The lowest floor houses the orphan babies and toddlers; the second floor, which is level with the main part of our property, is the spacious dining hall for 350 or more children. The third floor is the dormitory for girls ages seven to eighteen, or whenever they graduate from high school. Their dormitory is dedicated to the memory of Lance Corporal Warren Jack Ferguson, U.S. Marines, who was also killed in action in Vietnam. The Marine Corps Reserve Officers Association shared in making this building possible.

Two fine apartments were built on the upper fourth floor for the missionary staff at the orphanage. These apartments have terraces overlooking the tops of the tall whispering pines and the wide, sandy beach.

What a balcony view the missionaries have up here of the dramatic sea! They look at the brilliant sunrises, as they are facing directly toward the east; the changing blues throughout the day that sometimes grow into peacock blue green; the seas running high in the winds, with the white manes of the waves foaming, as they race endlessly toward the shore; the fat white clouds in a paler blue sky; the sea air, sweet and cool. All this sea! All this sky! And they listen to the sounds of the surf, the waves like God's great organ, thundering against the shore. How soul-strengthening it all is!

Then, from the fenced-in terrace on the roof of the Hocmuth building are splendid views in every direction. Out to the west spreads the city of Da Nang, mostly a jumble of tin roofs—no skyscrapers as yet—but with some nice buildings and the tall spire of the French-built Roman Catholic Cathedral. On the horizon to the north and west are mountains, with mighty Bana towering up 5,000 feet, fifteen miles away. To the south are the sheer Marble Mountains rising up from the seashore. Twenty miles out to sea, on the east, is Cu-Lao Cham Island, and the measureless expanse of the South China Sea out to the horizon.

At night in the terrace the sky is a silken blue black, littered with swarms of stars. Lighted Vietnamese fishing boats are out on the ocean by the hundreds, catching fish by their lanterns and nets.

Truly our hearts rejoice at the goodness of our loving Lord who put it upon the hearts of these friends in America to give these children and missionaries this lovely home.

China Beach Orphanage is contributing to our Bible school, sending fine young people to be trained for the Lord's work. A number of girls will study later to become nurses and teachers.

We were delighted to welcome Miss Diana Reed from England, graduate nurse and graduate of the Bible-Missionary Training College in Glasgow, Scotland, in the summer of 1969. She had spent several months in deputation work in America under the United World Mission, and was so happy to come to represent Christ in Vietnam. We praised God for calling this bright, talented, and devoted full-time worker to join us here in this field, white with harvest, where the laborers are so few.

She and Simone Haywood, besides caring for the leprosy work, helped with the care of the 350 children at the China Beach Orphanage. They lived in the two choice missionary apartments up on the fourth floor of the Hocmuth memorial building.

Soon after Diana arrived, they had an epidemic of measles, a bout with the flu, together with sundry broken arms and cuts, keeping the two nurses going almost night and day.

One little baby brought to our orphanage at that time had been found by a GI in a trash can when she was only a few days old! The GI took her to the U.S. hospital ship, *Sanctuary*. She was kept on the ship for six months and was everyone's pet. The nurses on the ship were reluctant to give her up, but when she was well and strong they brought her to our China Beach Orphanage and Diana took special care of her.

The GI who had found the baby girl in the trash can, returned to the States and started adoption proceedings for her. Finally, after nearly two years for the paper work to be done, the young man and his wife were able to adopt little Thien An, meaning "Heaven's Grace."

Diana had to go to Minneapolis with two Vietnamese children for open-heart surgery, so she took little Grace along with them and left her in California with the GI and his wife. Grace is very happy in her new home there today.

In the fall of 1969, Dr. Stuart Harverson had to take his fifty-one Hrey tribal orphans from the station at Ha Bak, in Quang Ngai Province, as the Communists were closing in all around, and it was more and more dangerous in that area. These orphan children were the victims of communist brutality and the doctor had been caring for them for the past three years. But now it was getting difficult to provide supplies for them, and he thought it best to bring the children out of the interior to a safer place.

The marines helped the orphans begin their new life by letting them stay for five weeks in their barracks at the big U.S. military base, Chu Lai, near Quang Ngai city. They fed the orphans well there while Dr. Harverson looked for a place to settle the children permanently.

The children played on the sand in the bright sunlight and when the American lifeguard mounted his watchtower, the children all rushed to plunge into the warm sea.

The doctor had no outside staff with him caring for the orphans at Chu Lai, and one day he had to go to Tam Ky about twenty miles away on a visit. An anxious marine strode into the orphans' tent to watch "the poor little untended waifs." He was surprised to see three of the Hrey boys bringing in pots of rice, steaming hot, from a smoky cook tent, while the fifty children sat down in two long rows facing each other, with their bowls on the floor between them. They sang a verse of a hymn in parts, one of them gave thanks, and then they set to! The marine saw that the older orphans were caring pretty well for the group!

After a few days, the American units sent hot meals in from their mess halls, and also chocolate milk, ice cream, and grapes! The children had never tasted such delicacies before! One boy

Nurse Diana Read takes two children for open heart surgery and Tien An, our "trash can baby," to America.

186

showed the doctor an apple. "What should I do with this?" he asked. Doc took a bite and gave it back to him. He took a bite and returned it to the doctor! So it went, back and forth.

The children gained weight on the good food, especially the very small ones who had been so dangerously thin. The doctor had some of his medic-evangelist young men flown out from Ha Bak to help keep things in order. As the children were living in a marine base, they had to be kept very tidy "as little 'sub-marines' should be."

One Sunday morning they had some baptisms in the sea, and one of the U.S. Marines from a major's Bible class was baptized by Dr. Harverson with the children.

That evening the major brought some of his Bible class men up to the orphans' tent and they all had Communion together. The orphans can sing many hymns and choruses in English. "It makes you feel good to hear them," said one marine.

Doctor Harverson and Gordon finally decided that the magnificent Crescent Beach across Da Nang Bay, where the new Happy Haven Leprosarium is located, would be an ideal spot for the Hrey Children's Orphanage. Divided by a river from the leprosarium, their beach would stretch for nearly half a mile, with plenty of good land and streams of fresh water. The unspoiled sweep of sand and the valley behind it reaching to the mountains make it a tropical paradise.

So, in November, 1969, a giant helicopter landed on Crescent Beach, not far from Happy Haven Leprosarium, and disgorged the fifty-one Hrey orphans and their meager little personal belongings. Four large army tents, army beds, mattresses, tables, and benches were donated by various units on the Chu Lai Base. Marines, air force, and also Philco-Ford engineers helped generously. Choppers came, swirling gigantic clouds of sand as they landed, bringing food, clothing, medicines, and nurses and doctors to help see to the needs of the children. Truly this was "civic action" at its best!

Some wooden army huts had been dismantled by marine volunteers, and they were soon reerected by our carpenter leprosy patients for the children when the materials were brought over by *Hope II*.

As the facilities were obtained to properly house the children, with a school and chapel besides, more needy Hrey children were brought in from the dangerous Son Ha area back in the mountains.

Soon there were eight wooden huts and a long cement dining room and kitchen. Sally (Mrs. Harverson) and the doctor had their own hut, or "hooch," as the American military men call it, and they fixed it up most attractively.

Two new missionaries joined them: a young pastor, Barrie Flitcroft, from Scotland, and his wife, Tillie, an experienced nurse from Ireland. Soon a big marine helicopter arrived at the Crescent Beach carrying a dismantled "hooch" on the end of a hook and line. They lowered it to the ground beside Doc and Sally's hooch, and this would be Barrie and Tillie's home on the beach.

Test pilots from the Red Beach helicopter base a few miles along the bay, began to help Barrie build their little house.

One day Barrie lay down for a midday rest on a bunk in one of the boys' dormitories. Soon a little Hrey orphan climbed up beside him, put his small arm around Barrie, and contentedly went to sleep. The Hrey orphans stole their way into these new missionaries' hearts.

Tillie helped with the girls. Her first task was to teach them personal hygiene and "the mystery of hair shampoo." They shrieked with delight at the sight of a head full of bubbles!

Nearly every Saturday, Barrie went in with the doctor by U.S. Army helicopter to the Hrey tribal regions around Son Ha, visiting the tribespeople there in the daytime. It was too unsafe to stay in the villages at night. Sometimes they'd take four or five of the orphan boys with them, armed with trumpets, trombones, and other band instruments given them by the Americans, and they'd travel by jeep, borrowed from a Vietnamese official, from village to village, playing hymns on the instruments and preaching the Gospel to the Hrey. There are several thousand professing Christians in the Ha Bak-Son Ha area, but also vast numbers of pagan tribesmen.

Sally and the doctor also have a small apartment on our mission property in Da Nang, and come in from the beach occasionally for supplies. One time when Sally was in, a typhoon struck the coast of Vietnam. Our boat, *Hope II,* didn't dare take the trip across the bay in the big waves. The wind was howling as the morning began to dawn. The floor of the doctor's "hooch" shook with the crash of the rollers on the beach. Rain poured down in torrents. The doctor put on his bathing suit, sandals, and a hooded army rain jacket.

Suddenly a Vietnamese woman's voice called from outside. "Doctor, Doctor, come and help Grandmother across the river!"

It was their faithful house helper, Chi Bay. Sally Harverson and she had caught the military train leaving Da Nang station before dawn, and they rode in a cattle car on it with a few Vietnamese militia. In an hour's time they reached our "request stop" for the train, on the hillside above our leprosy colony. But the train did not stop! It only slowed down. So Sally slid off the moving train and kept on sliding down the bank until the train had gone past! Then she and the house girl walked down through the leprosarium until they came to the river, but there the bridge had been broken by the rushing waters from the typhoon.

The water was up to the doctor's waist, so he carried Sally on his back until they reached the bank. Together they walked through the orphanage while the children gaped in surprised admiration at brave little septuagenarian Sally.

One sunny Sunday afternoon at Crescent Beach, a little Hrey girl cried, "The boy Ip has been bitten by a snake!" The doctor hurried to him. A small green snake, a bamboo viper, had bitten the boy's big toe while he was gathering wild limes. Nurse Tillie Flitcroft and the doctor treated him, injecting medicine. But he needed hospital treatment quickly, and there was no boat. They prayed, in simple faith, believing that God would send them a helicopter. The doctor changed into his town clothes, ready for the helicopter to come, and Tillie washed and dressed little Ip in clean clothing. Soon there was a helicopter flying overhead! The doctor waved it down! The young pilot had never been on the Crescent Beach before, but he saw Doc waving and he felt he should come down. He picked up

189

the doctor, the suffering boy, and nurse Tillie, and in five minutes they were at the U.S. Army Hospital receiving No. 1 priority treatment of anti-snake venom for the bite, and the boy's life was saved!

The young American pilot was greatly impressed. He said, "It was a miracle! I just felt that I had to fly over the beach and take a look. There was the doctor waving for me to come down!"

God is real and He is living. He says in Psalm 50:15, "Call upon Me in the day of trouble: I will deliver thee, and thou shalt glorify me." He means just what He says, and He will do all that He has promised.

By now there were 125 Hrey orphans at the Crescent Beach-Son Ha Orphanage, and the doctor tried to teach them the Bible lessons all together in one big class from the few Hrey books they had.

Then he struck on a better plan. He chose twelve older children to be "captains.' Each captain chose his "lieutenant" and together they chose eight "soldiers" to be on their team. Dr. Harverson said, "That solved all the problems of attendance and attention in meetings."

Each morning at sunrise the twelve little groups meet on the beach to sing and study the Bible. They have already studied most of the New Testament books and a book telling about Old Testament characters. After prayer and singing they take turns reading the verses, then each one memorizes a verse. The "captains" give a short message followed by another hymn and prayer. Even the six-year-olds can take their turn at participating in the meetings.

After breakfast they all attend the regular Vietnamese elementary school, and they have four Vietnamese Christian teachers. The older children study English and various musical instruments.

One day a U.S. Marine major walking on the beach half a mile away was startled to hear a trumpet playing "What a Friend We Have in Jesus." His heart was touched. The hymn of his childhood, played by a little tribal child on a secluded beach, stayed with him all that day and ministered to him.

As often as they could get a helicopter flight to Son Ha, the doctor, Barrie, and a group of orphans with their band instruments went. The tribespeople were startled by the boys' music of the hymns. They'd never heard such sounds in their lives! All they know are the tribal gongs and tom-toms to call on the demons. The boys had a good ministry in the villages.

As the missionaries and orphans walked through the hamlets, three of the boys stayed at one of the longhouses. They sat down on the veranda, played their instruments, and had a little meeting while the others in the party walked on to the next village.

The father in this longhouse had already bought a chicken to sacrifice to the demons because his little child was ill. The three orphans blew their trumpets, read the Scriptures in the Hrey language, and preached. The passage they chose was the healing of the woman bent double for eighteen years. The man of the house had asked the missionary party for medicine for his backache. Now he had received a forceful sermon on sin.

Before the missionary party left that village that day, a pocketknife was produced and the sacrifice strings, which the heathen use in making pacts with the devil, were cut off every wrist of the people in this longhouse. The bamboo demon altar was uprooted, thrown in a ditch, and burned. The father had prayed and his whole family was rejoicing in the Lord.

In the cool evenings and early mornings, pilots flying the northern approach to Da Nang Air Base looked down to a clear blue bay, and sitting on the pale beige sand by the water's edge, were the little groups of the 120 children of the orphanage, reading their Hrey Bible portions. This spoke to the GIs' hearts.

Gordon and I now had the desire to build a beachhouse for ourselves over on this beautiful Crescent Beach where we could go by the *Hope II* each week for two or three days to relax and recharge our batteries. We have no home of our own anywhere in the world. Our son Stanley and his wife, Ginny, and family would soon be taking over the directorship of the mission here, and they would be living in the Da Nang headquarters home where we had lived for seventeen years. We would be living in the mission house they had occupied on this property, and we would still be carrying on plenty of missionary work from there, but we also wanted a private home of our own. We would like to live out our lives among our people here in Vietnam if health and circumstances permit, and we want to keep busy in missionary work to the end of our days. We dearly love Vietnam and we've spent forty-three years of our lives here.

When we are out at Crescent Beach with the sea and mountains, our whole physical well-being seems to be refreshed; and we feel healthy and at ease in this enchanting outdoor life. We enjoy swimming in the clear, blue green water and hiking over the valley, as well as the fellowship with the leprosy patients and with Dr. and Mrs. Harverson and the Hrey orphans.

So in 1970 we began to build a home on Crescent Beach. An abundance of rocks for the foundation were taken from an ancient fort a few feet from our beach site. The U.S. Navy provided reenforcing steel bars for the concrete and dunnage lumber for the doors and windows. The sand was brought from a nearby creek and before we knew it, our split-level home on the beach was ready to live in!

A giant helicopter brought over several loads of nice second-hand house and office furniture from Philco-Ford engineers. They were leaving Vietnam and kindly gave these supplies for the leprosarium, orphanage, and our home.

We planted forty-five coconut palms around our beach house, and flowers are growing amazingly well in the sand, enriched with fertilizer. Up the sides of the house and the front and back verandas we have trained bougainvillea, brilliant and luxuriant in this tropical land in shades of purple, red, orange, and white, and lots of the velvety yellow-flowered alamanda vine. We have an abundance of hibiscus shrubs and rows of fragrant pink and white frangipani trees.

One of the outstanding bounties of our Crescent Beach is the abundance of fresh water. We dammed up a mountain stream and brought the water through three-inch pipes down to every part of the leprosarium, the orphanage, and finally to our beach house. It runs night and day with more than enough good water for everybody.

Of course, we must have pets at Crescent Beach, for Gordon and I love animals! We don't at all mind that tigers roam our valley. Two were shot just recently by the Vietnamese soldiers quite near our house. Most of the deer are being killed by ARVN soldiers, but the place is overrun by wild pigs that come rooting around our house in the middle of the night, after our vegetable garden and banana plants. Wild pigs are good game and the meat is delicious.

We enjoy the high-pitched crowing of the gaudy wild roosters as they challenge each other in the valley at the crack of dawn. At 5:30 a variety of lovely, singing birds welcome the new day in a rhapsody of joy!

Our Crescent Beach house soon became an extremely popular recreation center. We hardly ever had it to ourselves. The hour's trip across the bay on *Hope II* was half the attraction when the weather was fine.

Picnics, camp-outs, swimming parties, boat rides, and water skiing brought all kinds of people to us. Missionaries from various groups, American and Vietnamese officials and their families, high school students, and our orphans by the dozen, would ask to spend the day on our magnificent sandy beach.

We enjoyed entertaining doctors and nurses from the German hospital in Da Nang and groups of nurses from the city hospital and the Hoa Khanh Children's Hospital. So many of these people were giving us such priceless medical assistance in our work that we felt it only right to show our appreciation. In fact our greatest pleasure was watching so many of our friends thoroughly enjoying themselves.

We made a large cement table on the front veranda, and on Saturdays and holidays it was seldom without a crowd of happy holiday-makers eating their picnic lunches in the shade.

One day our ten-year-old grandson Kenny came striding in with an air of propriety. "This house," he said, "belongs to me."

"Only if you become a fourth-generation missionary someday," his grandma answered.

24

A Saga of Faith

A HANDSOME YOUNG Vietnamese couple, friendly, bright, and bubbling with enthusiasm, came to our Bible school in 1958. Cang, twenty-three years old, and his wife, Duyen (pronounced Zweeang), nineteen years old studied one year with us. Then they were appointed to a place called Bong Mieu, about twenty miles east of Tam Ky. They were to begin pioneer work among the Cua tribespeople and among the backcountry Vietnamese in the settlement there. It was a dangerous place even before the war broke out in force, with the Vietcong hiding in this area, the unhealthy climate, and hosts of malaria mosquitoes. Many Vietnamese died in this interior place next to the mountains.

Cang and Duyen's families were against their going to Bong Mieu. Even Cang himself didn't want to go. He held out against it for ten days. But Duyen said, "We must obey God. He wants us to open up this hard place. He is sending us and 'our God is able' " (see Dan 3:17).

Then, at last, Cang too felt it was God's clear order to go. The Book of Jonah, with this servant of God fleeing from his responsibility to Nineveh, spoke to Cang's heart. It took courage and faith, but they went out in unity of purpose.

The Bong Mieu settlement is surrounded by mountains, and a river runs through it. As Gordon drove the young couple to this place, they felt very lonely, inexperienced, and helpless. They were used to living near the big towns in nice homes. They shivered at the thought of the Vietcong enemy back in the mountains. They had no home here, and they wondered, "How shall we begin?"

They went to a more prosperous-looking widow woman, Ba

Mr. and Mrs. Dang Ngoc Cang and his wife, Duyen, with their children, showed great faith in the midst of great danger.

Bon, in the village and asked her if they could rent rooms in her home. But Mrs. Bon said, "No! You are working for the Americans, and I'd be afraid the Communists would come and burn down my house if I had you living here with me!"

Cang and his wife sat on their baggage outside the widow's home, praying, "O God, open a way for us!"

Then a Buddhist man came to them and asked, "Why are you sitting there outside? Come to my house and stay with my family." Cang and Duyen hurriedly gathered up their few belongings and went with him.

After getting settled in, Cang and his wife went out to witness for the Lord in the village. Cang went one way and Duyen another. That day, Cang prayed with three men and his wife prayed with two women. The first woman to believe and then become a leading Christian in the village was Ba Bon, the

195

widow who had refused to let the Cangs stay in her home! Today, fifteen years later, Mrs. Bon is one of our valuable housemothers in the China Beach Orphanage.

In one month's time after Mr. and Mrs. Cang had moved into Bong Mieu, the Lord had used them to win fifteen souls. Also they were able to buy a small house for about $40.00 (U.S.). It was only big enough for one bed and a small table. The lean-to kitchen's roof leaked so badly that Duyen had to wear a big cone-shaped, palm leaf Vietnamese hat while preparing meals when it rained.

The little settlement of Bong Mieu was full of Buddhists and other people who "had no religion." But Cang and his wife showed a lovely, cheery spirit to the people. It was truly a winsome Christianity, friendly, kind, and helpful, and the whole village became attracted to them and to the Gospel they preached.

The joint committee in Da Nang now could give them money to buy a good piece of land. Then Cang and his wife, along with the fifteen new Christians in Bong Mieu, all worked together to put up a church building on the land.

In five months' time it was completed, as was a small parsonage built of bamboo and thatch. By now they had 300 Christians, both Vietnamese and Cua tribesmen.

In the following year, they went witnessing in another villaage called An Trung, four miles away from Bong Mieu. The people there were eager to hear the Gospel, and one hundred people quickly believed on Christ.

In May, 1959, with Mr. and Mrs. Cang leading, the Christians were able to build a new church and house for a pastor there. They also built an elementary school, with three small rooms for children from eight to twelve years. Another pastor and his wife, Mr. and Mrs. Hap, who had been working among the Cua tribespeople at Tra Bong, came and ministered in this new church and school.

Cang and his wife lived at Bong Mieu for three years. Four hundred persons came to the Lord in that time. The young couple learned the great lesson that if they had refused to obey God's call to go to this backcountry village, if they had been too afraid to be exposed to the dangers of this hard place, then this wonderful harvest of souls would have been lost! They testified that they had learned that we must obey the Lord and go wherever He sends us.

In 1962 the Cangs returned to Da Nang for another year of Bible school. By now they had two little sons, Minh and Son, one three years and the other ten months old.

After a year of Bible school, in which Mrs. Cang was the best student of the year, they were appointed to go to Son Nam, another backcountry Vietnamese village fifteen miles west of Quang Ngai. They built up a small church there at Son Nam and opened another church at Tu My, four miles from Son Nam.

The people in these places were strongly Buddhist and they tried to trap the Cangs by asking them tricky questions in public. If they couldn't give bright, clear answers, they would "lose face" and be mocked by the villagers. But the Cangs trusted the Lord to help them answer the questions well and to give a good confession. The Lord brought them through the tests, blessed the meetings, and soon they had a new church in Son Nam with 150 Christians. The roof was of red tile, and they also built a parsonage.

Another preacher and his wife, Mr. and Mrs. Tue, came to care for the church at Tu My. Later, Tue was captured by the Vietcong in his ministry at our leprosarium, was taken up into the mountains and shot by the Communists.

The Cangs lived in Son Nam for three years. By June, 1964, it was no longer safe there. The whole area was crawling with Vietcong, who were determined to conquer all this backcountry section behind Quang Ngai. Battles raged night and day. The Cangs felt that they would have to leave the Son Nam Church or the Communists would capture and kill them. But they stayed on in great danger for four more months.

At last the Communists moved right into the Son Nam village. They were lenient with the Christians for the first month. During the second month they began to forbid the Christians to go to church. They persecuted Cang and his wife, jeering at God and our Saviour, Jesus Christ.

One night, five Vietcong knocked on the Cangs' door. Mrs. Cang told Cang to let her open the door, for if they saw her husband there they'd probably capture him. The Vietcong kept shouting, "Open the door! Open the door! Light a lamp quickly or we will throw a grenade into your house!"

Mrs. Cang was trembling, but she opened the door. She invited the Communists to come in and sit down. They were rough and ugly with her and told her that they wanted a drum. Mrs. Cang explained calmly, "Oh, this is a Protestant church, not a Buddhist pagoda. We do not use a drum in our church."

They shouted angrily at Mrs. Cang. Cang couldn't bear to stay hidden any longer. He came out and met the Communists, asking, "Don't you know that this is a Protestant church?"

They thundered back, "Of course we know. But we need a drum!"

Cang and his wife opened the door of the church and let them go in and look. They searched all around but could find no drum. They stalked angrily away. The Cangs were shaken up as they saw that the Communists were now in an ugly mood.

The next day, Sunday, the Cangs talked it over with the Christians, and they all prayed. The Cangs, pitying the Christians, courageously decided to stay on in Son Nam for a little longer. By the following month the Communists organized special meetings of their own every Sunday and forced everyone to attend. No one could go to church. They fenced off all the paths leading to the church! They also required Mr. and Mrs. Cang to work for them.

The Cangs were very troubled. Now there was no freedom of religion in the village. Cang built a bunker, as now the village was being attacked by the American and South Vietnam fighter planes, and the Cangs had to spend every night in the bunker. Mrs. Cang gave birth to another baby at this time of chaos in the village. The missionaries and joint committee in Da Nang told Cang that he and his family should leave Son Nam now. But it was very hard to leave the poor church flock.

Some of the Christians moved the Cangs' beds and few pieces of old furniture away by bicycle to the village of Ba Gia, a distance of four miles, near a military post of the South Vietnamese. The Cangs had been there for a week living in a little shack when a flood came. Many huts, including the Cang's, were adrift. They didn't know the people well yet at Ba Gia, but all were kind to them, helping them. No one stole any of their things. Other houses had many things stolen during the storms.

After the flood came famine. The Cangs had brought only enough rice for two weeks with them. Now they couldn't buy any. It was still raining and flooding. Some families had rice, but they wouldn't sell any.

The Cangs' little children kept asking their parents, "What shall we eat today?"

Cang answered, "Don't worry. Trust in God. He will give us food."

Cang walked from house to house all morning until noon, trying to buy a little rice. Then he met a kind woman who was able to give him four little tins of rice grain. Cang was very happy and when he started to pay for it, the woman said, "No! You don't remember me, but four months ago I went to your house in Son Nam and asked for medicine for my son. That medicine was good and it healed my son. You gave it to me free of charge. It was much more expensive than this rice."

This was enough rice for their family for two meals. They kept praying and trusting God, and the next day the rains stopped and the floods receded. Some Christians from Son Nam came to visit the Cangs and brought them a supply of rice. They knew the Cangs would be in great need. The passage of Matthew 6:25-34 was made real to the Cangs: the God who cares for the sparrows and lilies will surely care for His children too.

The Cangs lived in Ba Gia for five months. They went back to Son Nam every Sunday morning to visit with the Christians and try to preach the Word to them. Every time Cang went, he met North Vietnam soldiers who asked him many questions. Cang always said that his only knowledge was the Bible: "If you want to ask me about the Bible, I will explain it to you." The soldiers laughed at him and let him go.

Then the fighting came to Ba Gia. It was May, 1965. Guns

boomed night and day near the South Vietnam camp and near the Cang's hut. Many people were wounded. The Cangs had to live down in their bunker as much as possible, day and night. But both Mr. and Mrs. Cang helped the wounded, bandaging them, and giving them injections, working every day from morning to night, and risking their lives. One time Cang was so busy with the wounded that he went without eating for three days.

Death was all around them. Some children, the ages of their own little boys and girl, were wounded, with their legs broken. Whole families were killed. Cang knew that if they stayed there much longer, they'd be wounded or killed. So they decided to leave for the coastal city of Quang Ngai on their bicycle. Cang rode his wife and three children on the old bicycle, all at one time, the whole dangerous way from Ba Gia to Quang Ngai, twelve miles away. Many unburied bodies were lying along the side of the road! Many South Vietnam trucks were afire, their horns still blaring.

Three miles out of Ba Gia they came to the battlefront. The South Vietnam soldiers would not let them pass. "Go back! Go back!" they cried. "It is very dangerous!"

But Cang pleaded fervently with them to let their family through. He said, "We believe that God will protect us. We have God's Word, the 23rd Psalm!"

Finally the soldiers said, "You must ride very fast then," and they let the family pass. Cang bicycled swiftly over the twelve miles, with his wife and the children, and they were miraculously delivered by Almighty God!

In Quang Ngai, Cang went to the district chief. He explained their situation and asked him for help. The chief gave the Cangs three rooms in a refugee camp, enough place for his family and some Christians there. Soon Cang's little daughter came down with bad dysentery and was near death. They prayed and trusted, and God brought them through.

They were in the refugee camp for three weeks when Cang thought he'd return to Ba Gia to get some of their cooking utensils and furniture. He took with him a supply of medicines for those suffering at Ba Gia.

There were many difficulties on the twelve-mile trip. After riding about one mile out of Quang Ngai, he met some North Vietnamese soldiers. They asked, "Where are you going?"

Cang answered, "To Ba Gia to help the people there."

"How do you help them?"

Cang showed them the medicine kit he was taking and said, "There is no medicine in Ba Gia because the people can't get to Quang Ngai to obtain it."

The North Vietnamese agreed to let Cang through! This was another miracle. God was with Cang.

He arrived at Ba Gia and stayed there for three days, giving medicine to the people, and trying to find a way to get his cooking utensils, dishes, beds, and a table through to Quang Ngai. He prayed continually and asked God to open up a way. Then he went to Son Nam where they had lived before. He met the Christians there, and they wept because they were so happy to see him. They wanted him to stay with them, but Cang said he did not dare keep his family there any longer with war raging more and more fiercely all around.

He told the Christians that he had come to rent a boat so that he could use the rivers to get his household goods to Quang Ngai. Cang assured them, "We'll never forget you all."

Many wanted to leave with Cang as refugees, but the North Vietnamese would not allow them to go. They held them now as prisoners in their own village. A number of these managed to escape, however, to Quang Ngai, and there soon was a new Son Nam refugee settlement there. It is still there today, with a pastor and a little church.

Soon after Cang's visit, the new church and parsonage that the Cangs had built at Son Nam were destroyed by the war. The head deacon of the church and all his family were killed, except for one son, Khanh. In chapter 7 I told how twelve-year-old Khanh escaped, carrying a wounded pal on his back, to Quang Ngai, and then went on to the China Beach Orphanage to Da Nang where he is now in senior high school.

Cang rented a boat and went into Ba Gia, and the Christians there helped him carry his furniture and household goods to the ferry landing. Cang paid the people with the precious, relief-bringing American medicines from Quang Ngai. Then he started on his way back.

On the river he passed many Vietcong control stations. They shouted angrily at him and tried to take his poor furniture. Cang had a sewing machine given him by U.S. CARE to make clothing for the Christians and to teach young people how to sew. Some North Vietnamese women came to Cang's boat and checked everything. They said, "This sewing machine could be used for our Liberation Front people and they could use this furniture too!"

But the North Vietnam commander said, "No! You can't take these things from this man! That would be stealing!"

The North Vietnamese were going to keep Cang overnight, and Cang was very much afraid and prayed fervently that God would deliver him.

After fifteen minutes or so, a Christian man came running to Cang and hugged him, crying, "I was working in the field when I heard some people say, 'The Liberation Party has arrested a pastor.'" When he found out it was Cang, he had come running. He asked the Vietcong guards, "Please allow this man to come to my house. I will be responsible for him." It was a miracle that they allowed Cang to go!

In the farmer's bunker that night, Cang saw a Bible. The farmer said that he read it daily. Cang and he prayed together. It was impossible to sleep, for the guns were booming very near all night. About 1 A.M. two Vietcong came and said Pastor Cang could go since he wasn't involved in politics. They even gave him a travel permit to go through enemy territory to Quang Ngai by boat! God is indeed able to work miracles! And Cang was standing on the 23rd Psalm.

He got to Quang Ngai safely, sewing machine and all! His wife got a truck to carry all their furniture and belongings from the riverboat to their rooms in the refugee camp. How she and the children praised God for answering prayers for Cang! Radiantly happy, she made a simple feast in honor of Cang's return and called in all the Christians nearby for the celebration and testimony to the faithfulness of God.

The following week the Ba Gia military camp was captured and held by the Vietcong. Many houses were burned, including the shack the Cangs had occupied. Truly God had helped Cang to get their goods out in time!

The Cangs lived in Quang Ngai for five months. That fall they returned to Da Nang for their third year of Bible school. At the close of the year's study in 1966, they were appointed to the China Beach Orphanage. Cang was the supervisor, and his wife was one of the teachers in the school. She also taught sewing to a large class.

After one year at the orphanage, they were sent by the committee to Tam Ky, a city fifty miles south of Da Nang. The road from Da Nang to Tam Ky was stricken by the war. Trucks were wrecked on it by Vietcong mines, and many people were killed weekly. All the villages along the road were brutally attacked by the Vietcong, and houses, schools, and hospitals were burned.

When Cang arrived in Tam Ky, he found many refugee Christians there from the villages of Bong Mieu and An Trung. They had a joyous reunion! Cang was able to rent a poor bamboo house in the crowded city for his family. They lived in this shabby hut for seven months. They gathered for church services on Sundays with 200 of the refugee Christians.

Some American captains met the Cangs in their poor shack and saw their group of Christians. They were touched by the rugged sacrificial work of this cheery young couple among their own people. One of the Cangs' favorite verses was 2 Timothy 2:3, "Endure hardness, as a good soldier of Jesus Christ."

Mrs. Cang began to learn English with an American welfare group under Colonel Brierton. Being bright, she learned quickly and well. In three months' time she could speak English clearly enough to be understood by the Americans.

In 1968 Cang drew a plan for a church building in Tam Ky. He showed it to his wife, and she said, "Are you dreaming? We have no money and no land in Tam Ky!"

But Cang replied, "God is able! We need a nice church that will draw townspeople." He had faith that God "would bring it to pass." Cang prayed hard for some land. The government gave him some worthless lowland, old rice fields that would be flooded in the rainy season. To get any land in the refugee-crowded city of Tam Ky was humanly impossible, so Cang thankfully accepted this good-sized piece of lowland!

He felt God leading him to go to the Americans at USAID to ask if they could help him with the buildings. They had no program for building churches, but they could help Cang build a school. They asked Cang where he was planning to build. Cang showed them. They exclaimed, "This land is too low! It will be flooded in the rainy season. How will you fill it in? Also, it is dangerous to be so near to the American military compound. The Communists could come in and shoot at our American camp from here."

But Cang, looking steadfastly to God, went to the American chaplains at the big American base of Chu Lai, twenty miles south. They also came and saw the land and said the same thing: "The land is too low; you couldn't use it!" They told him they'd be happy to help with his church building if he could find better land. But this seemed to be the only land to be had for Cang in this crowded city.

Then Cang felt led to ask a Vietnamese major of the 104th Engineers of the South Vietnamese Army. The major was interested because Cang and his wife had a genius for making friends, they were so cheerful and courteous. The major said, "I came here a stranger to Tam Ky, but you visited me and have been so kind to me. I'll give you a detachment of ten trucks to be used in carrying soil for your land!" In one week the major's trucks had filled in all the land! Truly God had "brought it to pass," beyond their highest dreams!

American Colonel Brierton was very surprised and pleased when he visited the site with Cang and saw all the land filled in! He immediately gave metal sheeting and cement with which to build a school. It wasn't long before a school for 300 pupils was completed with good toilet facilities. There was also a classroom for teaching sewing. American Aid, CARE, gave them ten new sewing machines and they had pupils "graduating" every six months and going out to be tailors in the town.

This sewing program is still in full swing today, six years later.

The Chu Lai chaplains promised help soon for the new church.

Two American sergeants came and saw that the Cangs were living in a poor, shabby, thatched bamboo hut, with their growing family of charmingly polite and handsome little children. The sergeants told the Cangs that they themselves wanted to help build a modest cement house for the Cangs. They worked hard at it, and like a dream, the house was completed before the sergeants returned home to America!

Then the church was started. American engineers from Chu Lai base gave them cement, steel reinforcing bars, and sheeting. They paid the Vietnamese workmen who were building the church with donations from the chaplains' funds given by the GIs. In six months the church was built and benches were made for it.

The Cangs also opened another church at this time, three miles from Tam Ky, called Phu Tien. Soon 200 of the poor refugees in this area believed on Christ, and the Cangs got a school built with five classes for the needy children. Schoolteachers were hired, and another Vietnamese pastor and his wife, Mr. and Mrs. Son, went to minister in this new center.

In 1969 the Cangs decided to also open an orphanage at the Tam Ky center. Neighbors were bringing children whose parents had been killed in the war and asking the Cangs to help them. The U.S. Navy chaplain sent some food for the children, and some sponsors gave $5.00 U.S. a month. But this wasn't enough as the prices were rising high now in the war. Again the Cangs cried, " 'God is able!' He can work miracles and help us build an orphanage for all these helpless children." They knew their God and His power and faithfulness. Jesus would not turn sick and hungry little orphans from His door.

Cang drew up a plan for an orphanage and showed it to his church committee. They laughed and scoffed, saying, "We have no money. We couldn't build that!"

But Cang asked them, "Brothers, where is your faith?" Cang was the boss. He led the group and they all waited on the Lord.

One month later, the province chief of Tam Ky sent word

that he was planning to give out building materials for orphanages. This was the first time that a province chief in Vietnam had ever had such a program! So Cang sent in his request. The following week the government heads of the town requested Cang to come to a meeting. They asked him, "How much material do you need for an orphanage?" They gave Cang 600 bags of cement and 250 sheets of roofing iron. That was more than Cang had ever dreamed of!

Now they had the materials, but they needed money to pay workmen to start building. Cang was certain that God would supply.

In October, 1969, four German men came to Tam Ky and to the Cangs' home for a meal. They had just been to Da Nang and asked Stanley Smith, "Where is a very hard place for us to do social and medical work for the Lord here in Vietnam?"

Stanley answered, "Go to Tam Ky and help the Cangs there in their big projects of school, church, and orphanage." So they went to the Cangs immediately.

These four young men are a part of a group of German Protestant Christians who call themselves "Christ-Bearer Community." The men in this organization are called "Brothers" and the women are "Sisters."

One of these four Brothers who came to Tam Ky is a young Englishman, Michael Rogers, who speaks German fluently. He is the leader of the Brothers in Vietnam and their business manager. Another Brother is a medical doctor, Reinhard Beaupain. The third is a laboratory technician, Julius Scheidemandel, and the fourth, Gottfried Michel cares for their household.

Their program in Tam Ky is social work, helping refugees and the patients in the government hospital. They were thrilled to see the Cangs' big work opening up and that they could have a share in it. The Cangs helped the Brothers find a Vietnamese house to rent, right next door to their place. The Germans inquired about the new orphanage that they heard Cang was going to build, and they asked, "Do you want us to help with it? We have an Orphanage Assistance Program."

This was great victory of faith answered! The Cangs and

the church people had asked God and He, by His foreknowledge and provision had sent these Brothers all the way from Germany to help in their work at Tam Ky! The Cangs were indeed uplifted and encouraged, and they walked on air, praising the Lord!

The U.S. Navy chaplain at Chu Lai had been helping with supplies for the Tam Ky Orphanage. Now the Cangs had Michael Rogers write a letter to the chaplain to let him know that the German churches who help the "Christ-Bearer Community" were going to assist with the Tam Ky Orphanage.

Cang took the letter to the navy chaplain. He read it and rejoiced, exclaiming, "This is truly wonderful! I was very worried about your orphanage because in two months' time the Navy is going home to America. I did not know who would sponsor your poor children in the orphanage. I prayed much and asked God to please open the way for you. Now God has heard my prayers! Praise the Lord!"

Cang showed the orphanage building plan to Brother Michael and asked him to pray and request assistance in Germany for the building of this structure. They already had some materials from the Vietnam government and from the U.S. Navy. They needed money now to pay the contractor and workmen.

One month later, Michael let the Cangs and church committee know that the churches in Germany who support the Brotherhood had agreed to help build the orphanage. How the Cangs and the committee rejoiced and thanked the Lord! A big, two-story orphanage building was soon erected, and over fifty little children were brought in.

In 1971 the Cangs and the German Brothers were able to extend their work further. They built a boarding school and orphanage for some orphans and underprivileged children of the Cua tribe from Tra Bong District, about thirty miles into the mountains from Tam Ky. Again the churches in Germany, supporting the Christ-Bearer Community, undertook to sponsor this important program.

Very few people in the world have ever cared for the poor Cua tribespeople. Only four of us missionaries in United World Mission have ever visited them and had time to do anything for them. Two young ladies of Wycliffe Translators, Eva Burton and Jackie Maier, have been putting the Cua language into writing. Now here were these four German Brothers and the Christ-Bearer Community in Germany, building this Cua orphanage and school! This is also building goodwill among these tribespeople for the Western world. The Cua are a forgotten primitive people with 8,000 or more of them captured by the Communists and taken back far into the mountain jungles. Only about 3,000 Cua are left today in Tra Bong. Now the school in Tam Ky for the free Cua children makes good feeling between the yellow-skinned Vietnamese and these brown-skinned mountain people. This is very important. All the old ill-will between these races must be broken down.

So the Germans with the Cangs are doing a thrilling piece of work by bringing these neglected Cua children and Vietnamese children together in Tam Ky, all under the light of the Gospel. The Brothers are there as full-time workers, the doctors giving tremendous relief in the government hospital and caring for the health of the orphans and Cua children. They give malaria medicine, treatment for dysentery, infected sores, and preventive injections for many diseases. Michael oversees, very ably, a scientific raising of pigs, hens, chickens, and ducks, and sells eggs to help the orphanage.

In 1972 the Cangs enlarged their school, making another two-story building, and this school teaches a high school course now. There are 950 children from poor, underprivileged families who come to this school, including, of course, the orphans. In 1973 they enlarged the church. The building is packed every Sunday in church worship services, Sunday school, and young people's meetings.

So this is what God has wrought through Cang and Duyen. We are wondering if God may still have more amazing things for this couple to do for Him. A Bible-taught national couple like this is the key to the evangelization of their own people. We need many more bright young people like the Cangs who have faith that "God is able."

25

The Spring Offensive, 1972

On April 3, 1972, hundreds of North Vietnam tanks rolled across the 17th Parallel! It was the big invasion, the serious communist spring offensive. North Vietnam launched massive assaults on South Vietnam, first there at the Demilitarized Zone, aimed at taking Quang Tri; then at Kontum and other tribal centers in the central highlands, near the Laotian border, aimed at cutting South Vietnam in half from Kontum and Pleiku across to Qui Nhon on the coast; and at An Loc in the south on the Cambodian border, thirty miles from Saigon, aiming to take the capital city, Saigon, and the southern Mekong Delta. The offensive and battles lasted from April 3 on into August.

The North Vietnam troops and armored vehicles pushed into South Vietnam's northernmost province. Troops, tanks, and artillery were sent across the Demilitarized Zone. This was armed aggression against the Republic of South Vietnam, and the whole world was seeing it all vividly on the television screen! Suddenly the tanks were rolling down the road, right into the American living rooms!

The U.S. State Department branded the thrust across the DMZ, as an invasion of South Vietnam, and a flagrant violation of the 1968 "understandings" between United States and North Vietnam, that had led to the halt of the U.S. bombing of North Vietnam for four years.

The United States had already taken 500,000 of her troops home. Only 60,000 were left in Vietnam. Now it was up to the South Vietnam Army to defend the country with their ground forces. The United States would stand by with her strong air force and the Seventh Fleet.

But this was a *Blitzkrieg!* A communist armored drive! It

was a sudden shift from guerrilla to conventional warfare. The North Vietnamese broke through all the main South Vietnam defenses along the border. Streams of tanks hit the bases with a deep rumbling sound. This was a new weapon for the Communists to unleash in Vietnam. They were modern Soviet tanks with big guns. At first the South Vietnamese soldiers fled before the green steel monsters as they ground forward toward Quang Tri! All of the towns and bases on the ten-mile-wide border fell into the Communists' hands, and they still have them today, over one year later. These are Khe Sanh, the C.&M.A. center for the Bru tribe; Cam Phu, where our mission began work among the Bru in 1957; Cam Lo, where we had a nice brick church with over one hundred Christians since 1965; Dong Ha, a town of several thousand. All were now lost!

The city of Quang Tri with 40,000 inhabitants was badly threatened. Over 20,000 civilian refugees in one day jammed the main Highway No. 1, leading south, thirty miles to Hue. People "voting with their feet" went south fleeing Communism. The refugee numbers from Khe Sanh, Cam Phu, Cam Lo, Dong Ha, and Quang Tri would climb up to 100,000! Fifteen thousand refugees had already reached Hue.

There was a deliberate, terrible massacre of refugees by the North Vietnamese Army! As the northern troops saw the people fleeing from Quang Tri on Highway No. 1, they opened fire on them with their mortars and automatic rifles, killing 2,000 helpless civilian refugees. The poor people were moving on bicycles and motorbikes, many were trudging on foot, some were in carts loaded with their goods and pulled by old men and boys, and some were in busses.

But the busses were overturned, and huge columns of people were mowed down by the North Vietnamese machine guns. The dying were screaming and begging for water! North Vietnamese soldiers stripped the corpses, taking watches, money, clothes, and rice.

"Shoot anyone moving south!" was the North Vietnam order.

Many South Vietnamese soldiers were fleeing with the civilians! They were running before the streams of big Russian tanks. One South Vietnamese general battled with his own troops, hitting them with his steel helmet as they were fleeing from the advancing North Vietnamese.

Then the Americans came in with heavy air strikes and naval gunfire from destroyers offshore, bringing powerful destruction to the North Vietnamese. Ten thousand South Vietnamese troops were rushed from Saigon north to Quang Tri, and hundreds of truckloads of supplies streamed up Highway No. 1 from the south.

This wasn't guerrilla fighting. The enemy wasn't illusive now. They were out in the open, like swarms of ants coming out of their anthills. The U.S. B-52 bombers launched big sweeping operations on the Reds. The Seventh Fleet assembled four aircraft carriers and four destroyers off the coast of Quang Tri. These backed up 20,000 South Vietnamese military who had regrouped and reinforced to slow down the invasion.

After the first shock, the ARVN showed high morale in resisting the aggression. Strong South Vietnamese generals took charge, and the ARVN soldiers proved themselves in many impressive military achievements.

One day in the sand dunes south of Quang Tri city, sad mass burials were held for the Highway No. 1 victims. Some of the relatives were able to come and mourn.

Finally the invasion was broken! The Communists had taken Quang Tri city, but the South Vietnamese got it back again, even though the whole place is just rubble today. Quang Tri may remain just as it is today, as a lasting memorial to communist aggression. When the city is rebuilt, it may go up on another site.

The North Vietnam losses of men and material were catastrophic. This invasion had been a serious blunder for them. They had made a gross underestimate of the defensive fighting ability of the South Vietnamese troops. Hanoi lost 21,000 of its 44,000 troops sent to Quang Tri.

The Americans blockaded, by mining, the ports of North Vietnam, especially Haiphong Harbor, which stopped the heavy flow of Russian arms and also the Chinese supplies to the North Vietnamese forces. They also bombed North Vietnam, destroying their military installations, transportation networks, electric power, petroleum, iron, steel, and cement.

Finally the North Vietnamese were ready to begin negotiating in Paris. The Communists saw that their "war of national liberation" had not succeeded in South Vietnam because the South Vietnamese refused their so-called "liberation" which they knew meant slavery.

Through all this big offensive, our mission work was far from unscathed!

Gordon and I had just arrived back in Vietnam at the end of May, 1972, from a one-year speaking tour in America. We had had our health built up, and near the end of our furlough I had an operation for gallstones and my gallbladder was removed at the Santa Monica Hospital in California.

A month after my operation, Gordon and I flew from Los Angeles to return to Vietnam. On the way, we stopped in England for a ten-day visit with our relatives, the Vernon Hedderlys, and other friends.

Then we had a few delightful days in Germany with the Christ-Bearer Community whose four Brothers were working with the Cangs in Tam Ky.

We also visited the United World Mission headquarters in Madrid, Spain. Next we flew to Tangiers, Morocco, for two enjoyable weeks at Rabat with our son, Douglas, in the U.S.I.S. section of the American Embassy there, and his family.

We then hurried back to South Vietnam, as we knew the country was going through the throes of the Communist spring offensive and the refugee problem was big in Da Nang.

The desperate battles were raging for Quang Tri, Kontum, and An Loc, but we knew "the battle was the Lord's" and He would win! Omnipotence can answer any prayer, and we missionaries in Vietnam are working for God's Kingdom here. His Word says His "kingdom . . . cannot be shaken!" (Heb 12:28), and "Have faith in God!" (Mk 11:22). Many thousands of hearts in America, England, and Europe were trusting God for the day of deliverance for Vietnam.

Stanley and Ginny, Simone Haywood, Diana Reed, Dr. and Mrs. Harverson, and a former GI, Bob Martin, who would be with us in the bookkeeping work of the mission for two years, had seen the pouring in of 250,000 refugees to the Da Nang area with hunger, disease, families separated, loved ones lost. Two of our Kontum national pastors, Mr. Tho, a Vietnamese, with his wife and eight children, and Mr. Trien, a Katu tribesman, were taken captive by the North Vietnamese in the Kontum District.

The national preachers from all over our big mission field of 400 miles in length, came in to give firsthand reports on their churches during these heartrending times.

Khanh, eighteen years old, a bright student preacher from our Bible school, had been stationed with the Bru tribe up at Cam Phu near the 17th Parallel. The Communists sent in rockets and mortar shells on April 1, and Khanh and the Bru Christians all got into their underground bunkers. There were over 300 deep dugouts, with a network of tunnels, in this big resettlement area. Khanh was with seven Christian tribespeople in their bunker. They had to stay underground for two days and one night. One household was hit in another dugout, and the father was killed and two children were wounded.

Then Khanh felt that he must lead his people out to safety. They would refuse to be captured by the Communists and be forced to knuckle down under atheism. They would rather be refugees, leaving their land and homes, not knowing where they would be living in the future.

He and many Bru Christians, along with 2,000 other Bru tribespeople, left the Cam Phu area and walked the twenty miles to Quang Tri. They passed our Vietnamese church at Cam Lo on the way and saw many people dead on the road from the rockets and mortar shells.

Quang Tri was still safe, and Khanh and the Bru Christians stayed there a few days. They received some government rice and they had brought along salt, red peppers, and a few dried fish.

Then Khanh took all the Bru Christians to Hue by bus.

They got there before the worst of the refugee flight and the horrors, missing the awful slaughter on Highway No. 1.

At Hue, Khanh helped the Christians get some more rice from the government supply and after that, Vietnamese pilots flew the entire crowd of Bru tribespeople to Banmethuot, 300 miles south of Da Nang, where they are still stationed in refugee camps.

Then Khanh came to our mission compound in Da Nang and soon joined the army.

Preacher Pham told us about their experiences at the town of Cam Lo, three miles from Cam Phu. On March 30, the Communists sent in rockets all around Cam Lo. This was the warning that the North Vietnam soldiers had infiltrated by the thousands across the border in their big offensive.

On April 1 at 6 A.M., the frightened people began to flee from Cam Lo to the next town east, Dong Ha, ten miles away. They streamed steadily down the road by motorbikes, bicycle, and on foot.

At 8 A.M. that same day the communist soldiers flooded the ten-mile-wide DMZ area. They were all around our Cam Lo

Tens of thousands of refugees from Quang Tri province
crowded into former US bases at Da Nang.

214

church. Pham and his wife and their five little children were all inside the church, but God protected them from the enemy.

At 1:30 P.M. Pham took his wife and three younger children on his motorbike down to Dong Ha. They had to leave the two older boys, eight and ten years old, in their underground bunker beside the parsonage, next to the church.

Five minutes after Pham and his family left, a communist mortar shell hit the preacher's house, blowing it to bits! Pham's two sons down in the bunker were frightened almost to death. They ran out of the dugout and fled down the road toward Dong Ha after their parents. It is a miracle of God that they were not hurt!

Pham was afraid to stop at Dong Ha, so he took his wife and three small children on to the Christian and Mission Alliance church in Quang Tri, seven miles south from Dong Ha. As he came back from the seventeen-mile trip on his motorbike, he met his two young sons on the road! They had run three miles on the way to meet him, and were panting and trembling with fear. Pham took them back with him to Quang Tri, where the whole family was united in the preacher's house there.

The next day Pham returned to Cam Lo. There his house had been blown up and everything they had owned was gone. There had been many rockets all around the house, and the church had had some shells, but, miraculously, it was still standing.

Pham now took sick Christians and little children on his motorbike to Quang Tri. He made many trips on that day of April 2. The older Christians and well ones walked down the road the seventeen miles to the city. This was Easter Sunday, so when all the Christians got to Quang Tri, Pham had an Easter service for them that night, in the midst of war!

The following day Pham rescued many children from Dong Ha by his motorbike, taking them the seven miles to Quang Tri. The parents followed by walking. The Christians all stayed in the schoolhouse next to the church.

Many were being killed all around Dong Ha by the communist rockets. This was the hometown of little Vinh, the baby heart patient whom I had brought back with Cong from San

Francisco. But she was safe with all her family, for they had escaped to Da Nang.

But there was no trace of two other heart patients, Quit, a fourteen-year-old girl, and Anh, a seven-year-old boy, whom Gordon had taken to Minneapolis in the fall of 1969. They had had successful open-heart surgery there. Now they were lost! No word has been heard of them or their families for over a year. Quit's home was near the No. 1 Highway at the entrance to Quang Tri city. Anh's home was farther in from the main road. Pastor Pham had visited them from time to time in the past three years, and Quit had been to see us several times at Da Nang.

Pham and a Christian friend, with their two motorbikes, took Pham's wife and five children the thirty miles south to Hue. From there, another friend took them on to safety to Da Nang, sixty miles farther south. Pham himself returned to Quang Tri to care for the Cam Lo and Dong Ha Christians still there.

By this time, the Communists had taken control of all the DMZ at the 17th Parallel right through to Don Ha. They were very near Quang Tri. Pham took more of the Christians the thirty miles to Hue on his motorbike, and the rest, nearly one hundred, followed by bicycle or on foot. They just missed the dreadful massacre of the refugees by the Communists a few days later! Khanh and Pham had gotten all the Christians out just in time.

Pham's people were now getting very hungry. Many had had nothing to eat for three or four days. Pham, too, had had no food. No one would sell food. Everyone was running in terror. It was cold, rainy weather at that time up at Quang Tri and Hue, and the children were shaking with the cold because they had no sweaters or coats. Pham wept sorely for the suffering of his people and the thousands of others.

When the Cam Lo Christians got to Hue, they used their money to rent cars to get to Da Nang. It cost them a lot of money, but they were fleeing for their lives.

Arriving at Da Nang, they were given some bread and then some rice. The Vietnamese government had the Cam Lo and Quang Tri people all placed in large refugee camps, at the

American military camps. Most of the GIs had left for home. So Pham's groups of Christians and some Christian families of Bru, not sent to Banmethuot, were all at camps on the outskirts of Da Nang.

There was no more military neatness in these huge refugee camps. It was a vast, huddling mass of many thousands of dejected people, with many little shacks, lean-tos, and military tents added to the former American hooches. The refugees received some food and clothing from the government.

While Gordon and I were in England, the "Save the Children's Fund" and "TEAR", The Evangelical Association Relief, gave us sums of money for our mission to use for the refugees. So with some of the money we were able to help these two groups of Cam Lo and Bru Christians to build temporary school shacks, hire teachers, supply them with workbooks, pencils, soap, medicine, blankets, food, and many other things.

Pham held meetings for these two groups of Christian refugees every Sunday and on Wednesday and Thursday nights. We missionaries visited these congregations with him from time to time, and some more of the Cam Lo and Cam Phu refugees have believed on Christ during this year.

The North Vietnam Communists today are still holding all the DMZ border towns they captured in their 1972 spring offensive, even though cease-fire papers have been signed. So the Khe Sanh, Cam Phu, Cam Lo, and Dong Ha people cannot return home.

26

Tragedy at Dak Pek and Kontum

A-YEN, twenty years old, from the China Beach Orphanage and Da Nang Bible School, is a Jeh tribal worker up at Mang Blak. This is one of the fifteen resettlement villages for the Jeh tribal people in the Dak Pek area of the Kontum District near the Laotian border. Over the last five years this Mang Blak village became totally Christian. There were 1,467 people in the settlement, and they were all faithful to the Lord, meeting in their bamboo and grass church every Sunday and one night each week.

About five years ago the Mang Blak people had to go underground because of the communist mortars, grenades, and sniping. The people lived like rabbits, each family's "burrow" partitioned off with logs and sandbags. They couldn't come above ground long enough to make gardens or rice plots, or to fish in the streams, as the Vietcong guerrilla snipers would be hiding nearby, ready to shoot at them. Many had been killed in this way already.

In May, 1972, 1,500 North Vietnam soldiers came into this Mang Blak village and immediately captured 800 of the Christians and took them over the mountains into Laos, to be slaves or to be forced into fighting against the South Vietnamese. A-Yen's mother and six sisters were among those captured by the enemy. In 1965, seven years before, A-Yen's father, Mr. Ngo, who was an evangelist to the Jeh, was captured by the Communists and later killed.

These Christian tribal people, carried away by the Communists, will have a terrible setback. They can't yet read the Gospel of Mark translated into Jeh, and they will have no

218

teacher to lead them in the things of God. What will happen to these captured thousands?

The Viet Cong and North Vietnamese also killed many of the Jeh Christians in the village for no reason at all. They were exceedingly cruel and inhuman! A-Yen saw the soldiers cut off women's ears, and cut men and women into four pieces each! The atrocities of the Communists here among these poor helpless Jeh tribespeople were unbelievably fiendish. Even when little babies cried in distress and fear, they were slashed to death by the enemies' knives. I find it impossible to write more of the awful horrors that took place! But these Jeh people had to go through it!

Yet there are people in the United States and Canada who are blind as to what Communism is! These people look forward with *complacency* to a communist victory in Vietnam! We should hate and fear Communism as we hated and feared Hitler's Naziism.

The Communists threw bombs and grenades into the bunkers and completely destroyed the underground villages of Mang Blak and its bamboo church above ground.

About 600 Christians from Mang Blak were able to escape, running half a mile through secret tunnels to another underground village in the Dak Pek settlement. A-Yen was among these who got away.

A-Ron, another of the young Jeh student preachers from the China Beach Orphanage and Da Nang Bible School, was the tribal worker at this other village in the Dak Pek settlement. There were 2,000 or more Christians in this underground village. A-Yen and A-Ron saw 10,000 communist soldiers come into this Dak Pek center and wantonly kill 150 people. The rest of the villagers hid in secret underground tunnels, shaking in anguish and crying out to God.

For one week they dared not go up out of the burrows, so they had almost nothing to eat, only some leaves and very little water. They had to keep what water they had for drinking, so the people became very dirty, their skins scaly and dirt-caked. Their rude tunnels were dark mazes, crowded, bad-smelling, and filthy. It was horrible!

Of course sickness followed this starvation and filth. Stomachs were swollen from undernourishment. The people developed bad, choking coughs, rashes, and running sores. How terribly they needed soap and medicines! The half-naked mothers were painfully thin and couldn't feed their babies. Many infants died.

The communist rockets and mortar shells, 150 a day, came in all the time. One hit a woman underground, who was sitting near A-Yen. The rocket took off her head! Blood gushed all over A-Yen. The man sitting to A-Yen's right was badly wounded, but he did not die. Others in the bunker were seriously hurt. A-Yen, miraculously, wasn't wounded, but the shattering, appalling experience made him very sick for three days.

American planes tried to bring food and medicine to the people, but the rockets kept going off like thunder and the dust from their blasts was blinding! The planes couldn't see to land on the narrow little airstrip in the short valley surrounded by towering hills. So the planes would have to fly off without landing! The people received no food and no help!

What did they eat during those weeks of the spring offensive? Sometimes they'd be able to get the coarse stalks of banana plants, which are used for feeding pigs. The little children couldn't digest this coarse fibre, and their stomachs swelled up hard and many became very ill. The Jeh people also got a type of bamboo root, but this also made their stomachs swell. They ate larvae of beetles dug from the earth, any bees or wasps they could find, grasshoppers, rats, mice, spiders, or bats, any sort of creature that had flesh! Some ate the leaves of the tapioca plant, and some ate the *earth* of their underground bunkers! Men gnawed on pieces of *wood!* Many children and babies died.

How the people longed for some rice; just one handful of rice a day would keep them alive! Of course they yearned for a little fish or meat too.

None of the Christians gave up the Lord in these hard, bitter months of communist invasion. They just longed to hear A-Yen and A-Ron teach them more of Christ. They met in bunkers, surrounded by sandbags. Sometimes the communist bullets hit the walls as the people were meeting.

Soon A-Ron was taken by the government to be a soldier, and he learned to be a paratrooper and was serving up at the Quang Tri area. So A-Yen is left alone at Dak Pek with 3,000 or more Christians. He weeps because he feels so inexperienced and helpless.

To win the heathen to Christ takes the mighty turning power of God. God must be at work to cause the people not to be afraid to stop worshiping the demons. We have seen this great miraculous turning of the Jeh to God. It is startling and magnificent! Now these thousands of newborn believers in Christ must be built up in the Word. We need many strong national evangelists to teach them. But in this time of war, when most of the young men are taken to be soldiers, we only have A-Yen and two or three good Vietnamese preachers who go over from Kontum to visit the Dak Pek Christians from time to time.

How we miss Mr. Trien, the Katu tribal evangelist who was at Dak Pek working among the Jeh for years! He is the father-in-law of A-Ron. But the North Vietnam Communists captured him in May, 1972, and he is still in their hands today.

Mr. Tho and his wife and eight children from this district were also captured, and one year later we heard that Pastor Tho was killed by the Communists six days before the cease-fire on January 28, 1973. A Catholic priest who was just released told us that he, himself, buried Pastor Tho. These were all good faithful workers, much used of the Lord in this fruitful area.

When the offensive was checked, planes got through with food for the desperate people. With money from "Save the Children Fund" and "The TEAR Fund" from England, our workers were able to take in bags of rice, dried fish, *nuoc mam*, and other foods to nourish the people again, also some big cakes of yellow soap and helpful medicines. The Jeh were able to be above ground in the daytime to make their rice patches and vegetable gardens again. They could fish in the streams and start raising chickens and pigs once more.

They missed the hundreds of their Jeh tribespeople killed

Jeh tribe at Dak Pek fortified village were forced to live underground to escape enemy shelling.

and captured by the Communists. But A-Yen was ministering to over 3,000 believers at Dak Pek, besides there being thousands of Jeh Christian refugees over at Kontum and in other areas. His battered church was packed each Sunday and at the week-night meeting. Just recently more new Christians were baptized. A-Yen would humbly appreciate our earnest, prevailing prayers for him and his people.

When we think of how, ten short years ago, this great Jeh tribe was unreached with the Gospel, how wonderful it is that today, in spite of all the anguish caused by the communist attacks, practically all of the tribe have eternal hope in Christ.

This Jeh tribe was the tribe on the lowest rung of the human ladder in Vietnam, a people primitive, dirty, living in low, filthy, smoky longhouses, down on the ground, with no written language, uncivilized! Today there are 7,000 Christians among the Jeh people, practically all won to the Lord by the national evangelists, Thuong, Tuu, Trien, An, Chu, A-Yen, and A-Ron. The war brought this tribe, hard of access because of their living in high mountains and deep valleys, into the big refugee

222

centers of Dak Pek, Dak Sut, and Dak To in the Kontum District.

Pastor An, our preacher in Kontum, told us something of the nightmare experiences they had been having there. The workers and Christians in Kontum were surrounded by the Communists. The enemy was coming in from all sides, Dak Pek, Dak To, Ben Het, Tan Canh, Pleiku. The roads were cut off in every direction. In April the communist armies were just six miles from Kontum.

Every day the Communists launched fifty rockets or more on the city, destroying many planes and people. The first plane to be rocketed and go down had thirty people in it. All were killed. Then two big Air Vietnam planes were shelled and all the passengers in them lost their lives. After that, eight American planes were shot down and six Americans died in these, along with many Vietnamese.

Pastor An and his family didn't know where to go with the roads all cut off and the planes not able to get into the airport without being rocketed. It was a time of anguish and fear in Kontum in April, 1972. Still people waited at the airport for a chance to get on a plane between rockets because this was the only way out of Kontum. As they waited for a chance plane, many were killed by the rockets hitting the airport, so they made underground bunkers right there at the airport and waited in them for a plane to come.

Pastor and Mrs. An had started an orphanage of forty Jeh children on the church premises of Kontum. Mr. An gathered the orphans and many of the Kontum Christians into his parsonage and church. This section of the town seemed to be mercifully free of the rockets. Just once, a big shell burst about 300 yards from the church. Mr. and Mrs. An and all the Christians spent the time praying night and day, crying, "Help us! O God, help us!"

An was anxious to get his wife and children out of the town, as now the Communists were coming in nearer every day. They warned that when they entered the town, there would be street-to-street and house-to-house fighting. An went to the airport and pleaded with one American adviser there. Finally the adviser said, "Bring your wife and children and stay here in an underground bunker, and maybe a plane will be able to land." So An went with his family. Rockets came bursting in, some only thirty yards away. A plane came sweeping in, but a rocket nearly got it! It zoomed up swiftly and flew away!

The brown clouds of dust from the rockets were so blinding that the people couldn't see each other. An was afraid his six children would be wounded or killed. Two are charming four-year-old twin girls.

Finally, on April 28, one rescue plane landed in the dust of the rockets. It could only wait a few seconds and it could take thirty people on board. An's wife and six little children scrambled frantically to get onto the plane. Then it roared up and was away in the sky.

"Where is it going?" An asked the American adviser. The adviser was too excited and upset to know. Rockets were whooshing in, bursting all around. The people there could be hit any second!

Someone cried out, "The plane is going to An Loc!" That was a place to the south, near the Cambodian border, where the war was raging even more fiercely than at Kontum! Actually this plane was one being used in the rescue work of civilians at An Loc, but it had been called to come to Kontum to rescue some from this heavily besieged place too.

An went back to his house alone, full of distress and anguish. Would he ever see his wife and children again? Now he was desperate to get the forty Jeh tribal orphans out of the besieged city to safety. He sought out a young American working in the Vietnam Christian Service, Bill Rose, who spoke Vietnamese. The two men went to the American advisers, but the answer was, "All the American planes are in action, and there is no plane to get the orphans out!"

Two nights later the head American adviser in the plane service was able to let 300 Catholic orphans leave by a night plane when there weren't so many rockets. An heard the plane leaving in the night. He cried, "Oh, they must take our Protestant children too!" He went to the American heads and pleaded some more, "Please take our forty Jeh orphans and two older

Jeh women to care for them!" The Americans kindly said they would do their best, but An had to wait two more days.

By now the Communists were only two miles out of Kontum. The city was practically encircled. B-52 bombers were striking near Kontum, trying to smash the North Vietnam siege. North Vietnam tanks were swooping down on the city, but soon seven of these tanks were destroyed by the resistance of the South Vietnam troops and American air help.

An was sure that he and all the Christians and the forty Jeh orphans would be killed. He decided that he would try to go by helicopter to Pleiku, about thirty miles from Kontum, to meet one of the head Vietnamese generals there and ask him for a plane for the Jeh orphans. Mr. An met Gale Fleming, a C. & M.A. missionary from Pleiku, and Mr. Fleming promised An that if he could get the Jeh children to Pleiku, he would find some food to feed them all. Also, the Vietnamese general promised to get a plane to take the children on from Pleiku to Da Nang.

An returned to Kontum the next morning by helicopter and found that all the Jeh orphans had already left by plane for Da Nang! Bill Rose had taken them that night by plane, leaving Kontum at midnight. The plane got them to Da Nang at around 1:30 A.M., and the Vietnamese policemen at the airport helped Mr. Rose get the forty children and their two Jeh housemothers by truck over to our China Beach Orphanage. They were there safe and sound for one year. Now they are all back in Kontum again in their own new orphanage for 150 children which is being built at present.

An then went off to look for his wife and children. He returned to Pleiku by helicopter and then flew down to Nha Trang on the coast. There he found them, well and safe.

While An was away from Kontum, the battles raged bitterly for the city. Kontum, they said, was "like a constant explosion" from bombs, rockets, mortars, and artillery of both sides. The South Vietnam troops, with the help of American helicopters and their new anti-tank missiles, held the lines at Kontum. The 1,500 Communists were unable to capture the city. It was a proud testimony to the determination of the South Vietnam people. There was bitter house-to-house fighting, and 500 North Vietnamese dug in inside a school and some nearby houses. Some Communists climbed a water tower and sprayed bullets from there, but a U.S. helicopter knocked the tower out and killed the communist four-man machine-gun crew.

It was a massive communist offensive against Kontum and the city was almost destroyed. A total of 8,000 inhabitants of Kontum were killed in the struggle with the Communists. Some of the head American advisers perished in the battles.

Almost all of the lives of our Kontum Christians were spared. Somehow, by miracles, they were able to escape by plane or helicopter to Pleiku, Banmethuot, Nha Trang, or Saigon.

When Pastor An returned to Kontum, he found that everything had been stolen from his house, the church, school, and orphanage! That included his radio (very precious to them in this time of war), his old secondhand refrigerator, his motorbike, every stick of furniture, the church pews, the small pump organ, the orphans' beds, and the ten sewing machines the Americans had given the orphans so they could learn how to sew. Nothing was left! All of the mission buildings were damaged by about 30 percent, but they would be fixed up again.

The Christians and An's family returned to Kontum after four months. They worked hard to get the buildings repaired and their stolen things replaced. Mr. An and Mr. Tuu are ministering to several thousand Jeh tribal refugees and soldiers with their families in and around Kontum.

God is especially blessing in the building of a new Kontum orphanage for at least 150 children on a piece of land recently donated to the mission. It will be a tribal center as well, with accommodations for tribespeople passing through. It is hoped that there will be at least two foreign missionaries, including a nurse, to help in this important work.

27

Attack on Happy Haven Leprosarium

AROUND 1 A.M. on October 6, 1972, five Communists blew up part of the Happy Haven Leprosarium on Crescent Beach. They used satchel charges. One woman patient was killed and nineteen others were wounded. It was a vicious, wanton, terror attack. Why the Communists should single out these poor, defenseless, sick people with leprosy is beyond comprehension.

Gordon and I, together with Dr. Harverson, a chaplain, and other friends, had left Da Nang at 8:15 that morning on the *Hope II.* Gordon and I expected to spend the night in our beach house at Crescent Beach, for there were workmen to be overseen there.

As we drew near the shore an hour later, we saw Sally Harverson down on the beach to meet us, looking greatly worried. She called out, "Have you heard the news?"

We jumped out of the small boats taking us into shore from the *Hope II* crying, "What news?"

She exclaimed, "The Communists came here just after midnight last night and blew up many of the leprosarium buildings, killing one woman patient, and wounding nineteen others! Five of the wounded men are nearly dead, lying on stretchers now, over on the sand!"

As we stood speechless with shock, Sally added, "Just ten minutes ago, another bomb blew up one of the little schoolrooms, with a huge billowing of black smoke! No one was hurt there!"

This last was a delayed-action bomb, maliciously timed to go off when the twenty to thirty children were in school! But there was no school because of the attack in the night. The teachers and children were so upset and fearful with all that had happened that none of them were at classes. The bomb made a big crater, and the blackboard, desks, and benches were broken and scattered in pieces everywhere!

Gordon immediately ran into our beach house and got the little radio used by downed flyers in the jungle, which had been given to him by a departing American officer two months previously. It was only to be used in dire emergency. He ran out to the front of our house and called over the little radio:

"Calling Da Nang airport tower! This is Rev. Smith at the leprosarium, across Da Nang Bay. The leper colony has been attacked by the Communists. We have many wounded, needing evacuation. Please send a helicopter!"

Gordon repeated the message three times.

Then a voice responded clearly:

"Rev. Smith at the leprosarium. We read you. We are on guard. We have told the proper authorities. We are coming in to land. Tell us exactly where the leprosarium is."

Gordon replied, "We are straight across Da Nang Bay from

Schoolhouse for children of leprosy patients was blown up by time bomb set to go off while children were in class.

the city, at the foot of the Pass of the Clouds, on the road to Hue."

The visiting chaplain and Gordon began walking over toward the leprosarium, about a ten-minute walk along the beach, talking to the chopper which appeared overhead almost at once. It circled and then hovered down on a grassy spot in the center of the leprosarium village even before the two men reached it.

By the time Gordon and Chaplain Dean puffed up, a colonel of U.S. Army Intelligence, a sergeant, and two U.S.O. women had piled out of the helicopter with their belongings, and the men were loading some of the wounded on stretchers.

"We were on our way to Hue when we got your message," the colonel said.

Four stretchers of the worst cases, two of them had broken legs, were whisked up and off immediately to the American 95th Hospital at Da Nang Airport. Mr. Toi, Vietnamese head of the leprosarium, went with the wounded.

The Happy Haven was a pitiful sight! Gordon and I wept over the cruel attack. On the grass, the wounded were lying on a few stretchers or bloody mattresses with blankets covering them. Most of them were poor patients already badly mutilated with their leprosy, but now all of this suffering and misery was added!

In fifteen minutes the chopper churned in again and took two more stretcher cases and some walking cases, including the wives of two of our male nurses who were in Saigon at the time, taking special courses in leprosy. The young women were wounded in their legs and feet. Gordon accompanied this helicopter load to the Da Nang hospital.

He told us later that an ambulance rushed the wounded from the helicopter to the receiving ward at the airport hospital. A staff of U.S. doctors and nurses took in the poor people with leprosy, kindly cleansing and binding up their wounds.

One badly wounded man sorrowfully said to Gordon, "I'm going to die for sure."

But Gordon assured him, "No! No! you will be all right." And he was.

Some of the Vietnamese helpers and nurses were afraid of the people with leprosy, but the American colonel in charge of the 95th Hospital said they would do all they could to help. "Are there any precautions we should take?" he asked Gordon.

Gordon replied, "Just wash your hands with plenty of soap afterward."

The colonel said, "We shall not be able to keep the leprosy patients here for long, so I am asking the German hospital in Da Nang to take them."

Shortly afterward, an ambulance took several of the bad stretcher patients through the town to the German Malteser Hospital.

Gordon asked for a chopper to take him back to the leprosarium. They gave him a U.S. Army ambulance helicopter, and he took back the two women patients with him. They had been treated and bandaged and could hobble along by themselves. They were whisked back in ten minutes, and then they loaded the last of the waiting stretcher cases. They flew straight to the German hospital in town, landing on the helicopter pad on the roof.

Early that morning, one of the noncontagious leprosy patients had rowed around the headland of our beach to the main highway at Nam-O and took a bus into town to tell us the tragic news, but he had arrived fifteen minutes after we had left by boat.

He told our office, and our Vietnamese secretary, Mrs. Thanh Hoa, tried to find Simone Haywood, our nurse in charge of our leprosy program. She drove all over town, but Simone was at different hospitals where she had sick orphans so she didn't hear the news about the leprosarium attack until noon.

What had happened? Who did this terrible thing?

On the evening of October 5 two strange men in black pajamas were seen at the leprosarium beach with flashlights, hiding in and out of the bushes. The dogs at the colony barked frantically, running up and down the sand. The men disappeared in a sampan. They must have been assessing the leprosarium site.

At 1:30 A.M. an explosion ripped the small generator house on the orphanage side of the river, which separates the children from the leprosarium. Sally Harverson, who was there alone since the doctor was in town that night, was awakened but thought it was a warship firing into the hills, as they often do. But the 120 Hrey orphans in the Crescent Beach Orphanage where Sally lives, were all up and about and calling for Sally to go into the dining hall which was made of cement. There Sally and the orphans heard the series of seven more explosions at the leprosarium.

The Communists, after bombing the generator, raced across the river to the leprosarium to the six cement duplex houses, two of which had been built by the Swedish Red Cross and four by the Vietnamese Red Cross, costing $1,200 U.S. each. The Communists placed satchel charges in front of the houses. One charge didn't go off, but the other five damaged the houses beyond repair. One was only a pile of rubble. Patients were wounded, some so critically that they had to stay in the German hospital in Da Nang for five months and more.

Our Mercedes-Benz Unimog truck, a gift from the German Leprosy Relief in Germany, was standing at the back door of one of the duplex cement houses, between the back wall and the little outside kitchen. It wasn't harmed at all! The back door of the house was blown out against the car. We were so thankful that the useful truck was spared! The house next to the Unimog was blown down flat. Everything—the walls, roof, beds, tables, and all the furniture—was one tangled mass of rubble! The five men in this ruins were terribly wounded. Two had both their legs broken. One man was a patient who had had an eye blinded with leprosy, sagging out of its socket down onto his cheek. He had recently been operated on by a German eye doctor of the Malteser Hospital and had been fitted with a glass eye. He had been so pleased with how it had improved his looks. Now his life was in danger with his wounds and broken legs in the German hospital! But we wondered how anyone got out *alive* when we saw the terrible ruins and ground-up rubble of the house!

231

All the little flower gardens in front of each of the houses were blown up, and the leaves were blown off any trees that were left.

The men in the men's hospital ward, built with gifts from the staff of the German hospital ship *Helgoland,* had heard the six bombs erupting all down the line from the generator house. They knew their hospital would be next! Fortunately the Americans had just given the ward a number of high, iron hospital beds, so the men patients all got down and huddled underneath their beds.

The seventh bomb blew out the whole end of the men's hospital! It killed a woman of thirty years who had tuberculosis as well as leprosy, so she was in this section of the men's ward kept for the tubercular patients. She was too ill and crippled with leprosy to get out of her bed and under it, so her whole stomach was blown out! She lay covered up on her twisted bed with just her poor fingerless hand, covered with blood, sticking out from under the covers. She had been responding well to the treatment for tuberculosis, and the German doctors, who visit the leprosarium and help treat the patients, were interested in her case. Now she was gone! But she is in heaven where suffering and death are no more.

If the men patients hadn't been able to get under their beds, a number of them would probably also have been killed.

Then the communist terrorists sped on and threw a bomb into the treatment center that had been built in honor of Mimi de Fosse and Nellie Haebourg, the two Dutch nurses who had helped at the leprosarium for two years. The bomb blew out the back walls of the building, shattered cases of medicine, wrecked beds where the patients were examined and treated, and destroyed chairs and benches. Glass from bottles and mirrors was all over the floors. And since wounded patients had been brought in there in the night, for bandaging by candle-light, bloody rags were mixed up in the rubble.

The ninth bomb was the time bomb which had cruelly and inhumanly been set to kill the little well schoolchildren at 9:15 A.M.!

We stayed with the poor dazed patients until the last of the

232

wounded had left. Neither the women's ward nor any of the scores of little wooden huts full of patients had been hit. Mainly the new cement buildings had been attacked.

Six ARVN soldiers were at the leprosarium. They were young, small men, but experienced and courageous. They had heard the explosions during the night from their forts high up on the mountainsides above our beach, and they had hurried down at daylight over the wild growth, shrubs, and stones to investigate.

They found two grenades lying out on the orphanage section of the beach, near the bombed generator house. They picked these up and carried them away.

Another group of ARVNs from a fort up on a higher mountain above the main highway also came down and spent some time looking around. Then we loaded them all into our smaller launch and took them back around the headland to Nam-O, about four miles away, where they could reach the highway. The hikes up the mountainsides to their forts are exceedingly strenuous through coarse, tall grass, rocks, shrubs, and creepers.

Our boat party from Da Nang all walked back to our beach house for lunch.

Soon another chopper landed at the leprosarium. Gordon took a small boat back there and found that USAID information officers and two American army officers had come to make a report on the attack. Gordon showed them around, and they were appalled at the wantonness of the assault. They took photos of the damage.

Then another chopper came down at the orphanage, landing near our house. It was the American consul, Mr. Fred Brown, and U.S. Army Chief of Staff, Colonel Harrold. They had heard about our radio call for help and the attack on the leprosarium. They all assured us of their sympathetic assistance and said they would immediately provide us with a special radio, with several frequencies, to be kept with Dr. Harverson at the orphanage for use in emergencies.

At 3:30 P.M. our visitors, Gordon, and I left on the *Hope II* for Da Nang, taking Sally Harverson with us. Dr. Harverson stayed on.

233

By 5 P.M. Gordon was showering and thinking of a rest when the American vice-consul came and asked if Gordon would go back by helicopter to the leprosarium with six newsmen. Their chopper was waiting at a pad three blocks away from our house. Gordon hurriedly dressed and in ten minutes they churned in on the beach.

The news reporters represented *The Stars and Stripes,* Reuters, Agence France Presse, Associated Press, and two other agencies. There was still light so they took a lot of photos and made their notes. They interviewed Sally Harverson in Da Nang on their return. These pictures and stories were in newspapers and on television across America, England, and Australia.

That evening, Dr. Zerzavy, Public Health officer of USAID, and the German director of the Malteser Hospital in town came to our house to tell us that they could get tents for the patients to live in temporarily and more medicines and food for them. We would take these over by *Hope II* the next day.

So ended Friday, October 6, a day of infamy, another in the endless list of terror attacks perpetrated by the Communists in their all-out effort to subdue the people of South Vietnam. The poor leprosy patients had nothing to do with politics or Communists. It had been four years since they had been moved to their New Happy Haven at Crescent Beach, their third move in fifteen years, owing to the Communists. They thought they were safe at last.

Through the news media and the appeal put out through our letters to the United World Mission in Florida, many people sent funds to our mission headquarters in St. Petersburg, Florida, for the rebuilding of the leprosarium.

A new generator house and garage for the Unimog were constructed first. The duplex houses for eight people each have now been rebuilt, slightly larger than before. The new clinic dispensary, a kitchen, toilets, and baths are finished. Next is to be a four-room school building.

Some of the leprosy patients themselves asked to do the building, for there are good masons and carpenters among them. They will build it more slowly, but carefully, and they are giving one-tenth of the cost of their labor to the Lord as their tithe.

Most of the people at the leprosarium think that the terrorists were Communists who came over by a fishing boat from the village of Nam-O, ten miles from Da Nang. A big cache of hundreds of tons of rice and canned fish was found at this time deep underground near Nam-O. The communist armies wanted to come over the mountains to attack Da Nang, and the troops would live on hoarded stores of food like this.

The strangers who were seen scouting around the property in the dusk were probably leaders in this communist group. We asked for Vietnamese patrol boats to guard the shore of our bay and keep strange fishing boats from landing.

We kept asking why they attacked the leprosarium. They didn't touch our beach house or any of the orphanage buildings. Sally was the only white person out there that night and she was badly shaken for awhile. But she is also full of good Scotch courage and grit and was soon perfectly strong again.

Then the Communists came back a few nights later in another attempted raid. A fishing boat with five Vietnamese in it, armed with pistols and grenades, drew up near the orphanage at 9 P.M. Dr. Harverson had all the biggest Hrey orphan boys "armed" with big sticks, stones, and baseball bats given them by American soldiers. The boys stood on the beach and ordered the Vietnamese off! But what could sticks and stones do against their guns and grenades!

However, the five armed Vietnamese in their motor sampan went on up the shore to the leprosarium beach. Thirty patients were gathered there, also armed with sticks and clubs. The patients cried, "We dare you to land here!"

The communist fishermen called the leprosy patients names, cursing their parents, calling them "Lepers" and nothing but "driftwood, fit only for firewood that should be burned up." Then they went off in their motor sampan and stayed out in the bay, not far from the shore, for over an hour. The patients and older orphans kept strict vigil on them.

The intruders finally started their motor and chugged away

to the mouth of the bay by the rocky promontory, 800 feet high, running out into the sea at the end of the leprosarium. Some of the leprosy patients followed over the stones and rocks and kept watch on the fishermen there. About twenty other fishermen came in coracles (little round basket boats, like tubs, that have motors in them), and they seemed to be looking for an opportunity to land unobserved.

But lights from the many fishing boats out in the big bay showed up the coracles. Combined patients and tribal orphan guards in watches patrolled the entire beach all night.

Dr. Harverson also sent in a report to the American military heads in Da Nang. He entitled the report: "Previous Events before the Raid on the Leprosarium on Oct. 6th and the Attempted Raid on Oct. 10th."

> There were visits by the Nam-O fishing fleet, commencing several months ago. Often as many as 12 sampans, with their let-down scoop nets out in front (shrimp boats) came chugging round and round Crescent Bay all night, close in to shore and often stopping.
>
> In the evening these boatmen offered fish to the orphan children and tried to make friends. They told the children to steal orphanage supplies of cement and plywood and sell them to the Nam-O fishermen. The children replied that they were afraid of their head teacher, Mr. Hiep, and of Dr. Harverson.
>
> The fishermen scoffed, "Why are you afraid of Americans? They won't be here much longer in Viet-Nam. As soon as they leave, we will kill the Doctor and the head Vietnamese teacher. Then who will feed you? We'll take you all and teach you to be Communists. We'll burn up the lepers."
>
> These boatmen frequently threw grenades into the water near the shore to kill the fish. From where did they get all the grenades?

Gordon and I, when we were out at the beach, would see these fishermen throw five or six grenades every night. We felt badly that they were killing all the fish when the people with leprosy and the orphans were in great need of them for food.

The doctor wrote further:

236

As long as the railway line from Da Nang to Hue and Quang Tri was open it had good ARVN patrols. As the railway runs along the mountainside just above our beach, the Nam-O fishermen were held in check. Frequently ARVN patrols came through the Orphanage and Leprosarium and sometimes fired at the boats to restrain them. At any rate, the Nam-O folk were not encouraged to land when there might be ARVN patrols on the shore.

After the Communists blew up the railway bridge and lines early in 1972 and there were no more trains, the ARVNs hadn't been patrolling the shores anymore, and so the communist fishermen became bold and launched the first attack and then attempted another.

Dr. Harverson had his radio set up to call the military, and Gordon has three good battery pocket radios that can call in armed helicopters any time night or day. Dr. Harverson and the leprosy patients were given a lot of flares.

Since the attack, we've had Vietnamese Navy patrol boats guarding our beach nightly, and the ARVN troops are along our beach day and night. The railway has been built up again now, and trains are running from Da Nang to Hue and are well guarded by the ARVN.

28

The Cease-Fire

IT IS JANUARY 28, 1973.

All of a sudden the guns are silent! It is eerie and uncertain. The nightly booming of artillery ceased. The roaring of jets dwindled to almost nothing and the small-arms fire around Da Nang gave way to an uneasy peace. The cease-fire is here!

By now the U.S. Armed Forces had all gone from Vietnam. (We saw the Japanese and the French leave years ago.) We surely miss the many American officers and men who through the past ten years have been good friends to our work and staunch supporters. Now their great sprawling camps and bases are filled with tens of thousands of refugees, and the huge Da Nang air base seems almost deserted.

We are now in a quiet period of "wait and see." There are still some gun blasts in a few scattered areas. The barbed wire is being hauled away from the many streets and intersections in Da Nang, and the city is being cleaned up to look more presentable in a time of peace. Cement sidewalks with new trees have been put in all over town.

The train is running again between Da Nang and Hue, a distance of sixty miles. Traffic is starting to move once more on the main highways from the DMZ to the Delta. The trucks are arriving in Da Nang and Hue after the 600- and 700-mile run from Saigon, this time with no fears of mines and only an occasional ambush, when goods are hijacked and the drivers captured by the Communists.

Unfortunately there are still thousands of Vietcong and North Vietnamese in South Vietnam, but we hope and pray that they will gradually "fade away." We believe the South Vietnamese can now defeat any communist uprising, and South Vietnam will take its place as a strong, independent country.

Politically, we believe that this country is more unified than ever before. There is a new spirit of confidence in the South Vietnamese leaders, but there is still a deep distrust of all that the enemy says and does. So security is strict.

The hundreds of thousands of refugees in all the main cities are longing for the day when they can return to their homes, if they have any left. The Communists still hold a lot of jungle and countryside in South Vietnam, but comparatively few people. They have no cities or towns but they have a number of market centers.

Agencies are arriving with plans to build temporary towns all over the country for the refugees who formerly lived in the marketplaces and farmlands that the Communists still hold today.

We greatly mourn our losses of lives in the war. Many of our finest young men have been killed. One was Dat from our Da Nang church, mentioned in chapter 12. He was taken by the Vietnam Army and soon became a lieutenant. Then he was killed in a communist mortar attack on his company at Qui Nhon.

One of our recent Bible school students, Khoi, a young man from our orphanage who was making a bright, promising young preacher, was killed in one of the great battles for Quang Tri city. Dung, only eighteen, another Bible school student, was killed in the battle for Que Son, thirty miles from Da Nang. The deaths of these young men were great losses to our work.

Lieutenant Lanh, son of Mr. and Mrs. Lich, who had been in the Vietnamese Air Force for several years and had learned to fly a helicopter in America, was shot down by the enemy in a Chinook helicopter, as he was taking twenty-seven soldiers to An Lao. He had severe burns and died calling on the Lord Jesus Christ as his Saviour. A military funeral service was held for him in our Da Nang chapel, with an honor guard of four Vietnamese helicopter pilots standing by his flag-draped coffin for two days and nights. At the closing of the funeral service,

Eighty students from the Christian high school at the China Beach Orphanage marched in anti-Communist demonstration in Da Nang.

New skin clinic for leprosy outpatients was built at Da Nang.

Dak To Christians again were able to worship in chapel at new resettlement camp near Pleiku.

240

there was the thudding of drums, rifles cracked three times, and taps was sounded.

Mr. Lich, Lanh's father, the Vietnamese vice president of our mission and our noble co-laborer in the work for over fifteen years, died triumphantly in Christ last spring of liver trouble; it was a big blow to us to lose him! His reward now is glorious, we know, in the Kingdom of God.

Today Mrs. Lich is one of the housemothers in the China Beach Orphanage, especially caring for the teenage girls.

Again we pay tribute to the valiant martyrs of our mission, killed by the Communists. Their stories are told in *Victory in Viet-Nam* and in this book: Hiep, Mua, the Pkoh chief; Yong, Oai, Tà Long among the Bru tribe; John Haywood, from Birmingham, England; Tho, at Dak Psi, Kontum District, and Ngo, the Jeh worker, father of A-Yen; and Tue from our leprosarium.

"Except a corn of wheat fall into the ground and die, it abideth alone" (Jn 12:24). These lives were crushed out. But because of their sacrifice, indifference and hardness are broken, and God will call others to step into the gaps they have left.

Those who escaped from the Communists after they were captured are Tri, An, Huan, Ghe, a Hrey worker from Bato and all his family, among whom is Nuoi, a fifteen-year-old girl who has been to Minneapolis for successful open-heart surgery.

We trust that Trien, our Katu preacher to the Jeh tribe, and Mrs. Tho and her family of eight young children will be released by the Communists.

Of course, our minds have long been thinking about future plans. Some are sure to say, "Don't plan ahead too much! The peace may not last!" But if we had had this attitude through the years, very little would have been accomplished. So we look ahead with faith, not fear, and see the tremendous possibilities for the extension of Christ's Kingdom here in Vietnam.

As the Christian refugees are able to return to their home areas or to some new area, we shall have to help them rebuild their churches, schools, and preachers' houses.

With more students becoming available from our China Beach Orphanage and our churches, our Bible school will be in operation to train many more needed evangelists. Our Bible school in Da Nang should be one of the most important aspects of the work. It is imperative that well-trained workers be ready to take advantage of the many open doors into untouched areas both among the Vietnamese as well as the tribes.

Work is going on now at the new leprosy skin clinic on our mission compound in Da Nang. For years we have been using two little shacks, but now we have received gifts from the German Leprosy Relief Association and are putting up a two-story treatment center with plenty of space to care for the hundreds of out-patients who come to us from this area. Over the years, this clinic has been caring for 460 patients, and now, many more new patients are coming. One wing of the clinic will house the patients who have to be hospitalized temporarily or who spend the night away from the leprosarium.

We have the responsibility now of controlling leprosy in this big area. This is a much larger outreach in our leprosy program. By proposed radio and television publicity programs, our work will be tremendously extended. This dreadful disease must be stopped! There is a *way out* from this sickness now!

We are glad to have Simone Haywood here as a long-term missionary, and we have good Vietnamese helpers. But we need a big increase in our medical staff. A mobile treatment unit can now be used as the country opens up, and with this the nurses can go through the land and find the sick ones who are hidden away and bring them in for treatment.

We now are able to prevent and cure leprosy. We have the God-sent wonderful medicine. We know how the infection is passed on. Now we must get the patients and *stop* leprosy from being handed on to the next generation!

The heartbreak is that the people won't come for treatment! Why? It is like when Moses lifted up the brazen serpent in the wilderness, and whoever looked on it could be healed and live. But some people in that day refused! They scoffed at the remedy, or they were too lazy to look! They were too apathetic to come, or they were too far away to see the serpent, and they wouldn't let anyone bring them near.

So today, people are the same! They have the remedy for

leprosy given out carefully by nurses in the clinics. But many won't come. Also there are many who still don't even know about the remedy that can heal them. We have used Dapsone for years. Now we have the new miracle drug, Lamprene, made in Switzerland. Lamprene does not cause the severe reactions which often occur when using Dapsone. The drug turns the patient a dark purplish color, but it is extremely effective in special cases. This is a tremendous breakthrough in leprosy treatment.

Our new skin clinic for leprosy in Da Nang with its staff of trained nurses, laboratory, and treatment rooms, should help many thousands of leprosy sufferers to find healing for body and soul. Vietnamese doctors will operate on feet, legs, hands, and eyes. They transplant muscles and tendons from the arms into the paralyzed hands, or from the legs into the feet. Then the hands and feet become lithe again, strong, useful, and newly made!

When our patients need wooden legs and crutches they go to the new rehabilitation center here in Da Nang, built by American Aid, where they are taught how to use their new legs.

We have a shoe workshop with a sewing machine for leather at the Happy Haven Leprosarium, where the feet with bad ulcers are measured for a special insole. Then a special shoe is made of soft leather. As the patients wear these new kind of shoes daily, they are caring for their feet and their ulcers heal.

This is an impressive work! "It is marvellous in our eyes!" (Ps 118:23). The leprosy patient can sing, "He brought me . . . out of an horrible pit. . . . He . . . put a new song in my mouth" (Ps 40:2-3).

The people with leprosy are being "made whole." This is real drama! Don't let us be like the rich man in Luke 16:19-31 who did *nothing* to help the poor sufferer. What can you friends in the homelands do to respond to the poor "Lazarus" at our gate? You can make bandages, send bed sheets, pajamas, old clothing. Our patients need vegetable seeds for their gardens and flower seeds. Gifts of money will help us feed them.

What would you give to save a precious little child? This

243

child has leprosy but can be cured with Dapsone. If we treat him now, he won't ever be crippled. The complete care of that child for one entire year is about $120 (U.S.). Then he can play ball, laugh again, and be like any other child. He can help with household chores, keep chickens, ducks, help make gardens, study in school. He will be perfectly healed after a year's treatment and take his place as a healthy "whole" citizen in Vietnam.

And some of you young people can come as nurses and doctors, eager to help control this disease.

You, at home, are called "the Rope-Holders"! We missionaries are out here to save the perishing ones. If you let the rope go that binds us to you while we breast the dangerous current to save the perishing ones, then lives out here will be lost. If you fail, we missionaries, too, fail out here. We truly depend on you, under God.

We sing, "Rescue the Perishing!" and "Hark! 'tis the Shepherd's voice I hear," calling us to "Bring them in." We are to go and find these "other sheep" with leprosy who aren't in "the clinic fold" where they can be "made *whole*." We do all "in the name of Christ." Their diseased bodies can be totally cured! Leprosy is defeated. And Jesus Christ is the hope for their sin-diseased souls!

We are building an orphanage at Kontum. In the center of the orphanage will be a church, especially for these tribal orphans and visitors. Also there will be a clinic, office, and accommodations for transient tribes. There will be a special house for two missionaries who will be helping at the orphanage, along with Vietnamese doctors.

There are hundreds of orphans still waiting to be helped. Pastor Huan has twenty orphans of the Hroy tribe at Tuy Hoa. He hopes soon to take in twenty more. The government gave him two old storage buildings which he is now reconstructing to use as an orphanage.

In 1971 a new Christian high school was started at the China Beach Orphanage. It is now in full swing. Over eighty boys and girls attend. This school is about half a mile from the orphanage. It used to be a public school, and the government gave it to us to be repaired. It was unoccupied for some time, so the roof and windows were all vandalized and stolen. The pilots of the U.S. Jolly Green Giants (rescue helicopters) gave the money for the repairs before they left Vietnam.

We are very proud of these eighty high school students, and one day they all marched in an anti-Communist demonstration in Da Nang. All of the students of the city participated in this. Our young people looked smart in their school uniforms given them through gifts of money from a church in Texas. The girls wore white silk *ao-dais* over long white silk trousers, and the boys wore navy slacks and white shirts.

They carried big anti-communist slogans and signs and held their Vietnamese flag aloft, along with the name of their school, "Heaven's Grace." It was a proud day for their head teacher, Mr. Ai. He sent a warm letter of thanks and appreciation to the "Moms and Sisters" in Weatherford, Texas.

Two new missionaries have recently arrived. Yvonne Sontag, from Minneapolis, and Marlise Buchi from Switzerland. Yvonne is a nurse, working for two or three years or more, as the Lord calls her, at the China Beach Orphanage. Marlise has come as a long-term missionary loaned to us by the Worldwide Evangelization Crusade.

Our hearts well up in praise to God for permitting us to minister in His name to the people of this stricken country during the past ten hard years of bloodshed and tyranny. Whatever the uncertainties of the coming years in Vietnam, we know we can still march on victoriously in His wonderful name, "farther and farther into the night."

29

1974

THE COMMUNISTS are not keeping the truce. Since the cease-fire was signed on January 28, 1973, thousands of South Vietnamese have been killed. Continually they are being murdered, kidnapped, or wounded by the communist terrorist teams.

Reports say that over 200,000 communist combat troops are inside South Vietnam today. They have new weapons from Russia and China that are extremely accurate, including new tanks and guns. They have built good all-weather roads like the Ho Chi Minh Trail down which they boldly bring their supplies.

For several years Gordon's heart had been giving him trouble. The arrhythmia was getting worse, and the slightest exertion left him out of breath. We arrived back in the United States in February 1974, and a month later we were settled in at the Aldersgate Retiral Center, at Kissimmee, Florida. Gordon soon had a pacemaker implanted in his chest, and this made a tremendous improvement in his health. So, although now seventy-two years of age, we are able to make speaking tours in our secondhand motorhome.

On May 16, 1974, newspaper headlines read:

> North Vietnamese forces spearheaded by nine assault tanks captured a South Vietnamese district capital deep in Communist-held territory. All of the 3000 civilian inhabitants of Dak Pek and its 570 Jeh defenders were reported killed, wounded or missing.

Our young Jeh tribal preacher, A-Yen, and his new wife were captured by the Communists, along with those who were marched away over the border into Laos. We wept sadly over the terrible news of the loss of these 3,500 Jeh Christians whom

Gordon and our president, the Reverend Gerald Boyer, had visited in 1973.

That year, Mr. Tuu, our Vietnamese preacher among the Jeh, accompanied over 2,000 of the Jeh Christians to a safer area to the south near Phu Bon in Pleiku Province. There he has built a chapel and is caring for them as they clear virgin land and start life afresh.

The Communists are not only ignoring the cease-fire completely, but they have renewed their heavy pressure against many areas of South Vietnam. Their rockets have caused death and destruction, and a number of isolated South Vietnamese outposts and district towns that have become untenable, have been lost to the Communists.

The South Vietnamese are stoutly defending their country. The doors to missionary work are wider open today than ever in those areas outside communist influence, and the challenge to young missionaries to go to Vietnam is stronger. The call for medical personnel, Bible teachers, secretarial workers, young people's workers, practical mechanics, and others with a variety of talents such as music, is clear and pressing.

So many young people are saying, "We're waiting for God to call us."

Young people, God called you to serve Him the day you were saved. We are saved to serve. What does He say about the mission field? Listen:

"Lift up your eyes, and look on the fields" (Jn 4:35). "The field is the world" (Mt 15:38). Jesus said again, "I am the light of the world" (Jn 9:5). Then He said, *"Ye* are the light of the world" (Mt 5:14). "As my Father hath sent me, even so send I *you"* (Jn 20:21). "Go *ye* into all the world, and preach the gospel to every creature" (Mk 16:15). *"Ye* shall be [my] witnesses unto . . . the uttermost part of the earth" (Ac 1:8).

God's commands are clear. This Great Commission is still very much in force. The call for help from this needy land of Vietnam is loud and very clear. May we hear the sound of the feet of many young people going to Vietnam, taking up their cross to follow our Saviour, the Lord Jesus Christ.

247

Epilogue–1975

THE WHOLE WORLD knows in stark detail the monstrous tragedy of the swift collapse of Cambodia and South Vietnam. What can we say? As we mourn over the plight of hundreds of thousands of Christians now under Communist control, we can only cry out to God to have mercy upon .them. We have no illusions about the ultimate aim of these atheistic conquerors. History tells us that the Church of Jesus Christ will be a suffering Church, a martyr Church, when under the heel of Communism.

On March 14, 1975, President Thieu made the fateful decision to abandon the Central Highlands. This meant a great retreat of the military toward the coast. With hundreds of thousands of civilians joining them down the jungle road No. 7, the retreat turned into a rout lasting ten days; and the rout turned into a slaughter. Our preachers and many Christians made it to the coast. Nai was wounded and died on his arrival at Nha Trang.

Frightened soldiers and civilians from Quang Tri and Hue in the north poured in a mass exodus down Highway No. 1 to Da Nang. As the miles-long column of vehicles and barefoot walkers reached the Pass of the Clouds on the mountain highway above our Happy Haven Leprosarium and Orphanage on Crescent Beach, the Harversons, the orphans and the leprosy patients watched in awe and increasing concern.

On March 24, with the fall of Da Nang imminent, most of our missionaries were evacuated to Saigon. By now our Da Nang compound was crowded with 600 of our 800 orphans, and many of our preachers and their families were also there. Stan and the German Brothers tried for a week to hire a 900-ton vessel to take our people south, offering to pay $8,500 for the trip. It was to anchor in Da Nang Bay. Our mission boat, the *Hope II*, would ferry the people out to it; then, also with a load, *Hope II* would follow the larger ship to a safer place. The situation deteriorated so rapidly that this plan could not be carried out.

By March 27 a total evacuation of Americans and Vietnamese who had worked for them was to take place. For two hours Stan talked with the Vietnamese leaders and our mission secretary, Thanh Hoa; and they all wept together. He turned over all the mission money to them, enough to see them through for a while. The farewells were heart-breaking.

Stan, the Harversons, and the three German Brothers from Tam Ky drove to the airport and abandoned their vehicles. With thousands of Vietnamese refugees and soldiers clamoring to board the few planes available, it was impossible for the missionaries to get near them. It was a time of utter confusion and chaos.

Finally, after sitting on their suitcases for ten hours in the boiling sun, the American consul-general was able to direct them to a special truck some distance down the road which would take them to a waiting plane at another side of the air base. The already crowded Boeing 727 took them on board and flew to Nha Trang. On Good Friday, the 28th, they arrived safely in Saigon.

Da Nang soon was in utter anarchy. There was robbing and murder and looting, especially of American places. There was a desperate mass exodus to the Da Nang River, which divides the city, and the ocean beach, as thousands crammed onto barges and every available sampan and ship. Michael Rogers, of the German Brothers, had stayed behind to help our people; but he had been shot at several times and had to flee on a ship loaded even to the bridge with several thousand people. The three-day trip to Vung Tau with no food or water was an ordeal that many refugees did not survive.

When the victorious Communists raised their flag at the Da Nang city hall, the majority of our people—including the orphans and lepers—were unable to escape.

Pastor An of Kontum and four of his seven children made it to the United States. His little twin girls and a son were left behind in the confusion. Pastors Cang and Dich and their families also escaped to America, with one orphan from China Beach Orphanage. Of all the scores of thousands of refugees coming to this country, only a pitiful little group of our Christians succeeded in fleeing to safety.

The curtain has come down. No doubt it will not be long before the brainwashing and the terrible ordeals of will-breaking begin, with restrictions on worship and belief in Christ. Let us cry from the depths of our hearts, "Oh God, give them Thy grace to endure whatever is before them." They are counting on our prayers, and we must not let them down. As they pass through the deep trials, they will be hearing God's voice in the wonderful hymns which they have in their own language, such as:

"The flame shall not hurt thee; I only design
Thy dross to consume, and thy gold to refine.

"The soul that on Jesus still leans for repose,
I will not, I will not desert to his foes;
That soul, though all hell should endeavor to shake,
I'll never, no never, no never forsake!"

GEORGE KEITH
How Firm a Foundation

250

Appendix

COMPARATIVE TEACHINGS

BUDDHISM	CONFUCIANISM	CHRISTIANITY
1. Buddhists pray in a dead language. They chant words devoid of sense, vain repetitions to Buddha.	1. Confucianists burn incense, offer fruit and flowers before the ancestral tablet, and light candles. They talk to their ancestors.	1. Christians pray from the heart in their native tongue to God, the Father, and to Christ, the Son. They pour out their hearts as talking to a friend.
2. They worship the idol of Buddha, who was only a man.	2. They worship their ancestors whose names are written on tablets. These are only representative of former mortal men and women.	2. God says: "Thou shalt have no other gods before me . . . [or] any graven image" (Ex 20:3-4). We worship the true, living God, the Trinity: Father, Son, and Holy Spirit. He commands that we do not worship idols or people.
3. Buddhists never confess their sins or pray for a clean heart. They never see their sins as something which requires forgiveness.	3. Like Buddhists, they never ask for forgiveness.	3. We cannot come to God until our sins are washed away. Sin separates man from God. We must have our sins forgiven and have a clean heart. "If I regard iniquity in my heart,

BUDDHISM	CONFUCIANISM	CHRISTIANITY
		the Lord will not hear me" (Ps 66:18). "Without the shedding of blood there is no remission of sins." We are cleansed through the blood of Christ shed on Calvary's cross.
4. They never ask help from Buddha. He would not help if he could! He taught that we must depend on ourselves; we must *work* for our salvation. "Do good and you'll have good. Do bad and you'll have bad." To do "good" is to give alms to the priests and beggars, and set wild animals and birds free.	4. The people believe that if one is faithful in the rites before the ancestral tablets daily, the ancestors will help them. But the Confucianist classics say: "We do not know if the ancestors will help. We do not know if their spirits are alive or not!"	4. The Word of God says, "For by *grace* are ye saved through *faith* . . . not of works, lest any man should boast" (Eph 2:8-9). We Christians simply believe in the living Jesus and receive Him. He is all-powerful to save and help.
5. Buddhists believe in the transmigration of souls. People are born over and over, and die over and over. After death people become animals. If they are not too bad sinners, they become dogs, cats, mon-	5. Confucianists know nothing of what happens to the soul. They are profoundly in the dark about God. They know nothing about the future happiness or suffering in another world. They teach nothing about the	5. The Bible teaches that there are only two places for the soul after death, either in hell with the devil and demons, or in heaven with God and the angels. Souls of *unbelievers* in Christ are punished eternally

BUDDHISM	CONFUCIANISM	CHRISTIANITY
keys, cows, pigs, birds, or insects. Criminals turn into tigers, lions, snakes, dangerous beasts. Buddhists must never kill any living creature or insect. It may be a relative. The greatest sin in Buddhism is to take life. But they are not kind to animals. They have no sympathy for them. The fate of dogs and cats is piteous.	immortality of the soul. Confucianist classics say: "We know nothing."	in hell. Souls of *believers* in Christ live eternally in heaven.
6. The Buddhist heaven is Nirvana, which means "black-out into *nothingness.*" Buddha has now gone into Nirvana. Followers seek to enter Nirvana too.	6. Confucianist classics say: "We do not have sufficient knowledge to say *positively* that gods and spirits exist. We say *nothing* about them." They do not know if the dead teachers they worship, Confucius and Mencius, are living in another world. They have no proof. They don't know if they'll ever join the teachers they worship in another world. They say: "We worship them, but where are they?"	6. Jesus Christ is the second Person in the Trinity. He is eternal. He was "before the foundations of the earth." He came to earth, died to save us, but rose again. He is an eternally living Saviour. His followers will have eternal life with Him in heaven.

BUDDHISM	CONFUCIANISM	CHRISTIANITY
7. Buddhists treat polygamy lightly. If a Buddhist is rich enough, he may have three or four wives.	7. Confucianists practice polygamy also. It is common practice for a Confucianist to have many wives.	7. God commands: "Thou shalt not commit adultery" (Ex 20:14). It is great sin. A husband must have only one wife and vice versa.
8. A *woman* cannot get to heaven without being born again as a man. If she keeps the rites, vegetarian vows, and is faithful in giving alms, then she has hope of being born again as a man.	8. Girls and women are considered inferior to boys and men. Boys are first, and girls come far behind. They are happy when a boy baby is born. They say nothing at all when a girl baby is born. A girl must drudge and serve, be ignored, and repressed. A common saying is: "The word of one man equals the word of twelve women." "A woman's brain doesn't develop further after thirteen years of age. Women are like children." Confucius said: "One boy is a person. Ten girls are as nothing."	8. In Christianity, women are equal with men. "There is no difference before God—male or female." Salvation and eternal life are as free to woman as to man.

BUDDHISM	CONFUCIANISM	CHRISTIANITY
9. Buddhists fear death. They fear reincarnations.	9. Confucianists fear death. They are *in the dark* about the future life. They speak of the world of spirits as "The Dark World."	9. If we believe in Jesus Christ as our Saviour we are *sure* of heaven. We go straight to heaven when we die, and we have glorified bodies. There is no reincarnation of souls. We go to live with God eternally. "Death is swallowed up in victory" (1 Co 15:54).
10. The Buddhists realize that Buddha was just a man.	10. Confucianists realize that their great teachers, Confucius and Mencius, his student, were only men. The ancestors were only men and women.	10. If we say that Jesus Christ is only a man, God considers us to be very wicked. "He that honoureth not the Son honoureth not the Father" (Jn 5:23). Jesus *proved* that He was the Son of God here on earth, by miracles, feeding 5,000, walking on water, causing the dead to rise. He rose again and *was seen* ascending back into heaven.